The Moods of Homeric Greek

Homeric Greek has a particularly rich system of moods which are analysed afresh in this book in the light of recent theoretical interest in the semantic domain of modality. The domain is one of the most complex and interesting, since modal forms are used for the most 'subjective' of messages, expressing our beliefs, intentions, desires, abilities and wishes. Incorporating findings from the theory of grammaticalisation, this study considers the Homeric Greek modal system from a diachronic perspective and offers a radical revision of traditional accounts. Providing insights into both individual constructions as well as the overall system of modality in Greek, it will be of interest to general linguists, linguists studying ancient Greek, and also scholars interested in fundamental questions of meaning in Greek. The indices, where all the instances of the moods in the Homeric poems are categorised into types, also make it useful as a research tool.

JO WILLMOTT is a Research Fellow at Queens' College, Cambridge, and an Affiliate Lecturer in the Classics Faculty at the University of Cambridge.

CAMBRIDGE CLASSICAL STUDIES

General editors

R. L. HUNTER, R. G. OSBORNE, M. D. REEVE,
P. D. A. GARNSEY, M. MILLETT, D. N. SEDLEY,
G. C. HORROCKS

THE MOODS OF HOMERIC GREEK

JO WILLMOTT

Queens' College, Cambridge

CAMBRIDGE
UNIVERSITY PRESS

CAMBRIDGE UNIVERSITY PRESS
Cambridge, New York, Melbourne, Madrid, Cape Town, Singapore, São Paulo

Cambridge University Press
The Edinburgh Building, Cambridge CB2 8RU, UK

Published in the United States of America by Cambridge University Press, New York

www.cambridge.org
Information on this title: www.cambridge.org/9780521879880

First published 2007

Printed in the United Kingdom at the University Press, Cambridge

A catalogue record for this publication is available from the British Library

ISBN 978 0 521 87988 0 hardback

For M

CONTENTS

Acknowledgements   *page* ix
List of abbreviations   xi

1 Preliminaries   1
  1.1   Scope of the work   1
  1.2   The nature of the corpus   5

2 Theoretical framework   10
  2.1   Introduction   10
  2.2   Traditional accounts   11
  2.3   Recent advances   21
  2.4   Conclusions   35

3 Indicative   37
  3.1   Introduction   37
  3.2   Analysis   39
  3.3   Summary and conclusions   51

4 Subjunctive   53
  4.1   Introduction   53
  4.2   Epistemic   54
  4.3   Hortative   81
  4.4   Negative directive   90
  4.5   Summary and conclusions   110

5 Optative   113
  5.1   Introduction   113
  5.2   Morphological argument   114
  5.3   Conditionals   116
  5.4   Wish   124

5.5	Other meanings	138
5.6	Summary and conclusions	150

6	**Subordinate uses**	**153**
6.1	Introduction	153
6.2	Purpose	155
6.3	Iterative	174
6.4	Non-specific	184
6.5	Summary and conclusions	189

7	**Conclusion**	**192**
7.1	Introduction	192
7.2	New map of the indicative	193
7.3	New map of the subjunctive	194
7.4	New map of the optative	197
7.5	Final thoughts	198

Appendix 1: Formal markers	199
Appendix 2: Catalogue of mood uses	211
Bibliography	238
Index locorum	252
General index	257

ACKNOWLEDGEMENTS

This book could not have been written without the help of many people. It is based on my Ph.D. dissertation, which was submitted to Cambridge University in 2003. My supervisor, Geoff Horrocks, patiently read through innumerable drafts. He has been an incomparable support throughout the entire project. All members of the 'E' caucus of the Classics Faculty have sat through various seminars and improved my thinking with their questions, particularly James Clackson, who was another great support in these later stages. As my examiners, James Clackson and Gerry Wakker also provided many useful ideas of how to convert it from thesis into book.

James Diggle was my Director of Studies when I was an undergraduate, thesis supervisor for my M.Phil., and then entrusted several generations of his students to my teaching. In all roles his belief in me has been invaluable, as well as his suggestions, help and advice. I owe my position as Research Fellow in Queens' College largely to him, for which I must also thank the President and Fellows of the College, not only in appointing me, but also in contributing to such a productive and friendly environment. My students, too, in Queens', other colleges, and on the Bryanston summer school, have kept me on my toes, always forcing me to rethink my views on Greek language and linguistic theory, and generally being a lot of fun to teach and drink tea with.

Of course, the book would not exist at all without the editors of the series and Michael Sharp, the editor at Cambridge University Press. Many thanks are also due to Richard Hunter, who was at first the anonymous reader who made several useful suggestions all of which I tried to incorporate into the final version.

Finally, friends and family must also be thanked. In particular, James for being probably the only person other than my supervisor and examiners to read the whole of my Ph.D. My parents for being at the end of a phone. My Dad, for just the right amount of editorial advice. The Allwood family, for all their love and a place to get away. Helen and Kate for laughing at me and listening to me. And Tom, for help with words, phrases, and so much else.

ABBREVIATIONS

In most cases, bibliographical references in the text are made in the author–date format. However, in the case of grammars and books that were frequently quoted, the author's name alone was felt to be sufficient. These are listed below:

Abbott, E. and Mansfield, E. D. 1977.	*A Primer of Greek Grammar* (London: Duckworth)
Bybee, J. L., Pagliuca, W. and Perkins, R. D. 1994.	*The Evolution of Grammar: Tense, Aspect, and Modality in the Languages of the World* (Chicago: University of Chicago Press)
Chantraine, P. 1948.	*Grammaire homérique*, 2 vols. (Paris: Klincksieck) (2nd edn) (Unless indicated, all references are to volume II.)
Gonda, J. 1956.	*The Character of the Indo-European Moods* (Wiesbaden: Harrassowitz)
Goodwin, W. W. 1889.	*Syntax of the Moods and Tenses of the Greek Verb* (London: Macmillan)
Hahn, E. A. 1953.	*Subjunctive and Optative: Their Origin as Futures* (New York: American Philological Association)
Kirk, G. S. et al. 1985.	*The Iliad: A Commentary* (Cambridge University Press)

Kühner, R. and Gerth, B. 1898–1904.	*Ausführliche Grammatik der griechischen Sprache* (Hannover/Leipzig)
Leaf, W. 1900.	*The Iliad* (London: Macmillan)
Merry, W. W., Riddell, J. and Monro, D. B. 1886.	*Commentary on the Odyssey* (Oxford: Clarendon Press)
Monro, D. B. 1891.	*Homeric Grammar* (Oxford University Press)
Palmer¹ = Palmer, F. R. 1986.	*Mood and Modality* (Cambridge University Press) (1st edn)
Palmer² = Palmer, F. R. 2000.	*Mood and Modality* (Cambridge University Press) (2nd edn)
Schwyzer, E. and Debrunner, A. 1950.	*Griechische Grammatik* (Munich: Beck)
Smyth, H. W. 1956.	*Greek Grammar* (Cambridge, Mass.: Harvard University Press.)

The only other abbreviations used are BPP, which refers to works written by Bybee, Pagliuca and Perkins (unless otherwise indicated all references to BPP are to the work dated 1994), and LSJ, which refers to the Liddell, Scott and Jones Greek-English Lexicon.

PRELIMINARIES

1.1 Scope of the work

Modality, the grammatical domain expressed by moods, or modal verbs in English (may, must, will, can, etc.), is one of the most interesting semantic domains; we use these modal forms to communicate most 'subjectively', to express our beliefs, intentions, desires, abilities and wishes. In Homer, the subjunctive and optative are used to beseech the gods, to beg for something not to happen, to suggest a course of action, to speculate about what might be. Yet in spite of the obvious interest of the meaning of these forms, the domain of modality has only recently been paid much theoretical attention.[1] A reanalysis of the Homeric modal system is therefore overdue in the light of this recent theoretical interest, even though the uses of the moods have been minutely described in several standard grammars (Monro, Chantraine, Goodwin, Smyth). I will argue here that the traditional accounts need to be radically revised.

This book is both a close analysis of the various constructions in which moods are found in Homeric Greek, and also a case study in the theoretical description of a modal system. The analysis of the constructions discusses and takes issue with many of the assertions found in textbook grammars. Because of the nature of the constructions in which the moods are found (e.g. prayers (chapter 5.4), counterfactual conditions (3.2.4 and 5.3), prohibitions (4.4), descriptions of capacity (5.5.2), purpose clauses (6.2)), this discussion will not only be of interest to linguists concerned with the meaning of Homeric Greek, but also to those considering the poems from a literary perspective. Using findings from grammaticalisation and modern studies of modality that demonstrate

---

[1] The first full-length textbook on the subject (Palmer *Mood and Modality*, 1st edn) was only published in 1986.

the complexity of the domain, the modal system as a whole is here reconsidered, and the study thus also has conclusions which will be of interest to linguists considering ancient Greek and Proto-Indo-European from a theoretical perspective. Finally, I hope that the book will also interest linguists concerned with the description of modality in general. Most modality studies have discussed the use of modal verbs; in Homeric Greek modality is expressed primarily through moods, and important differences between the two types of systems may thus be highlighted.

This book is based on a Ph.D. thesis submitted to the University of Cambridge in 2003. There I used a corpus of the first six books of the *Iliad* for a preliminary survey of the different uses of the moods, sampling widely for extra data where necessary. For this book, all the examples of the moods throughout both Homeric poems have been analysed and categorised. While examples used for illustration might primarily come from my original corpus, these are always cross-referenced to any other examples elsewhere. An appendix of these examples, intended to be a useful research tool in its own right, may be found at the end of the book (see the index locorum).

The structure of the book, and the main arguments found in the separate chapters are as follows:

In chapter 2 the theoretical foundations of the book are laid. It consists of a description of traditional accounts of the Greek and Homeric modal system restated in terms found in the modern theoretical literature, and some preliminary theoretical reasons why such an account is implausible. Here many of the terms used throughout the book are introduced, particularly the concepts of the 'irrealis continuum' (and the terms 'realis' and 'irrealis'); 'epistemic', 'deontic' and 'speaker-oriented' types of modality; and the theories of 'grammaticalisation' and 'fuzzy set theory'.

Chapter 3 consists of a brief analysis of the indicative *qua* mood, necessary because the subjunctive and optative are often defined in relation to it. I analyse the whole spectrum of conditional clauses in which the indicative is found and argue that the mood is neither the most 'realis' nor an 'epistemically neutral' marker, but that it rather expresses 'positive epistemic stance'. The analysis provides an interesting overview of the different types of conditional clauses expressed by the indicative. The definition I propose also allows a more successful analysis of the use of the indicative in counterfactual conditional sentences than has previously been offered, explaining the difference between it and the optative in this context.

Chapter 4 is an analysis of the subjunctive in three parts, relating to the three major uses of the subjunctive in main and conditional clauses: epistemic, hortative and prohibitive. I argue that the main task in defining the epistemic use of the subjunctive is to distinguish it from the future indicative. I describe the theoretical difficulties of distinguishing between an epistemic mood and a future marker in general, and the formal difficulties of distinguishing between the subjunctive and future indicative in Homeric Greek. Taking these difficulties into consideration I claim that there is no evidence to suggest that the subjunctive is more 'irrealis' than the future indicative, as traditional analyses would suggest, and that the major difference between the two categories is one of distribution. I then consider the hortative meaning of the subjunctive and argue that these may be divided into two: invitation and autoprescription. I argue that these could have arisen from the epistemic meaning through 'conventionalisation of implicature'. I also demonstrate that in some of the examples previously given of this meaning, the subjunctive has been misunderstood. I argue that it expresses the true deontic meaning of intention in addition to the 'speaker-oriented' hortative meaning. Intention meaning is commonly found in future markers, confirming the claims made for the epistemic meaning of the mood. These conclusions have important consequences for our view of the 'subjunctive' and 'future' category in Proto-Indo-European. In the section on the prohibitive constructions I show that traditional accounts do not sufficiently account for the use of both the subjunctive and the imperative in this construction. Based on comparison with the cross-linguistic data, I argue that the subjunctive expresses a significantly different meaning from the imperative. This analysis allows us to understand the real meaning of prohibitions in a more sophisticated way.

3

In chapter 5 I consider the two major uses of the optative as traditionally defined but also demonstrate that the optative is more complex. The optative is traditionally described as a more remote version of the subjunctive, but I show that the claim is not supported either by formal marking or by its meanings. I suggest that, in conditional clauses, it would best be defined as a marker of 'negative epistemic stance' rather than 'most irrealis' marker. I argue that, in its use in wishes, it is not a 'weaker version' of the imperative but has specific semantic reference which has significant ramifications for our understanding of ancient prayer. I finally claim it is possible to distinguish other uses of the optative. I describe these meanings in detail and discuss the possible relations lying between these uses and the meanings that are traditionally distinguished. Of particular importance for translators and those considering the language from a literary perspective is the recognition that the optative expresses the ability or capacity of the subject.

While some of the uses of the moods in subordinate clauses have been considered in other chapters, in chapter 6 I look at what have been described as more 'grammatical' subordinate uses of both moods. It is in this context that the claim is most adamantly made that the optative is the 'past-time variant' of the subjunctive. I consider three constructions (purpose clauses, iterative clauses, relative clauses), and argue that the traditional claims do not stand for any of them, calling into question the traditional notion of the 'vivid subjunctive'. I argue that the use of both moods in these constructions can be explained with reference to their semantic meaning as defined elsewhere.

The conclusions are summarised in chapter 7 where I give the overall structure of the new 'maps' I propose for each mood, and outline their consequences for the general field of modality studies. There are also two appendices. In appendix 1 I give a brief explanation of the motivation for the lack of emphasis laid on the presence or absence of the modal particle and negator in the study. Previous scholars have claimed that they were used to mark the two types of modality that have traditionally been distinguished for the two moods, but I show that the evidence is not conclusive. Appendix 2 is a series of indices listing all the instances of the moods arranged according to the different types which are discussed throughout the book.

1.2 The nature of the corpus

As noted above, the corpus to be used for this analysis are the two epic poems of Homer, the *Iliad* and the *Odyssey*. It is of course impossible to conduct a linguistic analysis based on this corpus without addressing the particular problems presented by the language of these poems.

First, like any ancient language, we are not in a position to ask a native speaker about the acceptability or the semantic nuances of a given collocation. We must therefore rely on the text and our interpretation of it, while acknowledging that we can never capture exactly what it meant to its original hearers (Lightfoot 1975: 24). Even without the problems of subjective interpretation, we may not even be sure that the text as we have it now is a true representation of the poems as they were first written down. The long history of textual transmission has meant that the preconceived ideas of scholars may have actually shaped the language. A particularly clear example of this in relation to the study of modality is the treatment of the modal particle ἄν/κε: scholars have argued that it may be 'corrected' to other particles in the contexts in which they believe it should not exist (e.g. Bolling 1960: 34). A similar problem arises in the choice between the subjunctive and future indicative. Since the forms are often metrically equivalent, our interpretation of a particular form as either future indicative or subjunctive may well be based on prejudices about what the two categories 'mean' (see further chapter 3).

The above problems are faced by any linguist who uses ancient texts. But the language of Homer has a more specific problem: it is now generally acknowledged that it is the product of a long tradition of oral poetry.[2] There are several reasons why this makes it a far from ideal linguistic database. The 'formulaic' nature of the poetry leads to the possibility that a particular collocation may be used in

---

[2] The original hypothesis is found in Parry 1928, 1930 and 1932.

spite of not being perfectly 'semantically integrated' to the context (Bakker 1988a: 19). That is, metrical constraints could have led to phrases which are well formed in one particular semantic context being used in rather less appropriate contexts (Horrocks 1997: 18). Furthermore, elements from several different dialects are used, partly, at least, because of their metrical expediency. The language also has a diachronic dimension: older forms are fossilised in the language as newer forms would not fit metrically.[3] The Homeric language is thus an amalgam of different regional and temporal dialects, shaped by the constraints of the epic metre.

The existence of this diachronic dimension is perhaps the most serious problem for this study. It has been shown that the Homeric poems preserve elements that may well have entered a form of epic diction perhaps even before the division of the Indo-European proto-language into its various dialects, and almost certainly into a Greek tradition before the period of the Linear B tablets (Horrocks 1980: 4). In the several centuries between this earliest point and the final (significant) chronological slice to be incorporated into the language (normally taken to be eighth or seventh century Ionic Greek, see further Janko 1982 and West 2001), it must be assumed that the uses of the moods underwent several changes. We may not therefore be sure that the various uses of the moods we see in the Homeric poems were ever found in one synchronic period of the Greek language.

However, in spite of the peculiar nature of the language, I would suggest that these problems are not as serious as they seem. Although it is clear that the metre may have caused some rather unusual uses of forms, it has been pointed out that constructions have prototypical and peripheral uses in all styles of language (Bakker 1988a: 19). Non-prototypical uses of a particular construction may not therefore be dismissed as a 'metrical anomaly'. Stephens (1983: 76) further argues that the use of formulas will not be entirely linguistically unconstrained. That is, it would be surprising for formulaic adaptation to break a 'rule' of the language. It is probable that this problem of formulaic adaptation will

---

[3] Palmer, L. R. 1962: 97–106; Palmer, L. R. 1980: 93–7; Janko 1985: 8–19; Hainsworth 1988; Horrocks 1997.

be more visible in some contexts than others: it is perhaps less likely that the mood chosen in any particular main clause will be determined purely by metrical considerations, and more likely that a subordinate clause will be 'imported' into a context which is not entirely appropriate. For instance, we could compare the following use of a relative clause with a singular subject pronoun but a plural antecedent:[4]

O   οὐ γὰρ καλὸν ἀτέμβειν οὐδὲ δίκαιον
20.294 ξείνους Τηλεμάχου, ὅς κεν τάδε δώμαθ' ἵκηται.

It is neither polite nor right to maltreat the guests of Telemachus, whoever comes to this house.

The use of the relative clause in this context could be explained as governed by the formulaic nature of the text. However, there is likely to be some linguistic justification for it too: this can be understood as shifting the focus from the general to the particular – 'whoever the guests of Telemachus are, anyone who comes to his house should be treated well' (Monro: §283b). We will return to the particular problem of the interpretation of subordinate clauses in chapter 6.

Although it is well established that some archaic elements have been preserved in the language, there are also reasons to think that the diachronic nature of the language will not cause too many problems for our understanding of the use of the moods. The modal forms do not generally feature in the lists of forms that have been used to indicate whether passages are particularly early or late (e.g. Janko 1982: 71), and there are only a few examples of modal forms that are argued to be 'modern'. For example, μαχέοιντο found in 1.344 is said to have a modern ending (see Leaf ad loc. and Kirk et al. ad loc.). It was corrected by Bentley to μαχεοίατ', but the lateness of the ending is only one of the problems in its

---

[4] Throughout the book, all Greek examples will be from Homer unless otherwise indicated. A bare number refers to a book and line of the *Iliad*, a number preceded by O refers to a book and line from *Odyssey*. The text used is that of the Teubner edition (West, M. L. 1998) for the *Iliad*, and the Oxford Classical Text for the *Odyssey* (Allen, T. W. 1917), unless otherwise indicated. The line referred to is the line in which the particular modal form appears, not necessarily the first line quoted. Examples are accompanied by a translation. This is to aid the reader, and to explain the general context of the form in question: they have no aspiration to literary merit.

interpretation – see further section 6.2.2. The optatives φοροίη (O9.320) and φιλοίη (O4. 692) are also said to have the Attic vocalism (Palmer, L. R. 1962: 94), but the exact formation of the moods is in any case of little importance to my argument. Perhaps more importantly, some scholars have claimed that the use of 'vivid' subjunctives in subordinate clauses after a secondary main verb indicates that a passage is late (e.g. Leaf on 19.354). But as I will show in chapter 6, the evidence for this construction is very complex. At any rate, the study of grammaticalisation has shown that even truly synchronic slices of a language will provide evidence for various different chronological stages of development. For example, as will be discussed in chapter 2, the distribution of the modal verb 'will' in modern English provides evidence for its historical development. Homeric Greek may have a more obviously diachronic dimension, but it is thus only quantitatively, not qualitatively, different from other languages.

The particular nature of the Homeric language does not therefore cause insuperable problems for its use as a linguistic database. This is not to say that there will be nothing further to say regarding the diachronic aspect of the language. For example, it is interesting that all the certain examples of the future indicative in conditional clauses are found in the *Iliad*, the earlier of the two poems (Janko 1982: 228). I will return to the discussion of the possible significance of this distribution in chapter 4.

In any case, there are many positive reasons to use the Homeric language for a study of the meaning and development of the moods in Greek. Apart from Mycenaean, for which only a very limited set of verb forms is attested, it is the oldest available stratum of the language (Chantraine: §304). Perhaps most importantly, it has been claimed that the use of the moods is here less 'mechanical' than in Attic (Chantraine: §368; Hahn: §106). This suggests that a range of earlier meanings of the moods will be detectable in the Homeric language, even if these have become more grammaticalised and determined by context in the later language. Too frequently the Homeric language is seen against the back-drop of the better understood classical language, and the differences between it and the classical language are seen as 'peculiarities' (Goodwin: §434).

I will argue that these very peculiarities hold the key to properly understanding the modal system in Greek. Thus, although the language of the Homeric epics is perhaps not an ideal corpus to use for a synchronic analysis of a particular part of the grammatical system, the benefits of looking again at this earliest evidence for the Greek verbal system are clear.

THEORETICAL FRAMEWORK

2.1 Introduction

Over the last 150 years, many discussions of the moods in ancient Greek in general and Homeric Greek in particular have been published, both in grammars of the language, and in specialist monographs.[1] It might therefore be claimed that there is nothing new to be said on the subject. But there are various reasons why a reconsideration of the Homeric Greek moods can provide insights into this fascinating area of the grammatical system.

The first reason is that it may take account of the relatively recent proliferation of theoretical studies on modality, a category which was largely 'unfamiliar' to general linguists before the first edition of Palmer's important *Mood and Modality* (1986), as he notes in its preface. The traditional understanding of the ancient Greek moods may certainly be recouched in terms more familiar to the modern linguist, and this will be undertaken in section 2.2. I will show that the traditional understanding actually appears to accord very well with the 'standard' view of modality as outlined by Palmer. Indeed Palmer frequently uses ancient Greek data to exemplify his distinctions.

But in section 2.3 I will argue that this accord is illusory, thereby giving further reasons why a re-examination of the data will be profitable. The theory of grammaticalisation has shown that descriptions of grammatical systems have until now depended on a rather out-moded structuralist view of language which does not sufficiently take into account the diachronic dimension of language

---

[1] Grammars: Goodwin 1870; Smyth 1956; Kühner and Gerth 1898–1904; Monro 1891; Stahl 1907; Humbert 1943; Chantraine 1948; Schwyzer and Debrünner 1950; Abbott and Mansfield 1949. Monographs: Goodwin 1889; Hahn 1953; Gonda 1956; Lightfoot 1975. Hahn (§3–§18) provides a good discussion of earlier work, and also refers (§3) to Bennett (1910–14: 145–61) for more references.

change. I will describe the principles by which grammatical systems may more successfully be described in the light of findings from this theory. Recent studies of modality have also defined the different modal meanings with a greater degree of sophistication. Even before a detailed analysis of the Homeric data, it is clear that the modern version of the traditional account presented in section 2.2 is mistaken. Thus the theoretical foundations for this reanalysis will be laid.

2.2 Traditional accounts

2.2.1 Introduction

Traditional accounts of the ancient Greek moods, as found both in grammars and specialist monographs are inevitably rather outdated, since the theory of modality has developed since the original descriptions were formulated. They thus need to be restated in terms used in modern studies of modality. In this section I will show that, although there is no single view of the meaning of the moods, there is now general consensus on many aspects of the Greek modal system. This consensus, on both the relationship between the moods and the types of meanings expressed by the moods, requires surprisingly little adjustment to be formulated in terms of the 'standard' modern description of modality as found in Palmer (1986 and 2000). I believe and will show in subsequent chapters that these traditional accounts fail to accurately describe the meanings of the Homeric moods. Nonetheless, given that this understanding of the meaning of the moods is so wide-spread, it will be described in some detail here, and in effect will serve as the model against which I will be arguing in the rest of the book.

2.2.2 The relationship between the moods

The Greek moods are often explained in terms of the relationships that hold between them. At a basic level, these relationships are described in terms of binary oppositions. The first opposition is that between the indicative on the one hand, and the 'oblique' subjunctive and optative on the other (Hahn: §5; Chantraine: §305 and Gonda: 2).[2] This binary opposition is apparently confirmed by the term used for mood in Greek (ἔγκλισις), that is, an 'inclination' away from the indicative (Wackernagel 1926: 210).[3]

This understanding of the relationship between modal forms and the indicative is also found in one of the first theoretical accounts of modality in general. Lyons (1977: 794–6) links modal forms with non-factual meanings, and the indicative with factual meanings. (He actually uses the term 'factive', but Palmer (1986: 17–18) argues this term should be replaced with 'factual', since the term 'factive' is used in a different and more technical sense in Kiparsky and Kiparsky 1971.) The following examples illustrate some sentences which Lyons describes as 'modal':

1 He may have gone to Paris.
2 Perhaps he went to Paris.
3 It is possible that he went to Paris.

The definition of the indicative as factual has also been adopted for ancient Greek in the modern textbook *Reading Greek* (JACT 1978: 313).

But this view of the relationship between the moods is over simplistic, as we may see from more sophisticated analyses of both the Greek data and the theoretical field of modality. It has been widely argued for ancient Greek that the moods are not associated with non-factuality, but that they are rather more subjective. For example, Chantraine (§304) claims that moods 'introduissent une coloration subjective dans l'expression du procès'. Similarly, Smyth (§1759) claims that the moods designate 'the mode or manner (modus) in which the speaker conceives of an assertion concerning the subject', while Goodwin (§1) states that it 'shows the manner in which the assertion of the verb is made' (see further Gonda: 2 and Hahn: §6, with references to further literature). The importance of the speaker is also emphasised in many modern discussions of modality: the crucial criterion for determining whether or not a proposition will be expressed with a modal form in a given

---

[2] Also see Meillet and Vendryes 1927: 184; Humbert 1943: 84; Thomas 1938; Handford 1947.
[3] For etymology and first use of the term see LSJ s.v. and Schwyzer vol II: 302.

language is not the objective factuality of the event, but rather the attitude of the speaker towards that proposition.[4]

This definition of modal forms could still imply a binary opposition between the indicative on the one hand and the modal forms on the other. If this were the case, the indicative would be objective as opposed to the subjective modal forms. This appears to tie in well with the more basic definition of the indicative as 'factual'. However, it has been shown that the indicative is just as subjective as the modal forms. The subjective nature of the indicative is particularly clear for both ancient Greek and more generally in the case of the future tense, and indeed many scholars have wanted to class the future as a mood rather than a tense for this reason.[5] The nature of the future tense in Greek is certainly an interesting question, and I will return to it in section 4.2. But even in the past and present tenses, the indicative is not only used to describe objective facts.[6] This was recognised for the Greek indicative by Schwyzer (2.303), who characterised it as expressing 'was der Sprechende als wirklich aufgefasst wissen will' (see also Kühner and Gerth II: 382a). The involvement of the speaker in the choice of the indicative as well as the other moods suggests that the relationship between the moods is better seen as a continuum with one 'axis' of meaning rather than as a binary opposition. This conclusion is also suggested by the terminology used by ancient grammarians: after all, the indicative is also considered a mood (Latin *modus*).[7] Palmer (1986: 27) compares the difficulty of defining the difference between the indicative and the 'oblique' moods to Speech Act Theory. Assertions were originally held to be 'basic' while other types of utterance had special illocutionary forces. But in the end, Austin (1962: 132) realised that 'asserting' had its own illocutionary force.

Modern descriptions of modality as well as older descriptions of the Greek moods have thus recognised that the 'non-modal' indicative as well as more clearly 'modal' forms belong to one domain of

---

[4] See, e.g. BPP: 239; Lunn 1995: 429; Palmer[2]: 187.

[5] See Lyons 1977: 816; Palmer[2]: 104ff., chapter 6; Mithun 1995: 378; Romaine 1995: 396; Chantraine: §301; Hahn: §210.

[6] See Gonda: 3; Hahn: §15; Bakker 1988a: 33.

[7] Wackernagel 1926: 210; Schwyzer: 301, see also Wymann 1996: 44. Also see Hahn 1951 on the discussion of 'mood' by Apollonius Dyscolus.

modality. But the terminology used to further define this domain is not agreed upon. Some wish to use the term 'assertion', claiming that different modal forms reflect 'the extent to which the speaker is willing to ASSERT the truth of a proposition' (BPP: 239, see also Klein 1975). However, this definition is rather problematic as the terms 'assertive' and 'non-assertive' are used elsewhere in the description of syntactic contexts, with main clauses described as assertive syntactic contexts, and subordinate clauses described as non-assertive (BPP: 231). The semantically assertive indicative is often found in syntactically non-assertive constructions, for example in past-time temporal clauses:

6.173   ἀλλ' ὅτε δὴ Λυκίην ἷξε Ξάνθόν τε ῥέοντα,
        προφρονέως μιν τῖεν ἄναξ Λυκίης εὐρείης·

and once he reached Lycia and the rushing Xanthus, the king of broad Lycia gave him a royal welcome.

The dual use of the term 'assertion' means that another term proposed in the literature is to be preferred, namely 'irrealis'. Givón (1994: 268) has defined irrealis sentences as propositions which are 'weakly asserted as either possible, likely or uncertain . . . or necessary, desired or undesired'. Thus the term is itself defined in terms of speaker-assertion, but does not confuse the semantic domain with syntactic properties of the clause.

The term 'irrealis' is however rather controversial (Bybee 1998). A first problem is that 'irrealis' sentences are opposed to 'realis' ones, which apparently returns to the idea that there is a binary opposition between 'modal' and 'non-modal' sentences. This may be avoided by the use of the term 'irrealis continuum', on which realis forms may also lie (Akatsuka 1985: 1). Another problem is that the term 'realis' would appear to indicate objective reality whereas we have seen that it is the speaker's presentation of the proposition which is important. But this is merely a terminological issue which may be side-stepped by explicitly stating that 'realis' is connected with *subjective* rather than objective reality (Fleischman 1982: 522). For the present, the traditional understanding of the indicative may usefully be stated in these terms: the indicative is considered to be more realis than the other moods.

The idea of an irrealis continuum also well captures the relationship traditionally claimed to exist between the subjunctive and optative, although again this is more usually thought of in terms of a binary opposition. Essentially, the two moods are seen as parallel forms, with the optative a 'lesser' variant of the subjunctive. For example, Goodwin (§12) describes the optative as 'a less distinct and direct form of expression than the subjunctive'. Chantraine (§314) claims that the difference between the subjunctive and optative is one of 'attenuation': 'si l'on confronte le subjonctif et l'optatif, on remarque que le second . . . exprime l'idée d'une façon plus atténuée que le subjonctif'. Vairel (1979: 579) makes the perceived similarity between the two moods even more explicit, claiming that the optative is a 'double en mineur du subjonctif'. This understanding of the relationship between the subjunctive and optative is found in some of the earliest studies of the Greek moods: Delbrück (1871: 13), for example, discussed the 'near' subjunctive expressing 'will' and contrasted it with the 'remote' optative expressing 'wish'. Similarly, Wackernagel (1926: 230–8) stressed the essential parallelism of the two moods. Even Hahn (§31), who appears to deviate significantly from the traditional account with her claim that the subjunctive and optative were not originally moods but future tenses, claims that the difference between them is one of greater 'remoteness' for the optative. Palmer (2000: 13, 204ff.) appears to see the relationship between the two Greek moods in much the same way, when he compares it with the relationship between present and past tenses of modal verbs in English. With each of the following modal verbs the past tense is supposed to express the meaning with greater 'tentativeness':

will : would
can : could
may : might

The subjunctive in Greek is compared with the present tense, and the optative with the more tentative past tense. The relationship between subjunctive and optative is even believed to have morphological support, through the use of primary endings on the subjunctive and secondary endings on the optative.[8] For more discussion of this morphological claim see section 5.2.

The relationship between the subjunctive and optative may thus easily be expressed in terms of an irrealis continuum: the optative according to these definitions would lie at the most irrealis end, while the subjunctive is closer to the more realis indicative. Indeed, in one of the most recent studies of ancient Greek conditional clauses, Greenberg (1986: 247) chooses to describe the moods in just these terms, as represented by figure 2.1.

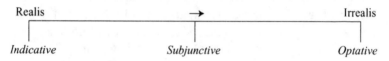

Figure 2.1 Greenberg's irrealis continuum

The traditional understanding of the relationship between the Greek moods thus only requires a little adaptation to fit in well with theoretical studies on the types of distinctions generally made in the field of modality.

2.2.3 The meanings of the moods

In the traditional accounts of the moods in Greek, the moods are not only described in terms of their relationship to each other, but in terms of the different meanings which they (specifically now the subjunctive and optative) have in various different constructions. Here again, the traditional description of the Greek moods appears to correspond well with modern categorisations of the types of meanings which are expressed cross-linguistically by modal forms.

The meanings of the moods are generally divided into two categories. For example, Chantraine (§306, §314) argues that the subjunctive has 'deux valeurs de volonté et d'éventualité', while the optative either means 'souhait' or 'possibilité'. Monro (§315)

---

[8] See Benveniste 1951: 16; Hahn: §8; Whitney 1892: 294; Monro: §317c; Shields 1988: 552.

calls the two types the 'quasi-imperative' and the 'quasi-future'. Examples of the first type are found in the 'jussive' subjunctive and the 'wish' optative, and examples of the second type in their 'possible' and 'potential' meanings. For example:

2.140 φεύγωμεν σὺν νηυσὶ φίλην ἐς πατρίδα γαῖαν,

Let's leave on our boats to our dear fatherland,

6.464 ἀλλά με τεθνηῶτα χυτὴ κατὰ γαῖα καλύπτοι,
πρίν γ' ἔτι σῆς τε βοῆς σοῦ θ' ἑλκηθμοῖο πυθέσθαι.

Let the earth pour down and hide my dead body before I hear your cries as you're dragged away!

1.184 τὴν μὲν ἐγὼ σὺν νηΐ τ' ἐμῆι καὶ ἐμοῖς ἑτάροισι
πέμψω· ἐγὼ δέ κ' ἄγω Βρισηΐδα καλλιπάρηον
αὐτὸς ἰὼν κλισίηνδε,

Her I'll send back in my own ship, and with my own crew. But I'll take the beautiful Briseis myself, going to your tent,

4.93 ἦ ῥά νύ μοί τι πίθοιο, Λυκάονος υἱὲ δαΐφρον;
τλαίης κεν Μενελάωι ἔπι προέμεν ταχὺν ἰόν;
πᾶσι δέ κε Τρώεσσι χάριν καὶ κῦδος ἄροιο,

Would you obey me, glorious son of Lycaon? Would you dare to shoot off an arrow at Menelaus? Then you would win glory and fame in the eyes of all the Trojans,

These two types appear to correspond to those described by Jespersen (1924: 320–1) in his early account of modality, where he divided modal forms into those with an element of will, and those without.[9] These types have subsequently been named 'deontic' and 'epistemic'. In his classic work on the subject, Lyons (1977: 681–2, 793) defines the two types as follows: 'Epistemic modality is concerned with matters of knowledge, belief'; 'Deontic modality . . . is concerned with the necessity or probability of acts performed by morally responsible agents.'

The two types of modality have many features in common. Both 'domains' are differentiated according to the same scalar axis of

---

[9] Even earlier, grammarians in the Universal Grammar, initiated by Lancelot, Nicole and Arnauld of Port-Royal had also divided up different 'verbal moods' (subjunctive, optative, concessive and imperative) into those expressing assertion (subjunctive) and those expressing will (the rest). (See Leclerc 2001: 70.)

possibility and necessity (BPP: 195; Coates 1995: 55). A distinction between strong obligation and weak obligation in the deontic domain (e.g. 'You must go now,' 'You may come in') corresponds to probability and possibility in the epistemic domain (e.g. 'It must be ready by now,' 'She may be in the office'). In many languages both domains are expressed by the same form.[10] Palmer (1986: 19) gives the following sentences as examples of this polyfunctionality of modal markers in English. All of them may be interpreted epistemically (the first gloss) or deontically (the second):

4 He may come tomorrow   = Perhaps he will/He is permitted
5 The book should be on the shelf = It probably is/Its proper place is
6 He must be in his office   = He certainly is/He is obliged to be

The fact that the distinction is often not formally marked, along with the other parallelisms between the two types, led Lyons (1977: 817) to question the need for two separate sub-systems. From a semantic point of view, however, the two functions of deontic and epistemic modality are quite distinct, and this semantic distinction often has some formal expression, even in languages which elsewhere in the system mark the two different functions with the same form (Coates 1983: 10; Palmer 1995). The following table shows how the English modal verbs interact with negation:

	Epistemic	Deontic
Necessary	John must be in his office	Mary must come tomorrow
Necessary not	John can't be in his office	Mary mustn't come tomorrow
Not necessary	John may not be in his office	Mary needn't come tomorrow

The modal verb is ambiguous in meaning only in the positive sentences. In the negative expressions, the two meanings are disambiguated and marked with different verbs. Palmer claims that another way of marking the different domains may be seen in modern Greek (Palmer[2]: 87, 92, 103). In both domains the same verb (μπορώ) is used to express possibility, but in the epistemic sense an impersonal form is found (sentence 7), while in the deontic sense the verb agrees with the subject (sentence 8):

---

[10] See Palmer[2]: 87. See also BPP: 195 and Lyons 1977.

7 μπορεί   να   είναι   στο   γραφείο   τους

bori	na	ine	sto	ɣrafío	tus
μπορώ+3SG+IMPFV	that	they.are	in.the	office	theirs

'They may be in their office'

8 τα   παιδιά   μπορούν   να   φύγουν   αύριο

ta	peðjá	borún		na	fíxun	ávrio
the	children	μπορώ+3PL+PRES+IMPFV		that	leave	tomorrow

'The children may leave tomorrow'

It has been argued that the two different senses are formally distinguished in ancient Greek too. For example, Chantraine (§306) claims that the 'subjonctif d'éventualité' is negated by οὐ and is accompanied by the 'modal particle' κε/ἄν, whereas the 'subjonctif de volonté' is negated with μή and is not accompanied by the modal particle, and the optative is meant to have parallel behaviour. Monro (§299 and §300) similarly distinguishes between the different meanings of the optative according to the presence or absence of the modal particle. However, the claim is not consistently confirmed by the data. There are several examples with the 'wrong' marking: the epistemic use of the subjunctive and optative without the particle, and the optative in wishes with a particle. For instance:

    Epistemic subjunctive, no particle:

1.262   οὐ γάρ πω τοίους ἴδον ἀνέρας, οὐδὲ ἴδωμαι

I have never seen such men, and I never will

Epistemic optative, no particle:

4.18   εἰ δ' αὖ πως τόδε πᾶσι φίλον καὶ ἡδὺ γένοιτο,
       ἤτοι μὲν οἰκέοιτο πόλις Πριάμοιο ἄνακτος,
       αὖτις δ' Ἀργείην Ἑλένην Μενέλαος ἄγοιτο.

If everyone thought this was a good idea, Priam's city might remain inhabited, and Menelaus might take the Argive Helen back home.

'Wish' optative with particle:

6.282   . . . ὥς κέ οἱ αὖθι
       γαῖα χάνοι

May the earth gape open and swallow him

Of course, commentators have tried to excuse these apparent anomalies. For example, at 6.282, Leaf argues that we should change κε to δέ, following Bekker's suggestion (Leaf ad loc.). But it seems rather unwise to change the text to fit a particular theory rather than considering that the theory might be mistaken. There are even some examples where sentences with apparently similar meaning are found first without a particle, and then with one:

14.191   ἦ ῥά νύ μοί τι <u>πίθοιο</u>, φίλον τέκος, ὅττί κεν εἴπω,
          ἦέ κεν <u>ἀρνήσαιο</u>, κοτεσσαμένη τό γε θυμῶι,

Would you listen, child, to what I will say? Or would you refuse, angry in your heart,

The inconsistency of the distribution of the particle has led me to ignore it in this study as a distinguishing factor for the analysis of particular lines. In appendix 1 this decision will be further justified and a different account of the 'meaning' of both particles and negators will be offered. At this stage it suffices to say that, regardless of whether the distinction is formally marked, many previous accounts of the Homeric Greek moods have distinguished between two different meanings of the moods. Significantly, this distinction appears to correspond to a division that is seen as fundamental in modal systems cross-linguistically, so that just as with the relationship between the moods, the meanings of the Greek moods may easily be described in modern terms.

2.2.4 Summary

Traditional accounts of the Greek moods were formulated long before modern descriptions of the field of modality. But the beliefs of these traditional accounts may easily be stated in modern terms. The perceived relationship between the moods may be represented by an irrealis continuum: the optative more irrealis than the subjunctive, which is more irrealis than the indicative. The two meanings of the moods distinguished in traditional accounts appear to correspond well with the deontic and epistemic types described in modern theoretical studies. These two aspects of the traditional understandings of the Greek moods may be summed up by the following table:

	Deontic	Epistemic
Less remote	Subjunctive *Want*	Subjunctive *Likely*
More remote	Optative *Wish*	Optative *Unlikely*

Figure 2.2 Meanings of the moods and their interrelationship in traditional accounts

2.3 Recent advances

2.3.1 Introduction

The ease with which the traditional accounts may be restated in modern terms appears to confirm both the traditional accounts and the standard view of modality as described in the previous section. However, in the following chapters close analysis of the data will demonstrate that the traditional accounts are mistaken in significant respects. Given recent theoretical study into language systems in general and the field of modality in particular this is in fact entirely unsurprising. In this section I will describe some of the conclusions from these recent studies, showing that the diagrams presented above and the meanings assigned to the moods are theoretically implausible.

2.3.2 Grammaticalisation

The models of the domain of modality and of the meanings of the ancient Greek moods as drawn up in the previous section are neat, with distinctions between deontic and epistemic meanings, and the level of 'remoteness' that each form will express. Underlying these models is the assumption that language is essentially *structural*: that grammatical domains may be defined, delimited and divided, and that each individual marker in the system gains its meaning through opposition with the other markers (Bybee 1988b; BPP: 1). But the study of grammaticalisation (or 'grammaticisation') has revealed that this description of grammatical markers in terms of oppositions is at best unhelpful, and that language is messier than this mode of description would suggest. This theory, as elaborated in, for example, Bybee 1998b, Traugott and Heine 1991 and Hopper and Traugott 1993, has shown that all grammatical markers gradually develop and accumulate new meanings. Since grammatical markers tend to evolve out of lexical markers, they often retain some of their earlier meaning. A form which expresses one particular grammatical meaning will not therefore necessarily have the same range of meanings and uses as a 'comparable' form in other languages (Bybee 1988a: 362 ff.). The theory of grammaticalisation therefore emphasises the role of language change over language structure.

Of course, a diachronic approach to the description of Homeric Greek is hardly unusual. After all, grammars of Homeric Greek always assume a knowledge of the later Attic Greek dialect, and much work specifically on the moods is just as concerned with their 'origin' as their meaning in Greek. However, a new explanation is certainly required in this area: while the synchronic descriptions of the different uses of the Greek moods and their meanings are reasonably consistent, diachronic explanations are very varied.

Most early scholars attempted to find which of the two main meanings (deontic or epistemic) was the most 'primitive'. For example, Delbrück (1871: 13, 24–5, 27–30) claimed that the original modal meaning was 'will' or 'wish', and that the future or potential meanings were somehow secondary, while Goodwin (§372) was the first to offer the opposite explanation (Hahn: §6). Other scholars argued that it was pointless trying to find such an original meaning of the moods since there were good reasons to suggest that *both* meanings were original (Schwyzer and Debrunner: 320; Slotty 1915: §5; Kühner and Gerth ii: 201). Three more recent monographs on the Greek moods have suggested rather more radical approaches. Hahn (*passim*) has claimed that the subjunctive and optative were both originally future forms, while both Gonda (62 and *passim*) and Lightfoot (1975: 12 and *passim*) have claimed that each mood has an 'essential character' which links both the 'deontic' and the 'epistemic' uses.

The theory of grammaticalisation suggests that this last way of explaining the different meanings of the moods is misguided. In order to understand the problems of assigning an 'essential use' to a form we may compare recent analyses of English 'will'. The main use of this marker is to predict what will happen in the future, and it is therefore generally described as the marker of 'future tense' in English (Bybee 1988a: 362). For example:

9 It will rain tomorrow.

But 'will' also has various other uses which have no simple reference to future time, such as in predictions about the present and in commands.[11] For example:

10 That will be the milkman.
11 You will get your homework done now!

In a structuralist approach, the use of 'will' in these constructions would be explained by distilling the abstract meaning which connects all of its uses, just as Lightfoot and Gonda wish to distil the essential character of the subjunctive and optative in Greek. For example, Ultan (1978: 105) claims that the underlying factor is the inherent 'modality' and 'uncertainty' of future tenses: 'The reason for the preponderance of modal applications of future tenses must lie in the fact that most modal categories refer to differing degrees of uncertainty, which correlates with the element of uncertainty inherent in any future event, while past tenses generally refer to completed, hence certain, events.'[12] Bybee (1988a: 364) has shown that future markers in general certainly tend to develop a variety of modal meanings, for example desire, intention, obligation, necessity, habituality, general truth, characteristic behaviour, imperative, optative, hortative and supposition. But proponents of grammaticalisation have shown that it is not sufficient to explain this phenomenon by the 'modal' nature of all the meanings (Bybee 1988a: 362ff.). Such an explanation does not clarify why it is that

[11] See Fries 1927; Aijmer 1985; Bybee 1988a: 362ff; Enç 1996; Gilbert 2001. See also Gonda: 9 with references to further literature from Indo-European scholars. For a similar range of meanings for a future marker see Heine 1995b on German 'werden'.

[12] See also Fries 1927; Chung and Timberlake 1985; Dahl 1985.

particular future markers only develop *particular* modal meanings. A better understanding of the marker in question will be gained by a thorough consideration of each particular meaning and the path along which it developed. In this case, the origin of the future marker from a verb marking the desire of the subject appears to have constrained its development and distribution (BPP: 256).

It could be argued that this theory will not be relevant for a study of the Homeric Greek moods, since the actual historical processes which resulted in the attested subjunctive and optative forms are not available to us. Descriptions of the etymological origin of the subjunctive do not suggest a lexical origin for the morphological elements which characterise the mood. And although various lexical origins have been suggested for the optative, they are necessarily speculative.[13] But the theory of grammaticalisation is useful even in the description of forms whose lexical origins are unclear, since it reveals the fruitlessness of explaining all the different meanings of a form in terms of one essential meaning.

The theory also offers principles on which a diachronic study of a language may be based so that it will have more useful conclusions than the earlier studies of Greek which merely considered (and disagreed on) which meaning was more primary. Firstly, it has shown that the nature of the construction in which a grammatical form is crucial in assessing the development of any meaning. As an illustration of this principle we may consider the common case of past tenses developing an 'irrealis' meaning, seen in the following English sentences, quoted in Bybee (1995: 503):

12 If you *had* that job lined up, *would* Fulbright then pay up?
13 I think it unlikely actually, but he *might* do it today.

In the first, the past tense alone appears to mark counterfactual meaning, and in the second, the past tense of the modal verb apparently increases the 'remoteness' of the modality. The English past tense thus appears to have a 'modal' meaning, a meaning

---

[13] Rix (1986: 5) details the claims made by Bopp that the optative suffix should be connected to a root *ī- meaning 'wish, beg'. On the more widely accepted, if still speculative, theory that the suffix developed from a verb of motion, see Hahn: §88 with references to the relevant literature.

recognised for many past tenses cross-linguistically. This was previously explained as due to the greater 'remoteness' of past tenses compared with present tenses, for example in Joos 1964; Steele 1975; James 1982; and also Lightfoot 1975: 130. However, Dahl (1997: 99) and Bybee (1995: 513) have shown that we may not attribute the development merely to the meaning of the past tense. Past tenses do not generally indicate the hypothetical meaning on their own, but only in particular constructions or syntactic environments, for example in the conditional protasis or with modal verbs. The existence of these constraints may be seen from the ill-formedness of the following sentences where the past tense is used outside these constructions/environments:

14 *If I were younger, I *studied* Classical Greek.
15 *I think it unlikely actually, but he *did* it today.

It is therefore clear that it is of crucial importance to examine the role of the construction in which certain meanings have developed. This principle will be particularly useful in the description of the Homeric Greek moods in subordinate clauses. It will be shown in chapter 6 that these will be better understood by considering the development and meaning of the particular types of subordinate clause rather than formulating a synchronic grammatical rule for all the meanings of the mood.

Another observation made in studies based on the theory of grammaticalisation that will be useful for this study is that grammatical meaning often originates in the conventionalisation of conversational implicature.[14] It is in this way that Traugott and Dasher (2002: 36ff.) account for the conditional meaning of the English phrase 'as long as'. In Old and Middle English, the phrase had a spatial or temporal meaning, although the temporal use often also implied a conditional sense. For example, the following sentence is found in a text dated AD 850–950 (for full references for this and the following examples, see Traugott and Dasher 2002: 36–7):

---

[14] See Comrie 1985: 23–6 for a discussion of the difference between meaning and implicature, with references to previous literature. For conventionalisation of implicature see Traugott 1989: 50ff. She claims the concept first originated in Geis and Zwicky 1971. Also see Heine 1995b: 126; Gordon and Lakoff 1975; Crystal 1985: s.v. 'implicature'; Lyons 1977: chapter 14; Risselada 1993: 93.

16 wring þurh   linnene claδ on þæt eage *swa lange swa* him
    wring through linen   cloth on that eye as   long   as   him

    δearf sy.
    need be-SUBJ
    'squeeze (the medication) through a linen cloth onto the eye as long
    as he needs'.

This sentence could be read purely temporally, but also implies
that the medication should only be put on *if* the patient needs it.
Over time, it became more and more usual for this implication to be
associated with this construction, until, in Early Modern English
(1614), the conditional meaning is often more predominant than
the temporal meaning. For example:

17 They whose words doe most shew forth their wise vnderstanding,
    and whose lips doe vtter the purest knowledge, so *as long as* they
    vnderstand and speake as men, are they not faine sundry waies to
    excuse themselues.

Finally, by the mid-nineteenth century (1865), the conditional
meaning may occur without any temporal implications:

18 'Would you tell me, please, which way I ought to go from here?'
    'That depends a good deal on where you want to get to,' said the Cat.
    'I don't much care where-' said Alice.
    'Then it doesn't matter which way you go,' said the Cat.
    '- *so long as* I get *somewhere*,' Alice added as an explanation.

It will be argued in section 4.3 that the hortative subjunctive has
developed by a similar process of 'conventionalisation'.

The theory of grammaticalisation thus suggests that the table of
meanings expressed by the moods presented in the previous section will only be useful (if at all) from a synchronic point of view,
and that it ignores the links which hold between the various different meanings expressed by the moods. The theory also provides a
principled basis on which to consider the data again. Rather than
trying to find an abstract meaning which links together the different
uses of a particular grammatical form, the different uses should be
seen as different stages along a path of development. The particular
nature of that path will be constrained by the types of construction in which the form is found, and will also be affected by the
implicatures associated with the different meanings.

26

2.3.3 Modality studies

Recent studies in modality also call into question the claims of the grammarians with regards to the meaning of the moods. While the two types of meaning assigned by traditional grammarians to the ancient Greek moods appear to correspond well to the two 'fundamental' types of modality as defined in the standard textbook on the subject, a closer look at the constructions will reveal that this is not the case. Neither the 'deontic' nor the 'epistemic' types correspond to the definitions given.

We may first take the 'deontic' uses of the moods. The three constructions in which the subjunctive and optative are said to have deontic meaning are the hortative, prohibitive and wish constructions. For example:

2.236   οἴκαδέ περ σὺν νηυσὶ νεώμεθα

Let's sail off for home in our ships

24.779   ἄξετε νῦν, Τρῶες, ξύλα ἄστυδε, μηδέ τι θυμῶι
δείσητ᾽ Ἀργείων πυκινὸν λόχον·

Men of Troy, bring the wood into the city, and have no fear of a heavy ambush from the Argives.

2.417   πολέες δ᾽ ἀμφ᾽ αὐτὸν ἑταῖροι
πρηνέες ἐν κονίηισιν ὀδὰξ λαζοίατο γαῖαν.

and may many comrades fall head-first round him in the dust and gnaw the earth.

In these uses the moods are explicitly compared with the imperative: the subjunctive is said to replace the imperative (Goodwin: §8; Chantraine: §306), while the optative is said to be a 'weaker version' of the imperative (Goodwin: §12). Since the imperative is said to be the unmarked member of the deontic domain (Palmer[1]: 29), this apparently confirms the deontic nature of the constructions.

It certainly appears reasonable to describe the imperative and imperative-like constructions such as those seen above as deontic. After all, they all clearly express the will of the speaker, the main criterion behind the deontic categorisation (Jespersen 1924: 320–1; Palmer[1]: 10–18). And if we consider the following list of the features of prototypical deontic modality (as recently set out in Heine 1995a), many more reasons for the categorisation are apparent:

a. There is some force that is characterised by an 'element of will', i.e., that has an interest in an event either occurring or not occurring.
b. The event is to be performed typically by a controlling agent.
c. The event is dynamic, i.e., it involves the manipulation of a situation and is conceived of typically as leading to a change of state.
d. The event has not yet taken place at the reference time, i.e., its occurrence, if it does in fact take place, will be later than the reference time.
e. The event is non-factual, though there is a certain degree of probability that it will occur.

These features of deontic modality are all found in sentences with an imperative. For example, by uttering the sentence 'Ring me in an hour,' the speaker imposes his will on the hearer, who is to be the agent of a dynamic event. The event (ringing) has not happened yet, and if it does happen, it will be later than the moment of speaking. The occurrence of the event is not certain, but there is a certain degree of probability that it will occur.

But the description of these imperative-like constructions as deontic obscures the fact that their status is different from that of the deontic statements used to exemplify the different types of modality in section 2.2.3. They are all 'performative' utterances: they are not types of statements at all, asserting that a state of affairs is true, necessary or possible, but are 'doing' rather different things (Austin 1962: 6). With the hortative subjunctive the speaker exhorts the listener, with the prohibitive subjunctive the speaker forbids the listener, while with the optative the speaker makes a wish.

The status of these performative utterances within the domain of modality is rather problematic. After all, the definition of 'irrealis' as used above explicitly linked modal forms with assertions: 'the proposition is weakly asserted as either possible, likely or uncertain . . . or necessary, desired or undesired' (Givón 1994: 268). This suggests that we should not consider imperative-like constructions as truly 'modal' at all. Indeed, this is the approach of van der Auwera and Plungian (1998: 83), who dismiss them as 'illocutionary types' (see also Kiefer 1993: 2515). If we followed this approach, the performative uses of the Greek moods would not be discussed in a study of modality, but would only be included in a more 'pragmatic' description of how particular forms are used. But the approach is unsatisfactory, since it fails to acknowledge the strong links between deontic modality and imperative-like constructions as outlined above, as well as the links between these meanings and other modal meanings. These particular links are highlighted by the Greek evidence, where the same form is used with both speaker-oriented and other meanings. Even in English, where modal verbs are formally quite different from imperative verbs, it has been shown that illocutionary force plays an important part in differentiating the meanings expressed by the moods. Since Lyons (1977: 797), the meanings of modal verbs have been divided, not only into deontic and epistemic types, but also into subjective and objective types (see also Kiefer 1993: 2517). These types may be exemplified by the following sentences:

19 Subjective: You must do your homework now.
20 Objective: Sally must be more polite to her mother.

Verstraete (2001: 1517) has shown that the only difference between the subjective and objective examples is their illocutionary force. While sentence 19 has the illocutionary force of a directive (Searle 1979: 147), sentence 20 has the illocutionary force of an assertion. Sweetser (1990: 65–8) similarly describes the difference between subjective and objective modality as the difference between performative and constative utterances. We must therefore conclude that an 'axis' of illocutionary force has some relevance for the field of modality, so that it seems quite unjustified to follow van der Auwera and Plungian and omit the more clearly illocutionary expressions, such as sentences with the imperative, from a study of modality. BPP include these types in their model of modality, terming them 'speaker-oriented' (BPP: 179, see also Foley and van Valin 1984: 213). The reason that this model has not been more widely adopted is perhaps because of the problems that it causes for an analysis of the English data, imposing a different interpretation of two uses of the same forms, namely the subjective (= speaker-oriented) and objective uses of the deontic modal verbs that we saw exemplified in sentences 19 and 20 above. But the simple fact that it makes the analysis of English seem more complicated than the traditional approach is no reason to abandon the model – certainly it makes more sense in the case of the Homeric Greek moods.

The conclusion that the hortative, prohibitive and wish meanings of the moods in Homeric Greek are speaker-oriented rather than deontic is not only a question of terminology: it also has an important consequence for the diachronic analysis of these forms. It has frequently been shown that epistemic modal forms develop from deontic modal forms, and not the other way round.[15] If the Greek constructions under consideration here were truly deontic, then the meanings of the moods in these constructions would most likely be the original meanings. But speaker-oriented modality, on the other hand, develops from various different grammatical types. For example, it is cross-linguistically common for future markers to develop a directive use.[16] Indeed, I will argue in 4.3 that this is just how the hortative meaning of the subjunctive arose.

The claim that the Homeric Greek moods express epistemic meaning is similarly questionable. In the examples given above of the epistemic meaning of the moods, the moods are found in main clauses:

1.184   τὴν μὲν ἐγὼ σὺν νηΐ τ᾽ ἐμῆι καὶ ἐμοῖς ἑτάροισι
πέμψω· ἐγὼ δέ κ᾽ <u>ἄγω</u> Βρισηΐδα καλλιπάρηον
αὐτὸς ἰὼν κλισίηνδε,

Her I'll send back in my own ship, and with my own crew. But I'll take the beautiful Briseis myself, going to your tent,

4.93   ἦ ῥά νύ μοί τι πίθοιο, Λυκάονος υἱὲ δαΐφρον;
τλαίης κεν Μενελάωι ἔπι προέμεν ταχὺν ἰόν;
πᾶσι δέ κε Τρώεσσι χάριν καὶ κῦδος <u>ἄροιο,</u>

Would you obey me, glorious son of Lycaon? Would you dare to shoot off an arrow at Menelaus? Then you would win glory and fame in the eyes of all the Trojans,

---

[15] See Bybee and Pagliuca 1985; Traugott 1989, 1990; Sweetser 1990; BPP: 194ff.; Traugott and Dasher 2002: 118ff.

[16] See BPP: 273; Ultan 1978: 103; Fleischman 1982: 129; Heine 1995b: 120.

However, this is not the usual context for this meaning; certainly the relationship between this meaning of the two moods is clearest in conditional sentences. For example:

3.289   εἰ δ' ἂν ἐμοὶ τιμὴν Πρίαμος Πριάμοιό τε παῖδες
        τίνειν οὐκ ἐθέλωσιν Ἀλεξάνδροιο πεσόντος,
        αὐτὰρ ἐγὼ καὶ ἔπειτα μαχήσομαι εἵνεκα ποινῆς

But if Priam and Priam's sons refuse to pay once Alexander has fallen, then I myself will fight it out for the ransom

1.255   ἦ κεν γηθήσαι Πρίαμος Πριάμοιό τε παῖδες,
        ἄλλοί τε Τρῶες μέγα κεν κεχαροίατο θυμῶι,
        εἰ σφῶϊν τάδε πάντα πυθοίατο μαρναμένοιιν,

Priam and Priam's sons and all the Trojans would exult and rejoice in their hearts, if they heard the two of you battling like this,

The meaning of both subjunctive and optative in these contexts, and the relationship between the two moods will be considered in more detail in their respective chapters. For now, however, we must ascertain whether this is truly 'epistemic' modality, as defined in the grammar-books. The moods here appear to be expressing the belief of the speakers about events, and are in that sense epistemic rather than deontic. However, they do not fully correspond to the category as traditionally defined. Certainly, in this context the subjunctive is not directly comparable to 'may' and the optative to 'might', the two core markers of epistemic modality in English. Rather, the subjunctive is translated by the present tense, and the optative by 'would'. Whatever the translational equivalence, the preponderance of this kind of meaning in conditional clauses is also problematic. The status of conditional modality within the domain of modality is uncertain. Jespersen (1924: 320–1) includes conditionals under the uses of moods which 'contain no element of will', thus appearing to equate the modality with what is later known as epistemic modality, but then states that this categorisation is 'open to doubt' (Palmer 1986: 12). Modern theoreticians are similarly vague: while Givón (1994: 289) describes the moods found in conditional sentences on an 'epistemic scale', and Bybee, Pagliuca and Perkins (1994: 209) note that the forms used in conditional clauses generally *also* have epistemic meaning, van der Auwera and Plungian (1998: 91) consider the conditional a 'post-modal meaning'. Chung and Timberlake (1985: 250ff.) describe conditional modality separately from the deontic and epistemic 'modes', while Kiefer (1993) ignores conditional sentences entirely in his description of modality. The most explicit claim that conditional modality is somehow different may be found in Palmer (1986: 212): 'Modality in conditional clauses tends to be *sui generis* – the use of forms is not directly related to the use of other types of clauses at least in IE languages.'

It thus seems that conditional modality should be considered separately from the types traditionally distinguished for main clauses, although there is no consensus on its exact status or its relationship to the other types. In my analysis of conditional sentences to be found in the indicative and optative chapters, I will also argue that the moods express something different, which I will term the 'epistemic stance' of the speaker. This term was first introduced to describe different types of English conditional sentences (Fillmore 1990), but has also been applied to the use of moods in German (Mortelmans 2000).

I believe that the reason that the status of this type of modality has not been agreed upon stems from the bias in modality studies to considering English, where modality is primarily expressed by modal verbs. It is thus the types of modality expressed by modal verbs which have received most attention. In conditional clauses, however, modality is not expressed by modal verbs in English – here distinctions are made through use of tense. It is significant that Mortelmans uses the term 'epistemic stance' in order to describe moods in German, a language where both moods and modal verbs are used to express modality. Previously, moods and modal verbs have not been clearly distinguished in general studies of modality: for example, Palmer (2000: 4) claims that they are both simply means to 'deal grammatically with an overall category of modality'. This contrasts significantly with studies of German, where the two topics are treated separately ('as if they did not have anything in common' Mortelmans 2000: 191). The evidence from Homeric Greek suggests again that moods should not be analysed in the same way as modal verbs. Given that the categories of deontic and epistemic modality have largely been defined in terms of the uses of modal verbs in English, it is entirely unsurprising that the ancient Greek data do not correspond.

Findings from modern studies in modality also call into question the claim that the Homeric Greek moods express only two meanings. The claim was particularly credible when those two types were associated with the deontic and epistemic types of modality. This is said to be the fundamental distinction in modality, so if a language expresses two different types, we would expect it to express just these two types. However, now that the description of the two types as deontic and epistemic respectively has been questioned, we may also question the belief that the moods only express those two meanings. After all, in many languages many other types are distinguished. Even in English, where the deontic/epistemic contrast is clear, modal verbs are said also to express dynamic modality, expressing the ability of the subject (Palmer[2]: 9; see also Kiefer 1993: 2517). In this book I will argue that the subjunctive expresses deontic modality in addition to the speaker-oriented and conditional meanings that are described in the grammar-books (4.3.3), and that the optative also expresses objective deontic and dynamic meaning (5.5).

Modern studies not only challenge the number and correct definition of the types of modality that are expressed by the moods in Homeric Greek, but also the way in which these meanings are related. The tables used in section 2.2 suggest neatly delimited different meanings. But, just as the study of grammaticalisation has concluded for language systems in general, so analyses of modal systems have suggested that the different meanings may not so easily be pigeon-holed. For example, in her study of the semantics of the modal auxiliaries in English, Coates (1983: 10) has argued that while there are discrete distinctions between certain types of modality, the different categories are indeterminate. She therefore adopts an approach from 'fuzzy set theory' to describe her data. According to this theory, membership of a particular category may be defined by the possession of a certain set of characteristics. However, all examples of the category will not necessarily display all the characteristics. Rather, there will be certain examples which are closer to the 'core' of the category than others. Van der Auwera and Plungian and BPP have come to similar conclusions about the relationship of the different modal meanings, observing that modal forms tend to express more than one meaning, and that these meanings are generally connected on a diachronic pathway.[17]

The nebulous nature of the domain may perhaps most clearly be seen in relation to speaker-oriented modality, since in this sub-domain it is even difficult to determine what should be described as a separate 'meaning' and what should not. To make this point clear, we may consider the statement 'It's cold in here.' This may in certain circumstances have a meaning 'equivalent' to a directive ('Close the window'), for example if it was spoken by a duke to his butler (Gordon and Lakoff 1975: 83; Cole 1975: 260). This 'directive' meaning may of course be explained in terms of Grice's co-operative principle: in this case the principle of relevance (Grice 1975: 46–7). But the question is whether this kind of sentence should be described as 'modal'. At first glance the answer would appear to be simple: this kind of sentence does not need to be described as modal since its illocutionary force is clearly only 'indirect' (Searle 1975). However, it is not always so easy to differentiate between indirect and direct illocutionary force, as we may see by considering the English 'let's go' construction. It is often claimed that this construction is used as the first person imperative, which would suggest that it has direct illocutionary force (Quirk et al. 1985: 404). However, it has been shown that the construction only developed its hortative meaning gradually (Hopper and Traugott 1993: 10–14). The 'invitation' meaning was originally only a 'conversational implicature' found alongside its literal sense of a request for permission, which was then gradually more frequently associated with the expression, until it was seen as part of its true meaning, or 'conventionalised' in a similar process to that undergone by the phrase 'as long as' (see 2.3.2). The distinction between an 'indirect' imperative construction and a 'true' imperative construction is therefore only gradual, and the choice of how best to describe a particular construction will be rather subjective (Risselada 1993: 95; Bolkestein 1980: chapter 5). We will meet this particular difficulty again in the description of the hortative construction (see 4.3).

[17] See van der Auwera and Plungian 1998: *passim*; BPP: chapter 6.

2.4 Conclusions

In this chapter I have summarised the traditional understanding of the moods, and also described findings from recent studies which inform the theoretical basis for this new study. I have shown that the traditional descriptions of the Greek moods coincide remarkably well with modern theories about the meanings expressed by modal forms in general. These traditional descriptions as up-dated into modern terminology can be represented by figures 2.1 and 2.2:

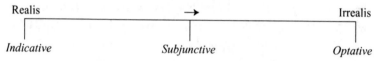

Figure 2.1 Greenberg's irrealis continuum:

	Deontic	Epistemic
Less **remote**	Subjunctive *Want*	Subjunctive *Likely*
More **remote**	Optative *Wish*	Optative *Unlikely*

Figure 2.2 Meanings of the moods and their interrelationship in traditional accounts

But in section 2.3, I have described the findings of studies in grammaticalisation and modality and proposed that these diagrams will be found to be over simplistic. They present an overly structural and abstract definition both of individual forms and of the domain of modality. That is, they have shown that it will be unhelpful and unrealistic to define all the different meanings of, for example, the subjunctive in terms of a particular place on the irrealis continuum. As for the domain, rather than being neatly divisible, it appears to consist of a web of meanings, related to each other along various axes. Modal forms are likely to express more than one of these meanings, though the categorisation of particular examples will not be straightforward.

These studies have also called into question the equation of the different meanings of the ancient Greek moods with the two fundamental types described in the textbooks. I have argued that the so-called deontic constructions express speaker-oriented modality, while the modality found in conditional clauses, although epistemic in some way, does not fully correspond to the category as usually defined.

In the following chapters, the different constructions in which the moods are found will be subjected to close analysis, and an attempt will be made to draw up a more plausible 'map' of the different meanings of the moods and the relationships holding between those meanings. The results of this close analysis will confirm that the traditional accounts have been mistaken, and will show that the real situation is both more messy and more interesting.

3

INDICATIVE

3.1 Introduction

The main focus of this study is to describe the meaning(s) of the subjunctive and optative. However, as noted in chapter 2, both moods are often defined in relation to the indicative: the indicative is positioned at the 'realis' end of the irrealis continuum. An understanding of the meaning of the indicative is therefore necessary for an understanding of all the moods. Of course, if the main aim of this study was a full description of the Homeric indicative, a far more detailed analysis would be possible and desirable. In this study it is only those aspects of the indicative that relate to its modality which will be considered. For this reason, the construction which I have picked to consider is the conditional clause, where all three moods are found, with clearly different meanings. The nature of the different types of conditional clause in which the indicative will be considered, in order to arrive at a successful definition of the mood.

Some difficulties in defining the indicative have already been mentioned in chapter 2 (2.2.2). In some accounts it is described as objective and non-modal. But most modern descriptions accept that it is as subjective as the other moods, and therefore should be included within the domain of modality. The problem which I wish to address here is where it lies within that domain.

The use of the indicative in assertions suggests that it is a 'realis' marker. Lyons observed (1977: 809) that 'there is no epistemically stronger statement than a categorical assertion'. According to Givón's definition (1994: 268), in realis assertions, 'the proposition is strongly asserted to be true'. However, there are other uses of the indicative cross-linguistically which cast doubt on this definition. In main clauses in English, the indicative is found with adverbial modifiers which affect speaker commitment in a similar way to modal verbs ('Tom is possibly singing' cf. 'Tom may be singing'), or which make the assertion stronger ('Tom is certainly singing'). The indicative is also used in conditional sentences, in many languages including English and ancient Greek. The proper description of conditional clauses has provoked centuries of debate.[1] But there is general consensus that neither protasis nor apodosis is asserted, and that speaker commitment is 'suspended' in these contexts (e.g. Dancygier 1988: 14–24; Verstraete 2001: 1520). The use of the indicative in this context therefore also jars with its definition as a realis mood.

These factors lead Palmer to conclude in the first edition of *Mood and Modality* (Palmer[1]: 29) that the indicative is not the epistemically strongest mood, but rather that it is 'epistemically unmarked or neutral, the expression of a proposition with no direct indication of its epistemic status'. Wakker (1994: 36, 112) similarly claims that Greek conditional clauses with an indicative express a 'neutral' value, where the speaker 'gives no indication as to the (chance of) fulfilment of the condition'. However, this definition is rather counter-intuitive, as Palmer himself acknowledges (1986: 86–7), since it implies that declaratives do not strictly assert anything at all. He therefore adds the following rider to his definition: 'it will generally be assumed that the purpose of the presentation is that he [the speaker] thinks it is relevant and probably true'. This 'rider' could be interpreted in pragmatic terms: indeed Grice's co-operative principle (maxim of quality) leads us to assume that the speaker will assert what he believes to be relevant and true (Grice 1975: 46).

A pragmatic explanation of the meaning of the indicative is however rather unsatisfactory. An analysis of the particular nature of the adverbial elements found with the indicative in English suggests

---

[1] For recent linguistic analyses of conditional sentences see the collections of articles in Traugott et al. 1986 and Athanasiadou and Dirven 1997b. On the relation of natural language conditionals to logical studies in particular see e.g. Comrie 1986b: 77; Podlesskaya 2001: 998; Wakker 1994: 24ff., 45, 105–6; Athanasiadou and Dirven 1996: 609, with references to previous works; Athanasiadou and Dirven 1997a: 64–70; Wierzbicka 1997: 20; van der Auwera 1997. On the different types of conditional clause see Athanasiadou and Dirven 1996: 610; Sweetser 1990: 117; Podlesskaya 2001: 1000. For the Functional Grammar perspective see Wakker 1992a; Wakker 1994: 91–2; Cuvalay 1995; Dik 1990.

that the definition 'epistemically neutral' is semantically too weak. While the adverbial elements modify the *degree* of speaker commitment, they never completely contradict a positive attitude to the proposition. They range from weak ('perhaps') through moderate ('probably') to strong commitment ('certainly'). Similar elements indicating a lack of commitment (e.g. 'doubtfully') do not exist, thus rendering the following sentence unacceptable: '*Tom is doubtfully singing'. This would suggest that the positive implication of the indicative is more than just pragmatic. After all, pragmatic meaning should be defeasible, which would mean that sentences like 'Tom is doubtfully singing' should be odd but acceptable. Since the positive meaning appears not to be defeasible from the indicative, it is more attractive to describe it as part of the semantic meaning of the mood. Indeed, Fillmore (1990: 142) has proposed that the indicative expresses the 'positive epistemic stance' of the speaker. Mortelmans (2000: 196) interprets this definition as meaning that, by using the indicative, the speaker assesses the proposition as being 'in line with her view of the world'. My analysis of the indicative in conditional clauses in Homeric Greek will lead me to conclude that the definition of positive epistemic stance is most successful for this language too.

3.2 Analysis

3.2.1 Introduction

I have grouped together the different uses of the indicative in Homeric conditional clauses into three types, which I have named 'realis', 'open' and 'counterfactual' and will analyse examples of these three types below. I will argue that there is no modal difference between the first two types, and that, in both types, the speaker is not epistemically neutral, but has a positive attitude to the event in question.

The use of the indicative in counterfactual sentences is perhaps the most difficult to explain. It refers to an event which did not happen, and therefore appears to express the opposite meaning to that found in main clauses. This use has therefore previously been described as a 'modal extension'. But I will argue that this meaning too can be explained in terms of the positive epistemic stance of the speaker.

3.2.2 Realis

Many of the examples of the indicative in conditional clauses are found in resumptive, obviously realised and concessive conditionals. In these contexts, the commitment of the speaker does not appear to be suspended, contrary to the usual definition of conditional clauses. These could therefore be taken to be the types of conditional clause where a realis indicative was first used, and the other uses could be described as developments from this original meaning. However, I will show that the commitment of the speaker *is* still suspended in these contexts, and that, for modal purposes, they should be considered no differently from the 'open' conditionals to be examined in section 3.2.3.

Comrie (1986b: 79) exemplifies the meaning of resumptive conditionals with the following exchange:

A: I'm leaving now.
B: If you're leaving now, I won't be able to go with you.

This may be glossed 'if what you said is true, and you're really leaving, then I won't be able to go with you'. The indicative thus reintroduces information already available in the linguistic or non-linguistic context and thus appears to be rather 'factual' (Wakker 1994: 126–7). A Homeric example of this type of conditional is found at 1.564:

1.564   εἰ δ' οὕτω τοῦτ' ἐστίν, ἐμοὶ μέλλει φίλον εἶναι.

If it is as you say, then it will be pleasing to me.

The 'factual' nature of the conditional clause is most clear in past time, when a resumptive conditional refers to something that actually happened. For example:

C: It rained last night.
D: Well, if it rained last night, they won't have slept outside.

Sentence D appears to be very close in meaning to the factive 'Since it rained last night, they won't have slept outside,' and the indicative thus appears to be realis in the conditional context too.

However, Wakker (1994: 127) has pointed out that statements that are known to be false by the speaker may also be resumed in this way, e.g. 'If three and four is eight then . . .' Thus the resumptive conditional is more a way of explaining one's reaction to something someone else has previously said, *without* necessarily agreeing that it is true. This may be seen in Comrie's exchange above (A and B), where the speaker is clearly hoping that the protasis will actually turn out to be untrue, so that he would be able to go with them. The Greek example of a resumptive conditional at 1.564 thus has two possible interpretations: perhaps the most natural interpretation is that the speaker accepts what has previously been said, but it could alternatively be used to indicate the doubt of the speaker, and thereby to threaten the interlocutor. In the first interpretation, the conditional clause is very similar to a causal sentence, which does entail the truth of the proposition: 'since what you've said is true, everything will be fine'. But in the latter interpretation, the possibility of the protasis being false must be entertained: '*if* you turn out to be speaking the truth, then all well and good. But if not, woe betide you.' Given that these resumptive conditionals have these two possible interpretations, it would appear that they are not the realis contexts they appear to be at first glance.

The same may be said about resumptive conditionals with past reference, which I described above as the most factual. This can be seen by the possibility of adding an 'attitudinal modifier' like 'really', indicating doubt in the proposition (Wakker 1994: 177–8). For example: 'If it really rained last night, why is the ground not wet?' The same type of attitudinal modifier is found in Homeric Greek indicative conditional clauses. For example:

7.359   εἰ δ' ἐτεὸν δὴ τοῦτον ἀπὸ σπουδῆς ἀγορεύεις,
         ἐξ ἄρα δή τοι ἔπειτα θεοὶ φρένας ὤλεσαν αὐτοί.

If you really say this truthfully, then the gods themselves have destroyed your wits.

O   εἰ ἐτεόν γ' ἐμός ἐσσι καὶ αἵματος ἡμετέροιο,
16.300   μή τις ἔπειτ' Ὀδυσῆος ἀκουσάτω ἔνδον ἐόντος,

If you really are my son, one of our blood, then let no one hear that Odysseus is inside,

Another apparently realis type of conditional clause is described as the obviously realised conditional. Wakker has glossed this type 'if X is true (and it clearly is), then Y is true' (Wakker 1994: 190–1, 233–5). An example of this type of sentence with the indicative in Homeric Greek may be seen in 1.503:

1.503   Ζεῦ πάτερ, εἴ ποτε δή σε μετ' ἀθανάτοισιν ὄνησα
    ἢ ἔπει ἢ ἔργωι, τόδε μοι κρήηνον ἐέλδωρ·
    τίμησόν μοι υἱόν,

Father Zeus! If I ever helped you of all the immortals in word or deed, fulfil me this prayer: honour my son!

The inference is that Chryses (the speaker) *did* help Zeus, and for this reason, Zeus ought to help him in return. This therefore again appears to resemble a factual statement rather than a conditional clause ('Since I kept on helping you before, help me now'). But again, there *is* still a disjunction, and this is *not* equivalent to a causal clause. The use of a conditional clause may be attributed to the rhetorical technique of Chryses: he does not want to appear to be bartering his previous duty for a favour from Zeus, and therefore uses the conditional and not the causal construction as a stylistic choice (cf. Wakker 1994: 234). Of course, because the indicative refers to an event in the past it may in some cases be used to describe events which did actually happen, as in 1.503. It is this type which appears to be most realis. But crucially, there is no difference between this sentence and one where the speaker does not know the truth of the protasis: e.g. 'If I pleased you, grant me this prayer.' In this sentence again, the speaker may imply that he thinks he *has* pleased him, that he has helped him so much that he *ought* to be pleased, but because this no longer refers to his own actions, the speaker may no longer know whether or not it is true. The 'truth-value' of the indicative is thus only implied in this sentence rather than being part of the meaning of the mood (Comrie 1986b: 79).

42

The third type of conditional clause which could be described as a rather realis context is the concessive conditional. Many scholars have claimed that they are not genuine conditionals, because the protasis is implied to be true and the apodosis is therefore entailed (e.g. König 1986: 231). For example:

4.55 εἴ περ γὰρ <u>φθονέω</u> τε καὶ οὐκ <u>εἰῶ</u> διαπέρσαι,
οὐκ ἀνύω φθονέουσ', ἐπεὶ ἦ πολὺ φέρτερός ἐσσι.

Even though I protest, and withold my consent, I won't gain anything in protesting, since you're much greater than me.

The protasis has here been translated as a concessive with 'even though', therefore implying that the protasis is true. This interpretation is supported by the participle φθονέουσ' in 4.56.

There is certainly overlap between concessive conditionals of the type 'even if **p**, then **q**', and concessives 'even though **p, q**'. However, it has been shown that concessive conditionals are genuine conditional sentences which do not necessarily entail either protasis or apodosis, or to put it in terms more relevant for this study, concessive conditionals are not (necessarily) realis contexts.[2] This may be proved by the use of the concessive conditional construction even when the speaker does not know whether the proposition in the protasis is true or not. For example:

21 Even if it rained last night, they'll be OK (I don't know whether or not it rained).
22 Even if he's finished by now, I'll be cross with him (I don't know whether he has).
23 Even if it rains on Saturday, we'll still go walking (I don't know whether it will).

Resumptive, obviously realised and concessive conditionals all appear at first glance to be realis contexts. The use of the indicative in these contexts could thus support the theory that it expresses realis modality. However, a closer examination of these contexts has shown that they are not as realis as they appear, and that the truth of the protasis is not asserted. These three types of conditional sentence should thus be considered no differently from the open conditional sentences below.

[2] See König 1986; Bennett 1982; Bakker 1988a: 206.

3.2.3 *Open*

Open conditional sentences are the 'classic' type of conditional sentence. According to many accounts, in open conditionals the speaker does not know whether the statement in the protasis is 'true' or not, but is just presenting the possibility to the speaker, or is mentioning it as the framework for describing the consequences.[3] Given that the indicative is used in open conditionals in many languages, this definition clearly calls into question the claim that the indicative is realis. If speaker commitment is 'suspended', then a realis marker would be inappropriate. The definition gives great weight to Palmer's view that the indicative is epistemically unmarked.

In English main clauses, it has been argued that this definition of the indicative is unsuccessful, because it does not explain the restriction of the indicative to epistemically positive statements. And it is my argument that the same holds true in conditional sentences: both linguistically and pragmatically speaking, I would argue that it is *not* the purpose of conditionals merely to present a proposition with no indication of the speaker's attitude towards it. This may be illustrated by the following example in Homeric Greek:

2.357   εἰ δέ τις ἐκπάγλως ἐθέλει οἴκόνδε νέεσθαι,
         ἁπτέσθω ἧς νηὸς ἐϋσσέλμοιο μελαίνης,

If anyone wants to go home, let him put his hand on his black well-benched ship,

Here the speaker only mentions the possibility of somebody wanting to leave because he thinks it is a *real* possibility. If we accept this explanation of open conditional sentences, the indicative in open (and so-called realis) conditionals may thus also be explained as expressing the positive epistemic stance of the speaker rather than the 'neutrality' of the speaker: 'if **p**, **q**' should therefore be glossed 'if **p** (and I'm reasonably sure that **p** is a possibility), then **q**'.

The same claim has been made in the 'Antecedent Possibility Theorem' of van der Auwera (1983). Unlike the traditional

---

[3] See Smyth: §2298; Comrie 1986b: 79; Wakker 1994: 32; Dik 1990; Dancygier 1998: 14; Tynan and Lavin 1997: 116; Podlesskaya 2001: 998–9.

account, which claims that speaker-assertion is suspended in this context, van der Auwera (1983: 298) claims that conditionals assert that **p** is possible. He supports this claim with three arguments. The first is intuitive: it makes sense that when somebody is speculating on the consequences of an event he accepts that the event might possibly happen. This intuition is accepted in several philosophical formulations of the meaning of conditional sentences.[4] The second reason is linguistic: many conditional sentences are introduced by a word marking possibility (Traugott 1985: 291). Thirdly, many languages include a modal particle indicating possibility in the conditional protasis – for example in Dutch the particle 'misschien' is often found (van der Auwera 1983: 300).

It might be argued that the 'untrue' resumptive type 'if three and four is eight . . .' considered above (p. 41) contradicts this claim. After all, here the indicative is used in a situation where the speaker knows the proposition to be false. But again, if we consider the pragmatic use of this kind of sentence we may see that the definition may stand. This kind of sentence is used to show the implausibility of another person's arguments. In order to do this, the speaker points out some ridiculous consequence of the speaker's beliefs, by taking the speaker's beliefs as his own. Even if done only sarcastically, the speaker adopts a positive epistemic stance towards the proposition for the sake of speculation.

It follows from this argument that I do not accept the generally proposed description of conditional clauses. If the indicative is a marker of positive epistemic stance it must mean that speaker commitment is *not* in fact suspended in this context. This analysis is supported, if not recognised, in modern accounts of conditional clauses. Amid all the debates about their proper interpretation, a consistent claim is that they may be divided into different types according to the different level of probability the speaker attaches to the utterance.[5] Future-referring conditionals are therefore divided into 'real' and 'unreal' types, as exemplified by the following English examples:

---

[4] See e.g. Ramsey, Stalnaker, Mackie, quoted in van der Auwera 1983: 299.
[5] See, e.g. Comrie 1986b: 88 ff.; Podlesskaya 2001: 998; Greenberg 1986; Harris 1986: 266.

24 If Tom gets home in time, I'll take him to the station.
25 If I won the lottery, I'd go abroad (or 'If I were to win . . .').

In 'real' conditionals, as exemplified by sentence 24, it is said that
the event described in the protasis is viewed as being possible:
it is a real possibility that such an event will happen. In 'unreal'
conditionals on the other hand, like sentence 25, rather less likely
possibilities are said to be entertained, in order to speculate on what
might happen. I will consider the meaning of 'unreal' conditionals
further in chapter 5. For now it will suffice to note that the two
types of conditional clause differ in epistemic terms. It therefore
again seems implausible to describe 'real' or 'open' conditionals
as 'epistemically neutral'. After all, these are surely *epistemically*
different from unreal conditionals. The meaning of real conditional
sentences fits in well with the definition of the indicative proposed
here, since the speaker appears to have a positive epistemic attitude
to the event in question.

The use of the indicative in open conditionals in Homeric Greek
again suggests that the indicative may not be described as a realis
mood, so that the irrealis continuum presented in chapter 2 is shown
to be implausible. Instead, it appears to support Palmer's view that
the mood is epistemically neutral. However, I have presented two
reasons which suggest that this definition is not strong enough, and
that the definition of 'positive epistemic stance' is to be preferred.
It remains to be seen whether this definition must be modified
in the light of the use of the mood in counterfactual conditional
sentences.

3.2.4 Counterfactual

The use of the indicative in counterfactual sentences has been found
difficult to explain, both for those who believe that the indicative is
a realis marker, and for those who believe it is epistemically neutral.
And it would at first sight also seem to be problematic for the claim
that the indicative expresses positive epistemic stance. After all, in
counterfactual sentences the speaker apparently describes events
that are known *not* to be true. For example (see Lang 1989 for a thorough discussion of all the Homeric 'counterfactual' conditionals):

2.156　ἔνθά κεν Ἀργείοισιν ὑπέρμορα νόστος ἐτύχθη,
　　　εἰ μὴ Ἀθηναίην Ἥρη πρὸς μῦθον ἔειπεν·

And now the Argives would have won their journey home, beyond what was ordained by fate, if Hera had not alerted Athena:

Counterfactual sentences have been described as more irrealis even than future-referring unreal sentences.[6] Most descriptions of the indicative thus discuss this use separately, as a 'modal' extension of meaning (e.g. Monro: §323ff.), a conclusion which is apparently supported by the presence of the so-called 'modal particle'. But we will see that this is in fact unnecessary, and that it is possible to explain the indicative in these contexts in the same way as in other types of conditional clause.

Theoretically, it is clear that we need to reassess the meaning of counterfactual sentences. The protasis 'if Tom had done X' in the sentence 'if Tom had done X, he would have done Y' is usually taken to mean 'Tom has not done X'. It is that meaning which has led to the indicative being seen as 'modal' in this context. However, Comrie (1986b: 88–93) has convincingly shown that this meaning is only part of the conversational implicature of these past conditionals, and that these sentences are no more irrealis than the open type exemplified above. Thus, sentences which are *not* definitely false are found with the same form. For example:

26 If the butler had done it, we would have found just the clues that we did in fact find.

In this sentence, the possibility that the butler did do 'it' is in fact an open possibility, as can be seen by the compatibility of the accompanying apodosis. Wierzbicka (1997: 30) has tried to counter this argument, claiming that these open readings are only found with positive examples while negative counterfactual sentences only imply the 'true' counterfactual meaning. Her example is, 'If they hadn't found that water, they would have died,' which she claims would only be uttered by a relieved search party, grateful

---

[6] See, e.g. Wierzbicka 1997: 28; Wakker 1994: 112. It should be noted that the term 'counterfactual' is used by some scholars to designate all 'unreal' conditionals, e.g. Greenberg (1986: 257). The term has here been restricted to past and present counterfactual sentences, since in future time no proposition is truly counterfactual: what would be called 'future counterfactuals' are really future conditionals which have a small likelihood of occurring.

that the water had indeed been found. However, I would argue that it is only because of the emotionally laden nature of the sentence that the alternative seems less acceptable here. If we return to a more 'neutral' whodunit scenario, the following sentence is quite possible: 'If he hadn't gone outside, he would have clean shoes – so let's go and check his shoes.' Even in the other situation, a sentence may be created where the protasis has a 'true' reading. For example, we may say, 'If they hadn't found that water by this point, they would have died, which would mean that their bodies would be visible from the top of that hill,' and for the statement in the apodosis to turn out to be true. The 'normal' counterfactual reading of these sentences is again only an implication.

It should be admitted that this kind of sentence, in which past time conditional sentences are ambiguous in meaning and the 'negative' reading of the protasis is defeasible, are rare. Certainly, the truth of the protasis is not similarly ambiguous in any of the Homeric examples, and they are perhaps rather too marginal a type to base a theory on. But whatever the status of the theoretical argument for counterfactual conditionals cross-linguistically, I would argue that it is possible to analyse the indicative in sentences like 2.156 in the same way as in the 'open' conditionals above. After all, even though they suggest that the event in question did not happen, that is surely not their focus. Rather they are used to point out that the event in question *could* have happened, that the event described in the protasis, and therefore its consequences in the apodosis, were real possibilities at one time. The speaker considers the world in which the events did happen as being a world very similar to the real world. 2.156 is indeed little different from the sentence, 'They *almost* won their return, but Hera stopped them.' As we saw above (3.1), it is useful to consider the meaning of the adverbial elements that may be used with the indicative: the use of 'almost' shows that the (English) indicative can be used to describe events which did not actually happen (McKay 1981: 40). But this does not contradict the definition of 'positive epistemic stance': with 'almost' the speaker asserts both that the event did not happen, but also that it had a good possibility of happening. The use of the indicative in counterfactual clauses in Greek may be interpreted in a similar way.

The claim that the indicative is somehow 'modal' in the context of counterfactual clauses has previously been supported by the observation that the optative is used in what appears to be the same type of sentence. For example:

5.311   καί νύ κεν ἔνθ' ἀπόλοιτο ἄναξ ἀνδρῶν Αἰνείας,
        εἰ μὴ ἄρ' ὀξὺ νόησε Διὸς θυγάτηρ Ἀφροδίτη,

And then Aeneas, the captain of men, would have died, if Zeus's daughter Aphrodite had not been quick to notice him,

Scholars have claimed that the optative was originally used in this construction but that the indicative is gradually replacing it.[7] This would suggest that the apodosis of counterfactual sentences is somehow 'modal'. However, I believe that the existence of these optative counterfactual sentences strengthens rather than weakens the claim that the indicative is expressing positive epistemic stance. I dispute the claim that the indicative is 'replacing' the optative in this environment, because there is a perceivable difference between the examples in which the optative is found and those in which the indicative is found, as we may see by comparing 5.311 with 16.617:

16.617   Μηριόνη, τάχα κέν σε καὶ ὀρχηστήν περ ἐόντα
         ἔγχος ἐμὸν κατέπαυσε διαμπερές, εἴ σ' ἔβαλόν περ.

Meriones – even though you're a dancer, my spear would have stopped you completely, if I'd hit you!

In both sentences the proposition in the protasis did not happen (Aeneas dying, Aeneas hitting Meriones with the spear). However, the speaker's attitude to the event in the two protases is rather different. In 5.311 the narrator is describing an event which we know to have only been a slight possibility, given Aeneas' genealogy. In 16.617, on the other hand, Aeneas is suggesting that it is a real possibility that he could have hit Meriones: it would hardly be an effectual taunt unless this were the case. Thus, just because the optative may be used in very similar situations to the indicative, there is no reason to describe the indicative in this context as any more irrealis than in the open conditionals above. Here too, it can be described as expressing the positive epistemic stance of the

---

[7] See Chantraine: §334; Horrocks 1995: 161; Wakker 1994: 210; Ruijgh 1992: 82–3.

speaker, and distinguished from the optative. The importance of the attitude of the speaker in mood choice may be further seen by comparing 5.311 with 7.104, which appears to be used in a very similar situation:

7.104   ἔνθά κέ τοι, Μενέλαε, <u>φάνη</u> βιότοιο τελευτή
      Ἕκτορος ἐν παλάμηισιν, ἐπεὶ πολὺ φέρτερος ἦεν,
      εἰ μὴ ἀναΐξαντες <u>ἕλον</u> βασιλῆες Ἀχαιῶν·

Menelaus, the end of your life would have appeared at the hands of Hector, since he was far mightier than you by far, if the kings of the Achaeans had not sprung up and taken you off:

In this sentence too, a possible event is being described which we know to be unlikely, given the genealogy of the person concerned. Nonetheless, the situation is rather different from that in 5.311. This is part of direct speech, and the indicative is thus again used to threaten the addressee: this sentence could be paraphrased in the following way: 'You really were a goner then. The only reason you're alive is because the king came to your aid.'

Of course, there is a crucial part of the indicative counterfactual construction which I have not so far discussed, and which could be argued to hold the key: the 'modal particle'. The presence of the particle in all apodoses of this type could be used to support the other interpretations of the indicative, in that it could be argued that we are not really dealing with the indicative in this context, but rather a separate category, the 'indicative-plus-modal-particle'. The meaning of the particle is particularly controversial and difficult, but for the sake of this claim, proponents would have to claim that it somehow 'carried' the apparent modality of the construction. But this is rather too simplistic: why would a category that had a realis or epistemically neutral meaning combine with a category that had a meaning of 'modality'? According to my interpretation, the particle and indicative can be understood as contributing componentially to the meaning of the construction. The indicative marks the positive epistemic stance of the subject. The particle, in combination with the presence of the protasis, could be said to mark the difference between the counterfactual indicative sentence and the normal use.

3.3 Summary and conclusions

In this chapter, I have considered the use of the indicative in Homeric Greek conditional clauses to reassess the definition of the mood. In the version of the irrealis continuum presented in chapter 2, the indicative lies at the most realis end of the spectrum. But the mood is often found with adverbial modifiers that make it synonymous with 'modal' sentences as traditionally defined, while in conditional clauses it is used even though the speaker-commitment to a proposition is suspended. This has led to a definition of the mood as 'epistemically unmarked' (Palmer[1]: 86). But this definition is problematic, in that it fails to capture the essential meaning of the indicative as seen in main clauses, which is to declare that a proposition is *true* in the speaker's opinion. It certainly fails to explain all the uses of the indicative in Homeric Greek, particularly in counterfactual sentences. These are described as the most irrealis of conditional sentences, and the indicative appears to describe an event which the speaker knows *not* to be true. This use of the indicative is generally described separately from its basic 'assertive' use, and is described as 'modal'.

I have argued in this chapter that the indicative in Homeric Greek may be more successfully defined as expressing the speaker's positive epistemic stance to a proposition. This explains its use in the whole range of conditional clauses. While most of the examples of the indicative occur in apparently realis contexts, such as 'resumptive', 'obviously realised', and 'concessive' conditionals, in all contexts the speaker-commitment is suspended, just as in the 'open' conditionals. What all these contexts do share is the speaker's commitment, if not to the 'truth' of the proposition, then to the possibility of it being true. I have argued that this is even true of the use of the indicative in counterfactual sentences. The falsity of the proposition in this context appears to be part of the implicature rather than the meaning of the sentence. The indicative is used to show that the speaker believes that it was a real possibility that a particular event could have happened, even if, in the real world, it did not. The use of the optative in the same context does not disprove this conclusion, by automatically implying that it is a modal context. Instead it shows that the same event may be described in different ways. The indicative focuses on the fact that the incident was possible. I will consider in more depth the meaning of the optative in the construction in chapter 5.

By defining all the uses of the indicative in one way, as expressing the 'positive epistemic stance' of the speaker, I might be accused of attempting to find a single abstract meaning which links various uses together. Such an approach to the description of modal forms was criticised in chapter 2. But in fact the claim is merely that the uses of the indicative are less different from each other than has previously been thought. That is, a comparison of the statements 'The eggs were cooked through' and 'If the eggs had been cooked through, they wouldn't have made us ill' was previously taken to mean that the indicative had two diametrically opposed meanings, one indicating that the speaker believes in the truth of the proposition, and one that he does not. It is in this scenario that an abstract meaning to link the two uses might be searched for. But it has instead been argued here that the meanings are not as different as has previously been thought. In both situations, the speaker could be described as having positive epistemic stance to the proposition of the eggs being cooked through. There is thus no longer any need to search for any 'linking' abstract meaning.

This conclusion will obviously have knock-on effects for our understanding of the other moods. It suggests that the three moods cannot be explained in terms of the one simple axis of the irrealis continuum. In the subsequent chapters my reanalysis of the subjunctive and optative further continues this break with the traditional accounts.

4

SUBJUNCTIVE

4.1 Introduction

In chapter 2, I described the traditional accounts of the subjunctive, according to which it is supposed to lie somewhere between the indicative and the optative, an understanding well captured by Greenberg's model of an irrealis continuum (see p. 35).

The traditional account also distinguishes two different uses of the subjunctive, 'epistemic' and 'deontic'. In both respects, this understanding of the subjunctive fits in well with modern research on modal markers and the meanings that they express. But I have already shown that the so-called deontic meanings of the moods have been misunderstood (2.3.3). In this chapter I will further criticise the traditional model, arguing both that there are intriguing uses of the subjunctive that have not previously been discussed, and that even those uses that *are* covered should be explained in a different way.

In the following sections, I will reanalyse different uses of the subjunctive to provide a new map of the meanings of the mood and their interrelationships. In section 4.2, I will consider the epistemic use of the subjunctive, said to be more 'irrealis' than the future indicative. To a certain extent, this description has already been called into question by the reanalysis of the indicative carried out in the last chapter. Here I will show that, although it is possible to draw a subtle distinction between future and more irrealis markers, the Homeric evidence does not support such a description of the future indicative and subjunctive. I will thus claim that the subjunctive was (originally at least) some kind of a future marker. I will however also describe the ways in which it is developing in a different way from the future indicative.

In section 4.3, I will consider the hortative use of the subjunctive, and will argue that it developed through the combination of the future meaning of the subjunctive and the first person, showing that there is a more complicated relationship between the different meanings of the mood than is suggested by the neat schematisations of the traditional models. I will also argue that many of the examples given to illustrate this use of the mood have been misinterpreted, since they are not performative but rather express intention, an objective deontic meaning. This conclusion thus further complicates the map of meanings.

In section 4.4 I will examine the negative directive construction. Previously, the subjunctive in this construction has been explained as 'replacing' the aorist imperative. Here I will point to several differences between subjunctive and imperative and will argue that it could more successfully be explained in a different way, which ties in with its description as a future marker.

4.2 Epistemic

4.2.1 Introduction

Monro (§315) described what I have called the 'epistemic' meaning of the subjunctive as the 'quasi-future' meaning. The subjunctive has this meaning in main, conditional and other subordinate clauses. For example:

6.459 καί ποτέ τις εἴπῃσιν ἰδὼν κατὰ δάκρυ χέουσαν·

And then someone will say as he sees you weeping:

3.289 εἰ δ' ἂν ἐμοὶ τιμὴν Πρίαμος Πριάμοιό τε παῖδες
τίνειν οὐκ ἐθέλωσιν Ἀλεξάνδροιο πεσόντος,
αὐτὰρ ἐγὼ καὶ ἔπειτα μαχήσομαι εἵνεκα ποινῆς

But if Priam and Priam's sons refuse to pay once Alexander has fallen, then I myself will fight it out for the ransom

1.242 τότε δ' οὔ τι δυνήσεαι ἀχνύμενός περ
χραισμεῖν, εὖτ' ἂν πολλοὶ ὑφ' Ἕκτορος ἀνδροφόνοιο
θνήισκοντες πίπτωσι·

But then you will not be able to ward off destruction, even though you are grieving, when many men will fall and die at the hands of man-killing Hector.

In these contexts the subjunctive is fulfilling a similar role to the future indicative, also used to refer to events in the speaker's future. The main issue to be discussed in an analysis of the epistemic meaning of the subjunctive will therefore be whether it is possible to differentiate between these two markers.

According to the model of the irrealis continuum we would expect the subjunctive to be more irrealis than the future indicative. And this expectation appears to be confirmed in a comparison of the 'characteristic' uses of the two forms. The future indicative is usually found in main clauses, whereas the subjunctive is usually found in subordinate clauses, such as 3.289 above. For example:

1.29   τὴν δ' ἐγὼ οὐ λύσω·

I will not free her.

The future indicative is here found in an assertion about future time, while the subjunctive in 3.289 is used in a conditional clause where the likelihood of that event happening is not so sure: there seems to be a clear difference in the level of 'realis' in the two sentences. However, as I will show, distinguishing between the subjunctive and future indicative is in fact difficult on both formal and functional grounds.

According to traditional accounts of the formation of the subjunctive, athematic verbs were originally marked by a short vowel in the subjunctive, while thematic verbs are marked by a long vowel, the result of the combination of the thematic vowel with the 'subjunctive' short vowel (Chantraine 1: §216; Buck 1933: 298). The long vowel soon takes over as the generalised marker of the subjunctive, even in athematic verbs, but there are many examples of the 'old' short vowel subjunctives in Homer, primarily in the sigmatic aorist, but also in the present, for example: ἴομεν, φθίεται (Sihler 1995: §535). The aorist subjunctive form is consequently impossible to distinguish from the future in most verbal paradigms (that is, with 'weak' verbs where the same root is used to form both aorist and future). Interpreting a particular form as either subjunctive or future indicative will therefore often rest on preconceptions about the different functions of the two moods.

The problem of formal distinction has been exacerbated by the early use of local alphabets such as Old Attic, where long and short vowels were not distinguished (Janko 1985: 34). The marking of vowel length in the text of Homer is therefore largely a matter of editorial convention. The formal confusion between future indicative and subjunctive forms has then been compounded by an inconsistency in the treatment of the vulgate by philologists. The inconsistency occurs in the description of 'potential' short vowel subjunctives: when forms with the short vowel are metrically different from the 'equivalent' form with a long vowel, they are recognised as possibly subjunctive, while forms where the long vowel version would be metrically the same as the short vowel version are described as unambiguously future indicative (Chantraine ı: §216). Thus δηλήσεται is thought of as ambiguous between the future indicative and aorist subjunctive reading because the alternative (δηλήσηται as found in 3.107) would make a metrical difference. On the other hand, τιμήσουσι is only taken as a future indicative, since the long-vowel subjunctive version is metrically equivalent (Chantraine: §332). The grammarians thus artificially distort the 'facts' of the language, which could have led to an overestimation of the number of future indicatives. In this study even forms like τιμήσουσι will be considered 'homophonous' between a future indicative and (short-vowel) aorist subjunctive, and therefore will not be used to support a particular semantic interpretation of the two moods.[1]

The formal similarity between the subjunctive and future indicative means that it is often hard to tell which mood a particular example is. But perhaps even more problematic for an analysis of the epistemic use of the subjunctive is the lack of an agreed definition of what the *functional* difference between an epistemic mood and a future tense-marker should be. In order to prove the traditional account of the difference between the subjunctive and indicative, we should be able to show that the subjunctive is more

---

[1] In the appendices only forms which are unambiguously subjunctive have been catalogued, unless a form ambiguous between present and subjunctive meaning is found with future meaning, or where a form ambiguous between indicative and subjunctive is found with hortative meaning. This last decision is disputable, given that the future indicative could independently have developed hortative meaning, but it follows the practice of the grammar-books.

'irrealis' than the future indicative. But it has been called into question whether such a distinction will be possible, both from an empirical and a theoretical perspective.

Empirically, the functional similarity between subjunctive and future tense categories has long been recognised in all Indo-European languages.[2] For example, in Vedic the subjunctive frequently has the meaning of a simple future, while the Latin future tense is supposed to have developed from the Indo-European subjunctive (Sihler 1995: §534, §501ff.). In the case of Greek conditional sentences, it has been argued that the subjunctive and the future indicative are *both* used to express future-referring 'real' conditionals (Goodwin: §447; Abbott and Mansfield: Syntax §180). Fortson thus concludes that the Indo-European subjunctive was a future tense (Fortson 1994: §5.52).

More importantly, theoretical descriptions of the future tense also suggest that there will be no such clear distinction between it and an epistemic mood. Tense is traditionally related to a time-line: a past tense refers deictically to the time before the utterance, a present tense to a time contemporaneous with the utterance (Comrie 1985: 2). Previously, the future tense would also have been described in the same way, pointing deictically to a time after the utterance. But it has more recently been argued that this was mistaken: while we can refer deictically to the past and present we may only make 'suppositions' about the future.[3] Based on various cross-linguistic studies of future meaning, BPP (1994: 244) have described the focal use of future markers as equivalent to a 'prediction on the part of the speaker that the situation in the proposition, which refers to an event taking place after the moment of speech, will hold'.[4] By emphasising the importance of the speaker, this definition reveals the blurring of mood and tense in this category.

---

[2] Palmer[2]: 105; Goodwin: 2; Handford 1947: 15; Jespersen 1924: 318.

[3] See for example Lyons 1977: 816; Palmer[2]: 104ff.; Mithun 1995: 378; Romaine 1995: 396; Chantraine: §301; Hahn: §210; BPP: 244; Dahl 1985: 103; Serbat 1975: 391 on various philosophical approaches; Lightfoot 1975: 17. The problematic status of the future was in fact commented on as early as Aristotle (cf. Lyons 1977: 814 and Prior 1967: 16: 'the sentence "there will be a sea-battle tomorrow" might be (because of the indeterminacy of the situation) "not yet" definitely true or false').

[4] This definition is based on the findings of Abraham 1989; Bybee and Pagliuca 1985; 1987; BPP 1991; Comrie 1985; Fleischman 1982; Heine, Claudi and Hünnemeyer 1991; Palmer[1]; Ultan 1978; Comrie 1989: 60; Dahl 1985: 103.

The functional similarity between future tenses and modal forms also works the other way: epistemic modal forms refer mainly to future time (Bybee 1985: 179). For example:

27 Adi may come out to the cinema this week.

In fact, it has been claimed on the basis of cross-linguistic evidence that modal markers will always refer to future events when no other tense indicator is present (BPP: 207; Palmer²: 33).

The overlap between modality and tense is sometimes formally expressed: in several languages future time-reference is expressed by what is elsewhere an epistemic mood and vice versa (Palmer²: 105). Markers that are described as primarily future tenses have often developed out of other modal markers, for example, English *will*, originally a desiderative verb. As we have seen in chapter 2, these forms can also then develop other, atemporal meanings. The modal nature of *will* has led many scholars to claim that English does not have a 'true' future tense at all.⁵ It is therefore perhaps no coincidence that there is formal as well as functional confusion between the future indicative and subjunctive in Greek.

As well as the problems arising from vowel-length, the evidence from suppletive verbs further suggests that there was some confusion between the subjunctive and future paradigms. For example, the supposedly future ἔδομαι, πίομαι and χεύω are all subjunctive in origin (Ruijgh 1992: 76). Similarly, in the paradigm of ὁράω, Ruijgh (*ibid.*) has argued that, at one stage, the subjunctive (ἴδῃ) was the only futural form, since the future from the aorist stem (εἴσομαι) was already in use as the future of οἶδα. It seems that both the 'subjunctive' and 'future' forms of verbs have the option of being used as the 'normal' future marker in the verbal paradigm.

Empirically and theoretically, then, there seem to be good reasons to suggest that both the future indicative and subjunctive were future markers, as indeed has been claimed by Hahn (*passim*).⁶ From a cross-linguistic point of view it would certainly be unsurprising if Greek had more than one future marker (Comrie 1989: 52; BPP 1991: 17; BPP: 243). And the description of both as future

---

⁵ Fries 1927; Fleischman 1982: 25; Brisard 1997: 271; Enç 1996; Palmer²: 104.
⁶ For other scholars who have made the same claim see Fleischman 1982: 190, fn. 7.

markers would not rule out the possibility that they expressed rather different notions. Certainly, other languages have more than one future marker. For example, English has two different ways of expressing future time, 'be going to' and 'will' – a 'go-future' and a 'simple future' in Fleischman's terms.[7] In an apparent parallel to Greek, it has been attempted to describe these also in 'modal' terms. Some scholars have claimed that 'will' is the more modal form, while the go-future has been described as 'a completely color- less "future tense" way of speaking, devoid of any emotion, desire, intention, resolution, compulsion, or the like' (Joos 1964: 23). This would appear to correspond to the distinction traditionally claimed for the Homeric subjunctive and future indicative respectively. But this description of the 'go-future' is in fact controversial: some have claimed that the 'go-future' is just as modal as the simple future, while others have claimed that it is *more* modal (see ref- erences in Fleischman 1982: 179, fn. 47). Of particular interest is that, even among those who admit that both the 'will-future' and the 'go-future' are equally 'future tenses', the exact difference between the two forms is disputed. The following are just some of the ways in which the 'go-future' has been distinguished from the 'simple future' (as discussed in Fleischman 1982: 4.4):

  i. Proximal vs distal futurity
  ii. Imminence
  iii. Intentionality
  iv. Localised action
  v. True vs false
  vi. Assumed vs contingent event
  vii. Statements vs predictions
  viii. Inceptive/inchoative vs simple
  ix. Present relevance

Fleischman (1982: 95–7) has elaborated the evidence both for and against all of these proposals and has concluded that only the last model well explains the difference between the two forms. It is not particularly relevant for our discussion to determine the exact meaning of the 'go-future' with respect to the simple future in English. Nonetheless, it is instructive to see how, even in a living

---

[7] Fleischman 1982: 17. See also Haegeman 1989; Bybee and Pagliuca 1987: 115–17; Coates 1983: 169–85.

language, differentiating between two future markers can be very difficult and prone to controversy. How much harder then to differentiate between the subjunctive and future indicative in Homeric Greek, with a limited number of examples, in one particular type of discourse, and with the added problem of the difficulty of identifying the relevant forms correctly.

Given the formal and functional similarity between the future indicative and subjunctive in Greek, and the possibility of having two future markers in one language, it is tempting to conclude with Hahn that the subjunctive and future indicative in Greek were both originally future markers. However, it has recently been argued that it is theoretically possible to distinguish between a future marker and an epistemic mood. This is perhaps unsurprising given the frequent existence of different forms to mark the different categories in various languages. Comrie (1989: 54) argues that in English it is possible to distinguish theoretically between the statements 'it will rain tomorrow' and 'it may rain tomorrow', even though both have reference to a future time and are thus inherently 'uncertain'. In the first sentence, he claims that the speaker vouches for the truth of the statement in the same way as when he says 'it rained yesterday'. Although the bases on which the speaker makes his judgement about the truth of the propositions may well be different, the level of commitment to the truth is thus the same. The 'future' statement may be distinguished from the 'modal' statement with 'may', where the speaker makes it clear that the eventuality is only possible. This suggests that 'future markers' and 'epistemic moods' may indeed be located at different points of the irrealis continuum. A similar situation has been observed in Central Pomo, which distinguishes a 'realis' from an 'irrealis' future (Palmer[2]: 189; Mithun 1995: 379).

Langacker (1991) has accounted for these two different ways of describing a future event in terms of an 'evolutionary model'. He suggests that the speaker 'conceives the world as being structured in a particular way, and reality as having a certain *evolutionary momentum* that constrains its future development' (Langacker 1991: 547). According to this model we may distinguish two different kinds of future markers: one expressing 'projected' reality, and the other expressing merely 'potential' reality. This terminology would appear to be useful in the description of the two types of future statement distinguished by Comrie: 'will' could be described as expressing projected reality, with 'may' expressing potential reality.

In the next section I will analyse the meaning and distribution of the future indicative and subjunctive in main, conditional and other subordinate clauses, and assess whether the first is a marker of projected reality and the second a marker of potential reality. In order to prove that this is the case it would be necessary to show that the two are used with different levels of speaker commitment. I will argue that this is not the case: in main clauses the evidence shows that both are used with the same range of meanings; in conditional clauses, although there is a difference in their distribution, this difference need not be explained as due to a difference in irrealis level.

4.2.2 Comparison of subjunctive and future indicative

4.2.2.1 Main clauses

The epistemic use of the subjunctive (usually aorist) in main clauses is described as a Homeric peculiarity which dies out in Attic Greek.[8] The epistemic use of the subjunctive is also found in apodoses (Goodwin: §452):

1.324 εἰ δέ κε μὴ δώησιν, ἐγὼ δέ κεν αὐτὸς ἕλωμαι
ἐλθὼν σὺν πλεόνεσσι,

But if he will not give her over, I'll go myself with an army and seize her,

There may be many more examples, but in other lines the aorist subjunctive is indistinguishable from the future indicative of the same verb, and the grammars therefore count them as examples of the future indicative.

There are some examples of both the subjunctive and future indicative which appear to confirm the suggestion that the difference between them is a difference in 'irrealis level'. For example, in 3.54 we find the subjunctive:

---

[8] Monro: §279; Goodwin: §284–6; Wackernagel 1926: 236.

3.54 οὐκ ἄν τοι χραίσμηι κίθαρις τά τε δῶρ᾽ Ἀφροδίτης

The lyre and these gifts of Aphrodite won't help you then

The prediction here is of necessity uncertain, and thus could be said to belong to a 'potential' rather than a 'projected' reality. This use of the subjunctive may be contrasted with the future indicative in 1.181:

1.181 ἀπειλήσω δέ τοι ὧδε·

I will threaten you thus:

This seems much more certain, since the speaker is sure what his own actions will be. He makes a very certain statement of intent, and immediately fulfills it.

But the future indicative is also found in predictions, as well as in the more certain statements of intent. For example:

4.238 ἡμεῖς αὖτ᾽ ἀλόχους τε φίλας καὶ νήπια τέκνα
ἄξομεν ἐν νήεσσιν, ἐπὴν πτολίεθρον ἕλωμεν.

We'll drag their dear wives and helpless children back to the ships, once we take their city.

This use of the future indicative is indeed unsurprising, given that prediction is said to be the focal use of future markers cross-linguistically (BPP: 244).

We could still maintain that the subjunctive and future indicative expressed potential and projected reality respectively if we could show that the certainty of the speaker differs in the predictions marked by the different moods. In this case it appears that such an argument could indeed be made: in the lines previous to 4.238, the speaker makes it clear that he is convinced that they will win, and the future will turn out as he predicts:

4.235 οὐ γὰρ ἐπὶ ψεύδεσσι πατὴρ Ζεὺς ἔσσετ᾽ ἀρωγός,
ἀλλ᾽ οἵ περ πρότεροι ὑπὲρ ὅρκια δηλήσαντο,

Father Zeus will never be the defender of lies – they were the first to break their oaths,

The future predicted in 3.54 by the subjunctive, on the other hand, is rather different: Hector is teasing Paris for his cowardice and wishing he had carried on fighting with Menelaus. He says that his beauty will no longer be able to help him when he is dead. We could claim that the future in this context, as expressed by the subjunctive, is rather less sure, since it is only an imaginary future.

But again the attempt to differentiate between the future indicative and the subjunctive in terms of lesser or greater degrees of irrealis breaks down on consideration of more evidence. A similarly 'imaginary' context to 3.54 is found at 4.305, where the future indicative is used:

4.305 μηδέ τις ἱπποσύνηι τε καὶ ἠνορέηφι πεποιθώς
οἶος πρόσθ' ἄλλων μεμάτω Τρώεσσι μάχεσθαι,
μηδ' ἀναχωρείτω· ἀλαπαδνότεροι γὰρ ἔσεσθε.

Let no man, so sure of his horsemanship and soldier's prowess, dare to fight it out alone with the Trojans, nor let him give ground, or you'll be powerless.

Similarly, a more 'certain' prediction is found in O16.437, where the subjunctive is used alongside a future:

O   οὐκ ἔσθ' οὗτος ἀνὴρ οὐδ' ἔσσεται οὐδὲ <u>γένηται,</u>
16.437

There is no man alive, nor will there be, nor will such a man be born,

Hahn (§108) claims that the only difference between the future indicative and the subjunctive here is 'one of vocabulary', not of mood. Similarly, Ruijgh (1992: 75) suggests that there is no difference of modal force between ἔσσεται and γένηται and therefore concludes that, in Homer, 'οὐδὲ γένηται a la même valeur que οὐδὲ γενήσεται en attique'.

As well as the future indicative being used in apparently 'subjunctive' contexts, the subjunctive is also found in the first person expressing the intentions of the speaker, only three lines after 1.181 above:

1.184   τὴν μὲν ἐγὼ σὺν νηΐ τ' ἐμῆι καὶ ἐμοῖς ἑτάροισιν
πέμψω· ἐγὼ δέ κ' <u>ἄγω</u> Βρισηΐδα καλλιπάρηον
αὐτὸς ἰὼν κλισίηνδε,

Her I'll send back in my own ships, and with my own crew. But I'll take Briseis in all her beauty, going to your tent myself,

The use of both the subjunctive and the future indicative to express the intent of the speaker is certainly interesting, and I will discuss it further in section 4.3. For now, it suffices to note that it is not possible to differentiate the two in terms of a difference in certainty.

1.184 and O16.437 demonstrate another characteristic which makes it hard to distinguish the subjunctive from the future indicative: the two are often found in parallel. We may compare 6.459 where the subjunctive is used, but the future indicative is found some lines later to refer to the same event:

6.459   καί ποτέ τις εἴπῃσιν ἰδὼν κατὰ δάκρυ χέουσαν·

And then someone will say as he sees you weeping:

6.462   ὥς ποτέ τις ἐρέει·

So he will say:

Hentze (1909: 131–2) discusses the above sentences in the context of his belief that the future indicative expresses a purely 'temporal' reference to future time, while the subjunctive expresses something more 'subjective', and claims that the event is viewed with some trepidation the first time it is mentioned, while the second time it is merely accepted as part of what will happen in the future. Similarly Gonda (75) has claimed that the first time the thought is 'hedged', and then stated more firmly. But although these offer interesting points of interpretation for the passage in question, these differences between the subjunctive and future indicative do not indicate that the future indicative refers to a projected future and the subjunctive to a potential future: the event is part of the speaker's projected reality whether he is worried about it, or expecting it, or just describing how it will happen in the future.

As well as lines where the subjunctive is in parallel with the future indicative, there are also places where the subjunctive is co-ordinated with past and present tenses of the indicative in such a way as to suggest that the only difference between them is a different time reference (Hahn: §108). For example:

1.262   οὐ γάρ πω τοίους ἴδον ἀνέρας, οὐδὲ ἴδωμαι,

I have never seen such men, and I never will,

Gonda (75) comments that the subjunctive is more 'modal' than the past or present indicative here – he would translate the subjunctive

'I don't expect to see' or 'I can't fancy them being seen again' as opposed to the straightforward 'I have never seen' of the past indicative. But this is precisely the difference that has been noticed between past and present tenses on the one hand and future tenses on the other: while the past and present tenses are more deictic, future tenses are inherently more modal. The observation that the subjunctive here is different from (and perhaps more 'modal' than) the past and present tense is not sufficient to prove that it is more modal than the future indicative.

One final way in which the distribution of the subjunctive and future indicative is said to differ is the frequent use of the subjunctive in negative propositions, while the future indicative is usually found in positive sentences (Hahn: §109; Gonda: 80). For example:

15.348   ὃν δ' ἂν ἐγὼν ἀπάνευθε νεῶν ἑτέρωθι νοήσω,
          αὐτοῦ οἱ θάνατον μητίσομαι, οὐδέ νυ τόν γε
          γνωτοί τε γνωταί τε πυρὸς λελάχωσι θανόντα,
          ἀλλὰ κύνες ἐρύουσι πρὸ ἄστεος ἡμετέροιο.

Whoever I find away from the ships, I'll plan death for him right here, and no kin or women will commit his corpse to the flames – instead the dogs will tear his flesh in front of our city.

Negative sentences are often claimed to be an 'irrealis' environment and this distribution could imply that the difference between the future indicative and subjunctive *is* a difference in the level of irrealis (Palmer[2]: 175–6). Gonda (80) claims 'it seems to be in harmony with the positive and assertive character of the future, and the idea of mental existence expressed by the subj[unctive] that the former often occurs in affirmative, the latter in negative sentences'. But although the subjunctive is apparently preferred in negative sentences, it is also found in positive contexts, as for example in 6.459 (see p. 64). This trend thus provides no clear-cut means of distinguishing between the two moods.

The evidence from main clauses suggests that both the subjunctive and future indicative are used with a variety of different meanings, ranging from more certain predictions or statements of intent to those with less certainty. Given the overlap in meanings, it does not appear justifiable to describe one as the marker of 'projected' and the other of 'potential' reality. There therefore seems to be no case for describing the subjunctive as any more 'irrealis' than the future indicative.

4.2.2.2 Conditional clauses

The subjunctive is preferred over the future indicative in conditional protases and thus it could be argued that, in spite of the apparent lack of difference of meaning between them in main clauses, there is a difference between the two categories. Cross-linguistic studies have shown that it is rare to find future markers in protases.[9] This might suggest that the subjunctive should indeed be categorised as a 'mood' and therefore separated from the future indicative.

It is certainly difficult to find many indisputable examples of the future indicative in the conditional protasis in Homeric Greek: of the various lines discussed in the grammars, I have found only 4.[10] This corresponds with a great many more certain subjunctives – I have noted 35 subjunctives in the protasis of specific conditionals in the first 6 books of the *Iliad* alone.[11] But the very existence of the future indicative in this situation means that the subjunctive may not be described as more of a mood than a tense, just because it is found in this context. Certainly, there is no rule *excluding* future markers from this context, and Russian indeed uses the future indicative here (Comrie 1982: 144).

BPP have argued that the reason why future markers are generally not found in protases is because future meanings typically develop in markers which (originally) have other, often modal meanings (BPP 1991: 19, 28; 1994: 208–9). In the context of a protasis this original meaning is brought out. That explains why, on the rare occasions when English 'will' *is* found in conditional protases, it has a sense of 'willingness' rather than a 'simple' future

---

[9] See for example BPP: 274; Dahl 1985; Comrie 1982; 1985: 117–21.

[10] 17.418; 24.57; 12.248 from Monro (§326.5). These are examples of the future indicative in a 'full conditional' with the apodosis expressed. Also 1.135 in a protasis where the apodosis is unexpressed.

[11] 1.090; 1.129; 1.137; 1.324; 1.341; 1.580; 2.364; 2.364; 3.026; 3.281; 3.284; 3.289; 4.098; 4.170; 4.170; 4.353; 4.353; 4.363; 4.416; 4.416; 5.129; 5.132; 5.225; 5.232; 5.258; 5.260; 5.351; 5.763; 5.821; 6.094; 6.260; 6.275; 6.309; 6.443; 6.527.

meaning, as we may see in the following example (BPP 1991: 28):[12]

28 If you will help me, we can finish faster.

BPP therefore conclude (1994: 274) that it is possible to find a true future marker in a conditional protasis, but only once its origins have been lost. Rather than showing that the subjunctive is more irrealis than the future indicative, the preference for the subjunctive in conditional protases could just suggest that it was a more 'mature' marker of futurity than the future indicative.

The meaning of the subjunctive in 'real' conditional clauses further supports the claim that it is no more irrealis than the future indicative. We may again consider the conditional clause at 3.289:

3.289 εἰ δ' ἂν ἐμοὶ τιμὴν Πρίαμος Πριάμοιό τε παῖδες
τίνειν οὐκ <u>ἐθέλωσιν</u> Ἀλεξάνδροιο πεσόντος,
αὐτὰρ ἐγὼ καὶ ἔπειτα μαχήσομαι εἵνεκα ποινῆς

But if Priam and Priam's sons refuse to pay once Alexander has fallen, then I myself will fight it out for the ransom

Here the speaker is speculating about something which he does not know about, and it could therefore be said to indicate that the subjunctive was somewhat irrealis. However, the events speculated about do seem to be 'in line' with the speaker's view of the world, the definition of a marker of *projected* reality. The conditional in 3.289 is thus very similar to the 'open' conditional in present time at 2.357 which has the indicative as discussed in chapter 3(3.2.3):

2.357 εἰ δέ τις ἐκπάγλως ἐθέλει οἴκόνδε νέεσθαι
ἁπτέσθω ἧς νηὸς ἐϋσσέλμοιο μελαίνης,

But if anyone wants to go home, he should put his hand on his black well-benched ship,

In both cases, the eventuality described in the protasis is seen as a distinct possibility, although the speaker does not know whether or not it will turn out to be true.

---

[12] See further Comrie 1982; Palmer 1983a; Jacobsson 1984; Tynan and Lavin 1997: 126.

The meaning of the subjunctive in conditional protases therefore seems to support the conclusion made in respect to main clauses. Indeed, many scholars believe that there is no distinction between the subjunctive and future indicative in conditional clauses, claiming that they both express 'real' conditionals (e.g. Goodwin: §447; Abbott and Mansfield: Syntax §180). I will show here that in Homeric Greek at least it *is* possible to distinguish between them, but that this does not mean that one should be considered more irrealis than the other.

We must first dismiss the claim, as made in Smyth (§2328) and Brunel (1980: 232), that the difference lies in the greater 'emphasis' of the future indicative. The future indicative is certainly found in sentences used to make a threat:

12.248 εἰ δὲ σὺ δηϊοτῆτος ἀφέξεαι, ἠέ τιν᾿ ἄλλον
        παρφάμενος ἐπέεσσιν ἀποτρέψεις πολέμοιο,
        αὐτίκ᾿ ἐμῶι ὑπὸ δουρὶ τυπεὶς ἀπὸ θυμὸν ὀλέσσεις.

But if you give up the fight, or persuade some other soldier to turn back from battle, you'll breathe your last, struck by my spear.

But the subjunctive appears to have also been used with this meaning: for example in 3.289, considered above (p. 67). Wakker (1994: 39, fn. 27) has argued that it is the context, rather than the mood-choice, which indicates that the conditional is imbued with threatening force.

I believe that the more important difference between the subjunctive and future indicative in conditional clauses lies in their distribution. At least three, and maybe all four of the certain future indicatives in conditional protases in Homer are found in what could be called 'resumptive' conditionals (see 3.2.2). Indeed Hentze (1909: 132) has argued that this is one of the primary uses of the future indicative in conditional clauses, expressing what he describes as 'Äußerungen des Mitunterredenden'. The three certain examples of the construction are 12.248 (seen above), 17.418 and 24.57:

17.418 ὦ φίλοι, οὐ μὰν ἧμιν ἐϋκλεὲς ἀπονέεσθαι
        νῆας ἔπι γλαφυράς, ἀλλ᾿ αὐτοῦ γαῖα μέλαινα
        πᾶσι χάνοι· τό κεν ἧμιν ἄφαρ πολὺ κέρδιον εἴη,

εἰ τοῦτον Τρώεσσι μεθήσομεν ἱπποδάμοισιν
ἄστυ πότι σφέτερον ἐρύσαι καὶ κῦδος ἀρέσθαι.

Friends! There's no glory in going back in our hollow ships – may the black earth
gape open here and swallow us instead. That would be a much better fate for us,
if we will give his corpse up to the horse-breaking Trojans, for them to drag it to
their town and take the glory.

24.57 εἴη κεν καὶ τοῦτο τεὸν ἔπος, Ἀργυρότοξε,
εἰ δὴ ὁμὴν Ἀχιλῆϊ καὶ Ἕκτορι θήσετε τιμήν.

What you say would be right, lord of the silver-bow, if you gods will set Achilles
and Hector in the same esteem.

12.248 takes up the threat that Polydamas made to Hector in 12.215.

17.418 may also be given a resumptive interpretation, although
it does not pick up actual words spoken previously. The sentence is
spoken by various indeterminate Achaeans, spurring each other on
to protect the body of Patroclus, and could therefore be translated
in the following way: 'If we really do give up this corpse (and I
take it from your present pathetic actions that we are going to) –
we should die here rather than trying to get back home.'

In 24.57 again we may not point to actual words that have
been spoken which the conditional resumes. But Hera is saying
that if the gods go along with the suggestion that Apollo has just
made, it would be as good as considering Hector as highly as they
hold Achilles, and it is thus again resumptive 'if you are indeed
going to consider Hector as highly as Achilles'. We may see this
resumptive force from the use of δή 'indeed' ('wenn denn': Hentze
1909: 140). Similar particles and words indicating that the speaker
doubts the veracity (or in this case the wisdom) of the event being
described, were found in the indicative conditionals considered in
chapter 3.

The fourth example of the future indicative in a conditional
protasis might also be described as 'resumptive', although here the
interpretation is unclear since no actual apodosis follows:

1.135 ἀλλ' εἰ μὲν δώσουσι γέρας μεγάθυμοι Ἀχαιοί,
ἄρσαντες κατὰ θυμόν, ὅπως ἀντάξιον ἔσται·
εἰ δέ κε μὴ δώωσιν, ἐγὼ δέ κεν αὐτὸς ἕλωμαι
ἢ τεὸν ἢ Αἴαντος ἰὼν γέρας, ἢ Ὀδυσῆος
ἄξω ἑλών·

No – if our generous Argives give me a prize, fitting my desires, so that it will be equal to what I've lost, well . . . But if they don't give me anything, I'll come to you, or Ajax, or Odysseus, and take *your* prize.

Hentze (1909: 133) has shown that the particles μέν . . . δέ prove that the first protasis may not be taken as a mere interjection, as has sometimes been claimed. But the interpretation of that protasis is unclear. Some scholars appear to describe it as a normal 'real' conditional, just like the subjunctive in 1.137, with an 'understood' apodosis meaning 'I will go along with their demands' (Leaf ad loc.). But Hentze argues that Agamemnon is not really entertaining the possibility as he would in a normal 'real' conditional since it has already been rejected by Achilles in 1.123:

1.123 πῶς γάρ τοι δώσουσι γέρας μεγάθυμοι Ἀχαιοί;

how will the generous Argives give you prizes?

Agamemnon is therefore repeating his previous demand, only to make a bigger demand in the next lines, thus suggesting that this is another example of the future indicative in a resumptive conditional. The interpretation of this line must remain unclear because of the lack of an apodosis, but it seems at least possible that this is the same as the other three examples, so that the use of the future indicative may be explained by the resumptive nature of the conditional.

It thus remains to discuss the significance of this different distribution for our understanding of the relationship between the future indicative and subjunctive. It could be argued that it supports the traditional interpretation. After all, the subjunctive is used in conditionals talking about possible events which *may* happen, while resumptive conditionals express what the speaker is convinced is *going to* happen. This is certainly the meaning of the resumptive conditionals examined above. But I argued in section 3.2.2, that resumptive conditionals are no more 'realis' than open conditionals. This argument is supported by the existence of resumptive conditionals in English where the speaker is known not to agree with the proposition in the protasis (e.g. 'But if three plus three is eight, what's four plus four?'). The use of 'attitudinal modifiers' with the indicative also supports the conclusion more specifically for Greek. For example:

O   εἰ <u>ἐτεόν</u> γ᾽ ἐμός ἐσσι καὶ αἵματος ἡμετέροιο,
16.300   μή τις ἔπειτ᾽ Ὀδυσῆος ἀκουσάτω ἔνδον ἐόντος,

If you really are my son, one of our blood, then let no one hear that Odysseus is inside,

It therefore seems reasonable to conclude that there is no such thing as a 'realis' conditional clause.

But if the distribution of future indicative and subjunctive in conditional clauses may *not* be explained in terms of different levels of realis, the distribution must be motivated in a different way. Perhaps it is connected with the 'bleaching' of meaning that BPP note when future markers are used in open conditional clauses. It could be said that resumptive conditionals are by nature the type most similar to main clauses, and could be thought of as 'quotations' of main clauses. The restriction of the future indicative to this context would therefore support the claim that the future indicative and subjunctive should be thought of as two future markers, differing in 'maturity', since resumptive conditionals require less bleaching of meaning than open ones.

It is noteworthy that all the certain examples of the future indicative in conditional clauses are found in the *Iliad* rather than the *Odyssey* (see section 1.2 for the discussion of the non-synchronic nature of the Homeric data). This could again be used to support the traditional interpretation of the moods, suggesting that the use of the future indicative in this context is 'phased out' at a time when conditional clauses were considered to be the reserve of a 'more modal' subjunctive. But the future indicative *is* found in conditional clauses in Attic Greek, if only occasionally (Goodwin: 530). This could suggest either that the lack of examples of the future indicative in the *Odyssey* is purely accidental, or that the future indicative was periodically used in conditional clauses and then avoided, according to the developing relationship between it and the subjunctive. It seems extremely likely that the relationship between the subjunctive and future indicative changed over time. The later developments will require further investigation, but in terms of the Homeric period it seems clear from the evidence of the conditional clauses that while there may be some difference between the future indicative and the subjunctive, this difference may not be explained in terms of the irrealis continuum.

4.2.2.3 Other subordinate clauses

The use of the subjunctive and future indicative in other types of subordinate clause confirm the suggestion that the future indicative and subjunctive do not differ in terms of their irrealis level. Just as in conditional clauses, the subjunctive is the usual marker of future time in subordinate clauses, and is found in a range of different contexts. In many of these contexts, the meaning of the subjunctive is comparable to the meaning we find in main clauses, expressing the projected reality of the speaker. For example:

1.242   τότε δ' οὔ τι δυνήσεαι ἀχνύμενός περ
χραισμεῖν, εὖτ' ἂν πολλοὶ ὑφ' Ἕκτορος ἀνδροφόνοιο
θνήισκοντες <u>πίπτωσι</u>·

But then you will not be able to ward off destruction, although you will be grieving, when many men will fall and die at the hands of man-killing Hector:

Here, the subjunctive is used in a 'non-restrictive' temporal clause that adds more information to the main clause, and the subjunctive has the same sense of 'prediction' that we saw in main clauses above (4.2.2.1).

The subjunctive is also found in temporal clauses which provide the temporal background for the main event (Bolling 1960). In this context the subjunctive appears again to refer to an event which lies in the projected reality of the speaker:

2.34   ἀλλὰ σὺ σῇσιν ἔχε φρεσί, μηδέ σε λήθη
αἱρείτω, εὖτ' ἄν σε μελίφρων ὕπνος <u>ἀνήηι.</u>

But keep this in your mind, and let no loss of memory overcome you when sweet sleep sets you free.

Many of the uses of the subjunctive in relative clauses may also be explained in the same terms. (See 6.4 for a discussion of relative clauses in general.) For example:

4.191 ἕλκος δ' ἰητὴρ ἐπιμάσσεται ἠδ' ἐπιθήσει
φάρμαχ', ἅ κεν <u>παύσησι</u> μελαινάων ὀδυνάων.

A doctor will treat the wound and apply medicine that will stop the black pain.

It is significant, though, that the subjunctive is not restricted to these meanings: the subjunctive is developing in these contexts, as we may see by examining the meaning of ὄφρα. The original meaning of this conjunction would appear to have been temporal 'while', since its correlative τόφρα also has this meaning (Chantraine 1980: s.v.; Bolling 1949). With this meaning it is found with various tenses. For example:

4.220 ὄφρα τοὶ <u>ἀμφεπένοντο</u> βοὴν ἀγαθὸν Μενέλαον,
τόφρα δ' ἐπὶ Τρώων στίχες ἤλυθον ἀσπιστάων·

While they tended Menelaus, good at the battle-cry, the Trojan ranks reformed with shields.

6.113 ἀνέρες ἔστε θοοὶ καὶ ἀμύνετε ἄστεϊ λώβην,
ὄφρ' ἂν ἐγὼ <u>βείω</u> προτὶ Ἴλιον ἠδὲ γέρουσιν
<u>εἴπω</u> βουλευτῆισι καὶ ἡμετέρηις ἀλόχοισιν
δαίμοσιν ἀρήσασθαι, ὑποσχέσθαι δ' ἑκατόμβας.

Now be swift, and ward off disgrace from the city, while I go to Troy and ask the old counsellors and our wives to pray to the gods, and promise them sacrifices.

As we expect, the subjunctive is found in future-referring sentences such as 6.113. In this sentence the subjunctive refers to an event that is predicted to happen in the future: the speaker is as sure as it is possible to be that the event will happen. This use is therefore again comparable to the use of the mood in main clauses. But the construction has also developed further meanings. For example:

1.510 τόφρα δ' ἐπὶ Τρώεσσι τίθει κράτος, ὄφρ' ἂν Ἀχαιοί
υἱὸν ἐμὸν <u>τίσωσιν</u> <u>ὀφέλλωσίν</u> τέ ἑ τιμῆι.

Grant the Trojans victory until the Achaeans repay my son, and raise him in honour.

1.515 νημερτὲς μὲν δή μοι ὑπόσχεο καὶ κατάνευσον,
ἢ ἀπόειπ', ἐπεὶ οὔ τοι ἔπι δέος, ὄφρ' εὖ <u>εἰδῶ</u>
ὅσσον ἐγὼ μετὰ πᾶσιν ἀτιμοτάτη θεός εἰμι.

Promise me truthfully, and bow your head in assent! Or deny me, since you have nothing to fear, so that I can know properly just how much I am the most dishonoured goddess of them all.

In 1.510, the construction has developed the meaning 'until'.[13] The occurrence of the event is thus no longer presupposed. The same is true of 1.515 where the construction has developed a purpose meaning. A similar development occurs with the conjunctions ἵνα and ὡς (see chapter 6 for further discussion of these developments).

While the subjunctive is found with a range of meanings in these subordinate clauses, the use of the future indicative is again very restricted. Most examples that are given in this context are not even unambiguously future indicative forms. The one instance of a temporal clause with the future indicative quoted by Chantraine (§333) could be 'corrected' to the subjunctive, as he admits, and as is indeed printed in the Teubner edition:

20.335   ἀλλ' ἀναχωρῆσαι, ὅτε κε <u>ξυμβλήεαι</u> αὐτῷ,
        μὴ καὶ ὑπὲρ μοῖραν δόμον Ἄϊδος εἰσαφίκηαι.

When you encounter him, retreat at once, so you do not go down to Hades' house before your time.

There are rather more examples given of the future indicative in purpose clauses.[14] But these examples too may be queried in some way. 9.251 (ἀλεξήσεις), O14.333 (πέμψουσι) and O1.57 (ἐπιλήσεται) have forms which are equivalent to a short-vowel subjunctive. In 8.110 (=16.242) and O17.6, the forms ὄψεται and εἴσεται are normally described as future forms. But we saw in section 4.2.1 that these are only the *suppletive* future forms of the verbs ὁράω and οἶδα and could therefore be subjunctive in origin (Ruijgh 1992: 76). Finally, Monro (§326.3) includes 1.344 (with a textual modification) as an example of a future indicative in a purpose clause. The reading Monro proposes, following Thiersch, is this:

1.344   οὐδέ τι οἶδε νοῆσαι ἅμα πρόσσω καὶ ὀπίσσω,
       ὅππως οἱ παρὰ νηυσὶ σόοι <u>μαχέονται</u> Ἀχαιοί.

He doesn't know how to think back and think ahead, so the Achaeans can battle safely by the ships.

Monro prefers μαχέονται to μαχεοίντο. The form μαχέοιντο is certainly anomalous, but it is unsatisfactory to use this 'corrected'

---

[13] There is a similar development in Elizabethan English: 'He shall conceal it whiles you are willing it shall come to pass' (*Twelfth Night* 4.3). See further Goodwin: 234.

[14] Chantraine: §301, 402; Kühner-Gerth: §553, Anmerk 4; Monro: §326.3.

form as evidence for the existence of a doubtful construction (see further 6.2.2 for discussion of this line).

From the several possible examples of the future indicative in purpose clauses, we are therefore left with only two that seem formally secure:

1.136 ἀλλ' εἰ μὲν δώσουσι γέρας μεγάθυμοι Ἀχαιοί,
ἄρσαντες κατὰ θυμόν, ὅπως ἀντάξιον ἔσται·
εἰ δέ κε μὴ δώωσιν, ἐγὼ δέ κεν αὐτὸς ἕλωμαι
ἢ τεὸν ἢ Αἴαντος ἰὼν γέρας,

No – if our generous Argives give me a prize, fitting my desires, so that it will be equal to what I've lost, hmm . . . But if they don't give me anything, I'll come to you, or Ajax and take *your* prize,

O   αὐτὰρ ἐμὲ προέηκε Γερήνιος ἱππότα Νέστωρ
4.163   τῷ ἅμα πομπὸν ἕπεσθαι· ἐέλδετο γάρ σε ἰδέσθαι,
ὄφρα οἱ ἤ τι ἔπος ὑποθήσεαι ἠέ τι ἔργον.

Nestor, the horseman of Gerenia, sent me with him as his escort, as he longed to see you, so you could give him some advice or help.

In section 2.2.2 we considered the future indicative in line 1.135 and concluded that the meaning was difficult to interpret because the sentence was unfinished. The same may be said for the future indicative in the ὅπως clause in the next line. Chantraine (§402) has interpreted this as a purpose clause, but Kirk et al. (ad loc.) argue that it may be interpreted in a different way: '(let them give it) fitting to my wishes in such a way that it will be a just equivalent'. Thus, although this is a certain example of a future indicative in a subordinate clause, it does not confirm the claim that the future is used in purpose clauses. This leaves us with O4.163, and when it is seen to be unique, Savelsberg's suggestion that ὑποθήσεαι is a rare form of subjunctive (Merry, Riddell and Monro ad loc.) is rather attractive. Alternatively, van Leeuwen suggests a similar 'correction' to that suggested for 20.335 above, replacing ὑπο-θήσεαι with ὑποθήεαι (Kirk et al. ad loc.). Goodwin (§565–9) thus concludes that the use of the future indicative in purpose clauses is non-Homeric.

But the existence of the future indicative in any type of subor-dinate clause is interesting, even if Goodwin's conclusion about purpose clauses is correct. In most examples, the future indicative is found in the context of an indirect question.[15] For example:

O   ὡς ἄρ' ὃ γ' ἔνθα καὶ ἔνθα ἑλίσσετο μερμηρίζων
20.28[16] ὅππως δὴ μνηστῆρσιν ἀναιδέσι χεῖρας ἐφήσει
         μοῦνος ἐών πολέσι.

So he turned this way and that, pondering how he could lay a hand on the suitors, one man against so many.

This is the most 'realis' of future-referring contexts, since the future event is almost presupposed: the only thing that is not known is *how* exactly it will turn out. This could again suggest that the future indicative was more 'realis' than the subjunctive. However, the subjunctive is found in very similar circumstances at 2.3:

2.3   ἀλλ' ὃ γε μερμήριζε κατὰ φρένα, ὡς Ἀχιλῆα
      τιμήσηι, ὀλέσηι δὲ πολὺς ἐπὶ νηυσὶν Ἀχαιῶν.

But he pondered in his heart how he could exalt Achilles, and slaughter many Achaeans at their ships.

The choice between future indicative and subjunctive in this context often depends on editorial decision. For example, the OCT prints the following text at 17.144:

17.144 φράζεο νῦν, ὅππως κε πόλιν καὶ ἄστυ σαώσηις

Now plan how you will save the town and citadel

But some manuscripts give the future indicative reading (σαώσεις), and the Teubner edition prints this. It is thus impossible to draw any firm conclusions about the distribution of the two forms in this context.

The future indicative is also found in the context of relative clauses. For example:[17]

---

[15] Also 1.136; 1.211; 2.252; 4.14; O13.376; O20.39.
[16] Here the future is found after a past tense main verb, rather like the so-called 'vivid' use of the subjunctive. See Goodwin: §344, and Merry, Riddell and Monro ad loc., who compare 12.59. Merry and Riddell and Monro suggest the future indicative could be 'corrected' to the optative ἐφείη on the basis of O20.386, a near-formulaic repetition of the line, where the optative is found in some MSS.
[17] Also 1.518; 2.231; 22.71.

17.241   οὔ τι τόσον νέκυος περιδείδια Πατρόκλοιο,
         ὅς κε τάχα Τρώων <u>κορέει</u> κύνας ἠδ᾽ οἰωνούς,

I do not fear so much for the body of dread Patroclus – he will soon glut the dogs and birds of Troy,

It could be claimed that, because this is a non-restrictive relative clause, only loosely connected to the main clause, this is the most realis of relative clauses. But we saw above (p. 73) that the subjunctive is used in 4.191 in a non-restrictive relative clause exactly parallel to the future indicative in these examples.

The evidence suggests that the future indicative is restricted to the most realis of contexts in these 'other' subordinate clauses. But the subjunctive is found in very similar environments, so that there is no straightforward way of predicting whether the subjunctive or the future indicative will be used in a particular case.

4.2.3 Conclusion

In this section I considered the 'quasi-future' uses of the subjunctive in order to assess the traditional claim that the Homeric subjunctive is more irrealis than the future indicative. I have shown that the task of differentiating between them is difficult on both formal and functional grounds. There is a great deal of homophony between the two forms, and many so-called futures are really subjunctive in origin. The functional confusion is even more marked, which might perhaps be unsurprising: recent discussions of future markers in various languages have argued that they are more 'modal' than past and present tenses, both because the role of the speaker is more obvious and because there are no 'truths' in the future. Future markers also often have other 'modal' meanings, even if their primary use is to predict events in the future. Furthermore, epistemic moods often only have future time reference. These observations could lead to the conclusion that future markers and epistemic modal markers cannot be distinguished. Here I have claimed that there is an important difference between markers which express a 'projected' future and those which express a 'potential' future. This provides a theoretical distinction against which the meanings of the Homeric Greek future indicative and subjunctive have been measured.

In main clauses, the comparison of the non-homophonous examples suggested that the difference between them is *not* that between a marker of 'projected' and 'potential' reality. Both forms are used in predictions where the speaker is unable to be sure about the likelihood of the occurrence of the event, and both are also used to express the firm intentions of the speaker. Both therefore seem to be used with a range of meanings, which could all be described as 'in line' with the speaker's view of the world. In conditional clauses too, the meaning of the subjunctive in real conditionals suggests that the subjunctive is no more irrealis than the future indicative. The context of conditional clauses does show that there is at least a distributional difference between the two forms. At least three, and possibly all four, of the certain future indicatives are found in so-called 'resumptive' conditionals, which reintroduce a piece of information available in the linguistic or non-linguistic context. Since these are almost 'quotations' of a main clause (if only an 'understood' one), this is a much less 'developed' meaning than the meanings of the subjunctive in conditional clauses. This suggests that there *was* an appreciable difference between the two categories, though a different one from that traditionally described. This conclusion is confirmed by the use of the subjunctive and future indicative in other subordinate clauses where the future indicative is again restricted to the most realis of contexts, while the subjunctive has developed wider uses.

Of course, it has long been known that the subjunctive and future indicative, in Greek as well as in other Indo-European languages, overlap in many of their uses. In the past this has led scholars such as Hahn to class the subjunctive in Greek as a future tense. The solution suggested here is rather more sophisticated: I have argued that the subjunctive is no more irrealis in meaning than the future indicative, while acknowledging that the very domain of the future is more irrealis than other tenses of the indicative, thus showing that both subjunctive and future indicative share features which we might want to describe either as 'tense-like' or 'mood-like'. Furthermore, unlike Hahn, I am not claiming that there is no difference at all between the two forms.[18] I have shown that

[18] See Lightfoot 1975: 18 for this criticism of Hahn.

there *is* a difference in distribution in conditional and other subordinate clauses: the future indicative is apparently only found in 'resumptive' conditional clauses and indirect questions, while the subjunctive is found in many types. This suggests that the subjunctive is the older form, developing more and more modal uses, while the future indicative, perhaps a 'younger' future marker, is still relatively restricted.

It thus seems appropriate to describe the Homeric subjunctive as occupying a 'transitional' position, between future tense and true mood. This transition would appear to have reached some kind of end-point in Attic Greek, where the 'future' meaning of the subjunctive is *only* found in subordinate contexts.[19] At that stage we may say that it truly has developed into a 'subjunctive' form. There is a similar development of future markers in Spanish, where a synthetic future marker is gradually being replaced by a periphrastic form (BPP: 235). In Mexican Spanish, as reported by Moreno de Alba (1977), the synthetic future is found with many more 'modal' functions than the periphrastic future. In the Iberian dialect of León this development has progressed even further so that the synthetic future is reportedly only used in subordinate clauses (Urdiales 1966).

As a coda to this argument, it is interesting to note that some scholars have claimed that the sigma marking the future indicative is the very same 'perfective' sigma we see in the aorist subjunctive.[20] If this origin is correct it suggests that there could originally have been one paradigm of forms expressing essentially future meaning (with all the modal meanings that this entails), which only later split into the two paradigms known to us as the future and subjunctive. The distribution of the two forms certainly supports the suggestion that there was a split between an older and a newer form, with the 'subjunctive' having developed more modal meanings and the 'future indicative' expressing the more basic meaning. Once the subjunctive 'lost its meaning' enough to be used in all these different types of subordinate clause it could have been seen as having strayed too far from the more 'tense-like' original use to be considered as part of the same paradigm.

[19] Monro: §279; Goodwin: §284–6; Wackernagel 1926: 236.
[20] Hewson and Bubenik 1997: 29; Hahn: §87; Schmidt 1986: 33; Kurylowicz 1964: 115.

But although this account of the formation of the subjunctive supports the findings I have proposed here for the meaning of the mood, it is not uncontroversial. The idea that the future indicative has developed from a marker which originally expressed perfective meaning is itself unremarkable: the use of a perfective form as a future tense has typological support from Slavic languages (e.g. Russian, Ukrainian, Byelorussian, Polish, Czech and Slovak), where the perfective non-past is used as a future marker (Hewson and Bubenik 1997: 39). And future meaning is certainly unsurprising for a form used to refer to an event which is seen as complete and non-past at the time of speaking (Comrie 1976: 66–7; Jakobson 1984: 49). But other scholars have claimed that the suffix marking the Greek future cannot be derived from an original *-s-, instead arguing that there must have been a laryngeal in the suffix (*-H$_1$s-) (Sihler 1995: §457). There certainly appear to be differences between aorist and future formation, as seen for example in the verb τείνω, whose aorist is ἔτεινα, but whose future is τενῶ.

The alternative explanation for the future suffix is that it derives from an original desiderative marker.[21] This claim is apparently supported by the meaning of such forms in Indo-Iranian, and possibly Latin.[22] *Prima facie* a desiderative marker is of course a good source for a future marker: we may compare the desiderative origin of the NE future auxiliary *will*. There is also some support for the theory within Greek, from the meaning of the future participle, frequently used to mark the purpose of the speaker (Chantraine: §299). There is also the category traditionally termed 'mixed aorists' which have convincingly been shown to have been built to the future stem, and which Roth (1974: 7) claims express desiderative meaning (see also Leumann 1953: 206, Magnien 1912 II: 1). But this theory too faces some problems: the desiderative meaning in Indic is only found in highly characterised verb forms, and the Latin evidence is based on two forms whose formation is highly disputed. And the 'intention' meaning seen in the future participle

---

[21] Sihler 1995: 507–9; Chantraine: §440. See also Meillet and Vendryes 1927: 183 and 199; Buck 1933: 279; Schwyzer and Debrunner I: 787, all quoted in Hahn: 61, fn. 116.

[22] Sinler 1995: §457. Indo-Iranian: *jighāsati* 'wishes to slay', *īpsati* 'wishes to obtain', *bibhitsati* 'wishes to slay', *śikṣati* 'wishes to be able to', *bhikṣati* 'wishes to share'. Latin: *viso* 'visit, wish to see', *quaeso*, 'beg'.

and 'mixed aorist' forms could have arisen from a future meaning rather than proving an original desiderative meaning.

In conclusion, the two theories on the origin of the future suffix depend on detailed evidence about the nature of verbal formation in Indo-European which there is no space to go into here. In any case, the argument proposed here, that the future and subjunctive are functionally very similar but that the distributional difference between them is gradually increasing, may be made independently of the claim that the two forms are also formally related.

4.3 Hortative

4.3.1 Introduction

The hortative meaning of the subjunctive is found in the first person singular and plural, where it is described as 'supplying the place' of a first-person imperative.[23] The comparison with the imperative highlights the performative nature of the construction discussed in 2.3.3. For example:

2.236   οἴκαδέ περ σὺν νηυσὶ <u>νεώμεθα,</u>

Let's sail off for home!

O   ἀλλ' ἄγεθ', ὑμῖν τεύχε' <u>ἐνείκω</u> θωρηχθῆναι
22.139   ἐκ θαλάμου·

But come, let me bring you weapons from the store-room to arm yourself with.

Grammarians give occasional examples of this meaning in other persons too (Chantraine: §306; Monro: §275b). However, they may be shown to be not truly hortative. For example:[24]

13.47   Αἴαντε, σφὼ μέν τε <u>σαώσετε</u> λαὸν Ἀχαιῶν
         ἀλκῆς μνησαμένω, μηδὲ κρυεροῖο φόβοιο.

My two Ajaxes – you will save the Achaean army if you remember your strength and forget the threat of icy death.

In 13.47 Poseidon certainly *wants* the two Ajaxes to save the Achaeans, and it is perhaps this 'will' which has led the

[23] Goodwin: §255; Chantraine §306; Monro: §275a.
[24] Also 1.205; 9.701; 21.60; O1.396; O4.80; O4.391; O10.507.

81

grammarians to class it in the same way as the first-person construction. But the Ajaxes want it too: Poseidon is not ordering them
to do something, but is rather explaining how their objective will
be achieved. In other examples given by the grammarians it is clear
that the speaker does not even *want* the event to happen, let alone
that he is ordering it. For example:

22.505   νῦν δ᾽ ἂν πολλὰ <u>πάθῃσι,</u> φίλου ἀπὸ πατρὸς ἁμαρτών,

He'll suffer much more, now he's lost his father,

Here Andromache surely does not want Astyanax to suffer in this
way, she is merely predicting that he will, epistemically. There is
therefore no need to claim that the subjunctive expresses hortative
meaning in anything other than the first person.

The description of this construction as a first-person imperative
must be examined in some detail, since the very existence of such
a concept has been disputed. Lyons argues that forms called first-
person imperatives are not really imperatives, because 'the subject
of these so-called imperatives does not refer to the addressee'.[25]
For example, in English, the grammatical subject of the imperative in 'let's go' is the second person, whereas in fact the speaker
includes himself in the exhortation, meaning that the real addressee
is 'us'. However, as we have seen in 2.3.3, although this construction may have started as a second person directive, in its developed
form it has lost any sense of being directed to that second person.[26]
Xrakovskij (2001a: 1031–3) has concluded that first-person imperatives do exist, on the basis both of the formal existence of special
forms for first-person imperatives in certain languages and also the
semantic criterion that obligations may be placed on other actors
as well as the second person. His cross-linguistic study shows
that first-person plural hortative constructions generally express
'invitation' while first-person singular hortative constructions only
express 'auto-prescription' (Xrakovskij 2001: 1031).

In the next section the Homeric Greek subjunctive in the first
person will be shown to express just these two meanings. I will
argue that these meanings could have developed from the future

[25] Lyons 1977: 747. See also Justus 2000: 165 and Sihler 1995: 601.
[26] Hopper and Traugott 1993: 10–14; Davies 1986: 230. See also Faarlund 1985 for a
discussion of a similar development in Norwegian.

meaning I have claimed for the subjunctive in section 4.2. But this does not exhaust the interest of the examples of the hortative construction: in section 4.3.3 I will show that many of the examples categorised by the grammars as hortative are not performative. Thus the subjunctive appears to have a third, true deontic meaning.

4.3.2 Analysis of hortative meaning

The plural construction, as exemplified by 2.236 (see above 4.3.1), is more commonly found than the singular. Goodwin (§256) claims that, in this construction the subjunctive 'generally expresses an exhortation of the speaker to others to join him in doing or not doing some act'. This is just the 'invitation' sense we expect in a first-person plural imperative construction as defined by Xrakovskij (2001a: 1033).

It is not difficult to derive this directive use of the subjunctive from the future meaning of the subjunctive observed in section 4.2. As mentioned in 2.3.3, it is cross-linguistically common for future markers to develop a directive use.[27] We may see a similar use of the second-person future indicative in later Greek.[28] For example:

πάντως δὲ τοῦτο δράσεις

but by all means do this

Aristophanes *Clouds* 1352

The development of a future marker to hortative marker in the first person receives more specific cross-linguistic support from the construction in modern Hebrew (Malygina 2001: 271). This cross-linguistically common development is unsurprising given the similarity between the two constructions. Future markers include the component of 'action incomplete at the moment of speech', which is also part of the characteristic semantics of imperative forms (Xrakovskij 2001a: 1035). But we noted in 2.3.2 that it is not enough to note that two related constructions share some element of meaning. Rather we should trace the development from one to the other.

---

[27] BPP: 273; Ultan 1978: 103; Fleischman 1982: 129; Heine 1995b: 120; Kibardina 2001: 325.
[28] Chantraine: §306; Monro: §275b; Goodwin: §69.

The restriction of the development of this particular meaning to the first-person plural suggests that the 'meaning' has arisen through a 'conventionalisation of implicature' present only in the first-person plural (see 2.3.3). We may perhaps see a comparable development in the English expression 'shall we dance?'. This expression is literally a question about the possibility of a future event. At face value it is exactly the same as a question asking about the future actions of a third person, for example 'will he ring tonight?' However, because of the difference in person, the two sentences are associated with two different implicatures. When asking about a third person's actions, it is most likely that the speaker and addressee do not know how he will act. The question 'will he ring tonight?' may therefore only be interpreted epistemically, since the speaker does not know whether the third person will ring, and is asking for the addressee's opinion on the likelihood of it happening. This meaning is particularly clear in sentences with an inanimate subject. For example, the sentence 'will it rain tonight?' may only be interpreted as a question about how likely the addressee thinks the event to be, with the implication that the speaker does not know. The situation is rather different in the first-person plural. Since speakers generally know what they will do in the future, or at least what they intend to do, the implication of asking about a future action of two or more people including the speaker will often be that the speaker intends to do it and wants to do it, and is wondering whether the second person will do it as well. Such a statement of 'wondering' will easily be interpreted as an invitation, particularly when the action is a joint one, like dancing. Thus it is the interaction between the meaning and the person which provides the development of a new use.

This speculative explanation of the development of the construction is supported by the occasional printing of question marks in these sentences. For example, the OCT prints the following at 5.34:

5.34 νῶϊ δὲ χαζώμεσθα, Διὸς δ' ἀλεώμεθα μῆνιν;

Shall we stay clear and escape Zeus's rage?

However, the question mark is only editorial, and indeed is not printed in the Teubner edition. In any case, not all the examples

84

of the hortative subjunctive are interpreted as questions. Nonetheless, the restriction of this meaning to the first-person plural does suggest that it has arisen because of the particular inferences associated with the first person plural. Even stating future acts of a group of people of which the speaker is a member could have the implicature that the speaker 'wants' those acts to happen and is therefore inviting the group to do them.

It was mentioned in section 2.3.3 that the nature of speaker-oriented modality will mean that it will be difficult to assert whether a particular use is merely pragmatic and context-driven or whether it has become so conventionalised that it may be described as a separate meaning. Here the invitation meaning of the subjunctive is found rather frequently, so that although it is plausible that the 'meaning' began as only an indirect implicature, the meaning now appears to be generally associated with the first-person plural, when uttered in appropriate circumstances. It is thus attractive to describe this as a separate meaning, rather than just a pragmatic use.

In the singular construction, we expect from Xrakovskij's cross-linguistic study (2001a: 1031) that a first-person imperative will express the meaning of 'autoprescription', that is an order to oneself. Several of the examples of the construction in the grammars could indeed be interpreted as fitting this definition. For example:[29]

O   ἀλλ' ἄγεθ', ὑμῖν τεύχε' ἐνείκω θωρηχθῆναι
22.139   ἐκ θαλάμου·

But come, let me bring you weapons from the store-room to arm yourself with.

There are also a few examples of the plural subjunctive apparently expressing this meaning rather than the invitation meaning considered above. For example:[30]

3.283   εἰ μέν κεν Μενέλαον Ἀλέξανδρος καταπέφνηι,
    αὐτὸς ἔπειθ' Ἑλένην ἐχέτω καὶ κτήματα πάντα,
    ἡμεῖς δ' ἐν νήεσσι νεώμεθα ποντοπόροισιν·

If Alexander kills Menelaus, let him keep Helen and all her treasure, and let us depart in our seafaring ships.

---

[29] Also 9.121; 22.416; 22.450; 23.071; O6.126; O9.37; O13.215; O22.139; O22.429; O23.73.
[30] Also O24.485.

It would be possible to explain the development of the 'auto-prescription' meaning in the same way as the invitation meaning considered above: statements about the future in the first person may occasionally have the 'conversational implicature' that the speaker is urging himself to do it.

4.3.3 Analysis of non-hortative meaning

The examples of the hortative construction considered above fit the pattern that we expect from the cross-linguistic study of directive constructions, as well as fitting in with the semantics of the subjunctive as we have observed in section 4.2. But several of the examples given by grammarians to illustrate the construction in the first-person singular do not appear to be hortative at all. In this section I will examine these examples in more detail, and will argue that they provide a further layer of complexity to the map of the subjunctive.

Monro (§275a) describes many of the first-person singular examples he groups as 'quasi-imperative' as expressing the 'resolve' of the speaker. For example:[31]

O   εἰ δέ κε τεθνηῶτος ἀκούσω μηδ' ἔτ' ἐόντος,
2.222 νοστήσας δὴ ἔπειτα φίλην ἐς πατρίδα γαῖαν
          σῆμά τέ οἱ χεύω καὶ ἐπὶ κτέρεα κτερεΐξω
          πολλὰ μάλ', ὅσσα ἔοικε, καὶ ἀνέρι μητέρα δώσω.

If I hear he's dead, no longer alive, I'll go back to my beloved home, raise a grave-mound for him, and add to his burial honours as much as he deserves, and give my mother to another.

It is clear that this is not truly hortative as Telemachus is *not* here imposing his will on himself. The difference between this sentence and a true hortative construction may be seen in the report that would have been made of this statement. While a hortative statement would be reported 'Telemachus ordered himself to bury his father' *vel sim.*, the statement in O2.222 would be reported 'Telemachus said that he wanted to/was going to bury his father.'

How then should we describe the modality of this sentence? It fits into neither of the categories previously thought to be expressed

---

[31] Also 9.121 and O12.383.

by the subjunctive: Telemachus is not imposing his will on himself (speaker-oriented modality) or making an epistemic statement about his future actions ('I reckon I'll build him a mound'). Instead the subjunctives in O2.222 express the *intent* of the speaker: the speaker intends the non-factual, future action described to take place (if the condition in the protasis is also fulfilled), and is himself the potential controlling agent of that action. The subjunctive in this meaning is not speaker-oriented, but is rather truly deontic, sharing the prototypical features of deontic modality as set out by Heine (1995a: 29, and listed in section 2.3.3 p. 28), but not the performative illocutionary force of the speaker-oriented constructions.

In addition to the epistemic and speaker-oriented meanings described in the traditional accounts, the subjunctive thus has a further meaning. The 'discovery' of this new meaning is entirely in harmony with the conclusions reached about the nature of the subjunctive in the epistemic constructions. The sense of intention has been shown to be fundamental to future markers: indeed BPP have argued that all future markers will pass through a stage where they express the intention of the speaker.[32] The true deontic meaning of the subjunctive is thus just what we expect to be expressed by the mood, having concluded that it should best be described as some kind of future marker.

It is again unsurprising that this deontic use of a future marker is not confined to the subjunctive, but is also found with the future indicative:

4.39   ἄλλο δέ τοι ἐρέω, σὺ δ᾿ἐνὶ φρεσὶ βάλλεο σῇσιν·

I will tell you one more thing, and I urge you to take it to heart:

Here too, the verb refers to a non-factual event that will happen later. The speaker wants it to happen, and it will be carried out by a controlling agent (the speaker), which will lead to a change of state.

The existence of this deontic meaning appears again to be partially determined by the combination of the meaning of the

---

[32] BPP 1994: 256: See also Ultan 1978; Fleischman 1982; Coates 1983; Dahl 1985; Heine 1995b: 126.

subjunctive or future indicative marker with the grammatical category of 'person'. In the first-person singular, dispassionate epistemic speculations about how things will turn out do not occur as readily as in other persons. That is, there is a marked difference between the statements 'It's going to rain later' and 'I'll pick you up at half past three.' The first statement is clearly epistemic, and could be 'glossed' as 'I believe it's going to rain later.' The second sentence may not be glossed in the same way. The speaker is not stating his beliefs but his intentions: 'I intend to pick you up at half past three.' Because of the nature of future time, both are referring to events whose occurrence is epistemically uncertain. But the first-person sentence has elements of deontic modality, because it is understood that the speaker wants the future to turn out in that way. This is not to say that the first person may not be used in the epistemic sense. For example, the sentence 'One day I'll be as old as you' would not necessarily be interpreted as a statement of the speaker's intention or desire, but rather as an epistemic judgement about the future, in which case it would be glossed 'I believe/I am sure that I will be as old as you one day.' But future markers in the first person are more commonly used with deontic rather than epistemic meanings. This provides further evidence that there is not as clear a cut-off point between epistemic and deontic modality as has been thought, and that the important axis to determine the meaning is the axis of person, as suggested by Heine (1995a: 26) in his consideration of the modal verbs in German.

The acknowledgement of the existence of 'true' deontic meaning for the subjunctive allows us to return to the question of the 'auto-prescription' meaning of the subjunctive apparently found in the first-person singular, and to consider it in a new light. We may question whether the meaning of 'auto-prescription' should really be classified as a separate meaning at all. The difference between an expression of intent and an order to oneself is really very slight, and may be accounted for according to whether the speaker really *wants* to perform the action. If the action is unpleasant, a statement of intent will more obviously be taken as an order to oneself (cf. 'I *will* put out the rubbish tonight'). When describing a 'pleasant' action which the speaker is clearly happy to do, this meaning is not apparent (cf. 'I will arrive by 8 o'clock'). But this difference is very small, and would seem to be determined by the pragmatic contexts rather than signifying a different meaning. In the examples previously classed as expressing auto-prescription, it is really only the presence of other imperative forms which encourages us to take the subjunctive in this way. We may therefore reconsider O22.139:

O   ἀλλ' ἄγεθ', ὑμῖν τεύχε' <u>ἐνείκω</u> θωρηχθῆναι
22.139 ἐκ θαλάμου·

But come, let me bring you weapons from the store-room to arm yourself with.

Indeed, it is more attractive to describe this as a statement of intent: 'Come then, and I will bring you weapons' rather than as a prescription to the speaker. In the first-person singular, then, we may conclude that any 'performative' meaning is more an implicature than a true meaning, at least in Homeric Greek.

4.3.4 Conclusion

The hortative uses of the subjunctive are very restricted. It is possible that they developed from the combination of future meaning and the first person. In the first-person plural the implicature appears to be so regularly associated with the construction that 'invitation' may be seen as a separate meaning expressed by the subjunctive. The examples of the construction in the first-person singular lead to some more interesting and complicated conclusions. Most of the examples given by grammarians are not 'hortative' at all. Instead they are true 'deontic' markers.

This conclusion clearly demonstrates just how wrong previous accounts of the moods have been in their attempt to strait-jacket the wide and varied uses of the moods into neat tables. We do not have a binary distinction between epistemic and non-epistemic meanings, but really a three-way system of epistemic, speaker-oriented and deontic. My new map of the subjunctive must also recognise that this system has a complicated relationship with person: both hortative and deontic meanings arise mainly in the first person, due to the particular properties of first-person statements, showing both that the different fields are not easy to distinguish, and that they interact with other grammatical categories.

4.4 Negative directive

4.4.1 Introduction

In the negative directive construction, the subjunctive is said to 'replace' the imperative just as in the hortative construction (Goodwin: §259). According to the well-known grammar-book rule, positive commands are expressed by the aorist or present imperative, whereas in negative commands either the present imperative or the aorist subjunctive is used, resulting in the following asymmetrical pattern of forms:[33]

Positive	Negative
present imperative	μή + present imperative
aorist imperative	μή + aorist subjunctive

In most previous explanations, scholars have claimed that the difference between the aorist subjunctive and present imperative in this construction is one of aspect alone, and the difference in mood has been deemed insignificant.[34]

The use of the subjunctive as a marker of the imperative would in itself be unremarkable given the meaning of the mood that we have described in section 4.2. As we have seen, the use of future markers with directive illocutionary force is common, and we could explain this new 'meaning' (or new illocutionary force) of the subjunctive in terms of a conventionalisation of implicature in a similar way to our explanation of the hortative subjunctive as outlined in section 4.3.2. The development is particularly unsurprising since it only arises in conjunction with the negator μή, which could be said to 'carry' some of the meaning of the construction (see further appendix 1 on the meaning of the negators).

---

[33] Monro: §328; Chantraine: §338–40; Smyth: §1835, §1840; Goodwin: §250, §259.

[34] For interpretations of the meaning of aspect in ancient Greek imperatives see most recently Sicking 1991; McKay 1986; Bakker, W. F. 1966; Louw 1959, and for Homer in particular, Friedrich 1974. For aspect in general, see Comrie 1976. McKay (1986: 44, fn. 13) explicitly denies the significance of the difference in mood: 'The substitution of subjunctive for imperative in ancient prohibitions does not affect the aspectual question,' as does Goodwin (§259): 'The distinction of tense here is solely the ordinary distinction between the present and aorist and has no reference to the moods.'

But in this section I will show that the distribution of aspect and mood in this construction requires further attention. The central question is this: if the difference between the imperative and subjunctive in this construction is purely aspectual, why could the aorist imperative not have been used instead? It is not enough to claim, as Moore did (1934: §158), that it is due to 'idiomatic convention' alone. I will suggest that previous attempts to answer this question have been unsatisfactory, and that the difference in mood *is* significant. In section 4.4.4 I will show that other languages grammaticalise two different types of negative directive sentences, and in 4.4.5 I will argue that it is more attractive to explain the Greek constructions in this way rather than viewing them as one unified construction.

4.4.2 *Previous explanations*

Chantraine (§340) claims that the aorist subjunctive was preferred to the aorist imperative in the negative directive construction because the two aspects 'developed' in two separate waves: the aorist (perfective) was developed first because the present (imperfective) 'conviendrait mieux à l'ordre qu'à la défense'. He must also claim that, at the time of this first development, there was a restriction against the use of imperatives in negative directives, and so the subjunctive was used. Imperfective negative directives developed later, by which time the original restriction was not operating any longer, and the present imperative could be used.

This claim can be criticised on many fronts. Firstly, Chantraine does not explain in any great detail the original system which the aorist subjunctive and present imperative replace. It would seem that he is here imagining a system which for some time did not have *any* formal way of marking prohibitions at all, which is rather implausible. Furthermore, both cross-linguistic evidence and internal Greek evidence contradict his claim that the imperfective aspect is less suited to negative directives than the perfective. In the Slavic languages, the branch of Indo-European apart from Greek where aspect is most entrenched, it is *perfective* negative directives which are rare (Boguslawski 1985: 225; Kucera 1985: 118). In Homeric Greek itself the present imperative is used much more commonly in negative directives than the aorist subjunctive (Stephens 1983: 69, fn. 2). If there ever was a preference for perfective negative directives in Greek, it has apparently been completely reversed by the time of Homer.

More plausible and useful suggestions to explain the skewing of mood in the construction base their arguments on the observation that in Vedic texts, *mā* (cognate with Greek μή) is not found with the imperative form, but only the 'injunctive' (Monro: §328; Szemerényi 1996: 263). The existence of this category and its true meaning has long been debated, but it seems clear that the form at least (augmentless past indicative) may be reconstructed for PIE.[35] The importance of the Vedic evidence lies in its demonstration that the use of both the imperative and subjunctive in this construction are innovations of Greek. But it still leaves unanswered the question why a single category should have been replaced by two.

Monro (§328) points to the rarity of the aorist imperative in Sanskrit and what he describes as the 'late origin' of the forms of the weak aorist imperative in Greek. He concludes that Greek originally had no aorist imperatives at all, and that the injunctive would originally have been replaced by the (aorist and present) subjunctive. Later a development took place whereby imperative forms were introduced into prohibitions, but since there was no aorist imperative, the replacement could only happen in the present aspect: 'In other words, the form μὴ κλέπτε came into use in pre-historic Greek as an extension of the positive κλέπτε, and superseded μὴ κλέπτης: but μὴ κλέψῃς kept its ground because the form κλέψον did not then exist.'

But this explanation also encounters problems. Firstly, it is a misrepresentation of the Sanskrit evidence: while in the classical language it is true to state that the imperative is almost always present in form, the same is *not* true of the oldest evidence. In Vedic, imperatives are formed to present, aorist and perfect stems.[36] Monro's second argument, that the weak aorist endings in Greek

---

[35] Sihler 1995: §416; Kiparsky 1968; Vai 1998: 54–60. The name is thought first to have appeared in Brugmann 1916: 520, 539 in a description of the Celtic form. According to Hahn (§55), the category was 'invented' by Delbrück. The different functions were listed by Whitney 1892: 221.

[36] Macdonell 1916: 118 §122a; Burrow 1973: 350; Stephens 1983: 69.

appear to be recent innovations, does not explain why imperatives were not formed to *strong* aorist roots, since these use the same endings as the present imperative. The claim that the ending is of late origin is also nowhere proved: Sihler merely claims that its origins are 'obscure' (Sihler 1995: §547.5). Finally, the argument claims that the Greek system is the result of two waves of replacements, when even one is hard to explain: there is no explanation given for why the present imperative should ever have replaced the present subjunctive.

4.4.3 *More than an aspectual difference?*

The claim that the difference between the aorist subjunctive and present imperative is purely aspectual is therefore made without satisfactory explanation of why the aorist imperative is not used instead. This automatically increases the plausibility of the alternative explanation: that there is a bigger difference between the two moods than previously thought. In this section I will review evidence which further supports this claim, considering the syntactic, semantic and even metrical distribution of the two constructions.

When discussing the use of the subjunctive in the negative directive construction I believe it is of central importance to note that certain subordinate clauses, namely the fear and negative purpose clauses introduced by μή, are generally agreed to have developed directly from the construction (Chantraine: §386; Schwyzer: 672). For example:

6.432 ἀλλ' ἄγε νῦν ἐλέαιρε καὶ αὐτοῦ μίμν' ἐπὶ πύργωι,
       μὴ παῖδ' ὀρφανικὸν θήηις χήρην τε γυναῖκα.

Wait, take pity and stay here on the wall, so you don't make an orphan of your child and a widow of your wife.

In this example we may indeed question whether this sentence really does involve a subordinate clause: it could instead be understood as two consecutive directives: 'have pity, do not make your child an orphan'. However, there are some examples where the negator has developed an undeniable subordinating use. For example:

10.348   εἰ δ' ἄμμε παραφθαίησι πόδεσσιν,
        αἰεί μιν ποτὶ νῆας ἀπὸ στρατόφι προτιειλεῖν,
        ἔγχει ἐπαΐσσων, μή πως προτὶ ἄστυ ἀλύξῃι.

If he outruns us, press him against the ship, away from his forces, and rush at him with your spear so he can't escape back to town.

The development of these types of clauses suggests that the subjunctive is not equivalent to an imperative in the negative directive construction, since the imperative construction does not develop such a use. Indeed, imperatives in all languages very rarely appear in subordinate contexts, if at all (Palmer[2]: 80). Although Elmsley (1825: commentary to line 543) has listed twelve examples in ancient Greek, these always appear to be some kind of anacoluthon and are anyway only post-Homeric.[37] It therefore seems erroneous to describe the subjunctive as equivalent to an imperative in this construction.

Describing the subjunctive as an imperative also does not capture the semantic range of the construction. This is most clearly apparent in the first-person subjunctive but an acknowledgement of a difference will also help to explain the exact meaning of some of the second-person examples. In the first person, the subjunctive has two clearly distinguishable meanings. The first meaning is just what we expect from the combination of the hortative meaning of the subjunctive and the negative particle. For example:

12.216   μὴ ἴομεν Δαναοῖσι μαχησόμενοι περὶ νηῶν.

Let's not go and fight them at their ships.

23.7   μὴ δή πω ὑπ' ὄχεσφι λυώμεθα μώνυχας ἵππους,
       ἀλλ' αὐτοῖς ἵπποισι καὶ ἅρμασιν ἆσσον ἰόντες
       Πάτροκλον κλαίωμεν·

Let us not release the horses from the chariots yet, but drive them past Patroclus and mourn him with horses and chariots.

---

[37] These examples are found at: Soph. *OT* 543; Eur. *Hec.* 225; *IA* 725; *Cycl.* 131; *Her.* 452; *Hel.* 322, 1249; *IT* 1029; Arist. *Eq.* 1158; *Pac.* 1061; *Av.* 54, 80. Some of these also in Goodwin: §253. Jebb first suggests the idea that this might be an anacoluthon in the commentary to *OT* 543 (Jebb 1893). He terms it a replacement of οἶσθ' ὡς δεῖ σε ποιῆσαι caused by the 'anxious haste of the speaker', although he does later also claim that there is 'no reason, in logic or in grammar, against this "subordinate imperative", which the flexible Greek idiom allowed'.

These sentences are hortative constructions of the type studied above (4.3). The speaker invites the group (including himself) to carry out a particular action, which in this case is negative. They could therefore be glossed 'I invite us *not* to go /release our horses.' But some of the first-person subjunctives have quite a different meaning:

24.53   μὴ ἀγαθῶι περ ἐόντι <u>νεμεσσηθέωμέν</u> οἱ ἡμεῖς·

Let him take care, or we gods will become angry with him, however brave he is!

As the translation shows, this is *not* an invitation to refrain from anger addressed to the first-person plural subject. Rather it is addressed to a third person, Achilles, warning him to take preventative action against the gods (the first-person plural subject) becoming angry with him (Gonda: 200).

Several of the second-person examples could be interpreted in the same way. For example:

23.428   στεινωπὸς γὰρ ὁδός, τάχα δ᾽ εὐρυτέρη παρελάσσαι -
μή πως ἀμφοτέρους <u>δηλήσεαι</u> ἅρματι κύρσας.

The road is narrow here, soon it will be wider. Don't harm us both by crashing the chariot.

In the translation offered here, the subjunctive has been interpreted as expressing a straightforward prohibition 'don't harm us'. But we may alternatively interpret it in the same way as 24.53: 'take care that you don't harm us'. In this situation the latter interpretation seems preferable as the addressee would surely not *want* to harm his passenger as well as himself.

The final reason to think that there is a difference that is greater than merely aspectual between the subjunctive and imperative comes from the metrical evidence. Stephens (1983:75) has shown that, while all the present imperative forms are metrically secure the aorist subjunctives are always metrically equivalent to injunctive forms. This suggests that the replacement of the aorist injunctive took place during the composition of the poem, since as soon as an aorist injunctive was used in a formula it would not have been possible to replace it except with a metrically identical form. The replacement of the present injunctive by the present imperative on the other hand appears to have taken place before the composition of the poems so that the present injunctive would never have been used in the epic diction. This provides evidence for two different 'waves' of development rather similar to those proposed by Chantraine and Monro (see 4.4.2, although note that in both their arguments, it was the aorist subjunctive which was held to be the more 'original' form). It is attractive to explain these two waves in terms of the two rather different meanings expressed by the different moods, as suggested by the syntactic and semantic evidence.

4.4.4 Cross-linguistic evidence for two different constructions

The syntactic, semantic and metrical evidence presented above suggests that the subjunctive and imperative are *not* equivalent in the negative directive construction. It is therefore interesting to note a recent cross-linguistic study which showed that several languages (e.g. Russian, Aleut, Tatar, Even and Armenian) grammaticalise two *different* negative directive constructions, which are called 'preventive' and 'prohibitive' (Birjulin and Xrakovskij 2001: 34). In this section these two types will be defined and exemplified so that we may then consider whether this distinction could be used to explain the use of two moods in Homeric Greek.

According to the basic definition, 'preventive' sentences order a 'non-performance of uncontrollable actions' while 'prohibitive' sentences order a 'non-performance of controllable actions' (Birjulin and Xrakovskij 2001: 34). An example of preventive meaning is 'don't fall over', while an example of prohibitive meaning is 'don't eat any more'. The agent is capable of 'obeying' the prohibition by choosing not to eat any more, while he is not (normally) capable of choosing not to fall over.

Since actions are generally either controllable or uncontrollable, this basic definition suggests that the choice between a prohibitive rather than a preventive marker will depend solely on the semantics of the verb in question. But in fact it has been shown that the difference lies rather in the way that the speaker wants to present the event. The difference may be understood by considering the exact semantics of the two 'prototypical' types. In preventive sentences the speaker is exhorting the addressee to take care for an event not to happen, and is therefore also usually advising him to take avoiding action: thus in the sentence 'don't fall over' the speaker could be seen as advising the agent to walk carefully so he does not end up falling over. Such a meaning may also be found with verbs that are strictly controllable: thus if the sentence 'don't wake the baby' were marked with a preventive marker it would really mean 'don't speak loudly, or else you'll wake the baby' (Birjulin and Xrakovskij 2001: 37). This would be distinguished from the straightforward prohibition which could follow, say, an offer to wake the baby ('no, don't').

Thus the preventive is generally used in contexts where caution is being advised, 'to warn the performer ... to be careful to avoid actions that may be hazardous for the performer, the speaker, or a third person/persons' (Birjulin and Xrakovskij 2001: 37) or 'a warning against some undesirable consequences of the listener's actions s/he does not take into account' (Kozintseva 2001: 258). We may see an example of this use of a preventive marker with a semantically controllable verb in the following Armenian sentence:

29 *De,*   *zekucir,*   *t'e*   *inč*   *es₁arel₂.*   *Tes,*
   well, report:IMP:2SG, that what do:PRF:2SG$_{1,2}$. Mind,

   čxabes,   *ha ...* *Teɣnyteyə kb̆rnem*
   NEG:cheat:SBJV:FUT:2SG (PREV), hey ... At once COND:catch:FUT:1SG
   'Come on, report what you've done. Mind you, don't cheat (PREV) ... I'll catch you at once.'

Perhaps because of this connection to 'hazardous' or undesirable events, scholars have noticed that the preventive may also be used in more emphatic prohibitions. For example, Kozintseva (2001: 258) notes the following Armenian sentence:

30 *Gna* *čk'vir,*   *minčev* *šnikə* *čberes*
   go   get.out:IMP:2SG, unless doggy COND:bring:FUT:2SG

   ačk'is₁čerevas₂
   NEG:show.oneself:SBJV:2SG$_{1,2}$(PREV)
   'Get out of my sight and don't show yourself (PREV) unless you bring the doggy here.'

The preventive marker implies that the event warned against is harmful, and thus appears to heighten the strength with which the injunction is made.

Just as preventive markers are found with controllable verbs, prohibitive markers are found with verbs that are strictly uncontrollable. This use perhaps arises from a desire to present certain actions as controllable, which would have the effect of forbidding it with more strength. For example, Kozintseva noticed that the prohibitive in Armenian is used to 'express a strong prescription for the performer to keep his/her situation under control' (Kozintseva 2001: 256), even when those actions are strictly uncontrollable:

31 *Ēli*   *čap'd*   *mi*   *korcu,*   *ay*   *tχa*
   Again   size:POSS2   NEG   lose:IMP:2SG (PROHIB)   hey   buddy
   'Don't you forget yourself (PROHIB) again, buddy.'

Similarly, the prohibitive is found in Armenian forbidding emotions, again strictly uncontrollable, to 'convey the speaker's wish to improve the listener's currently adverse emotional state' (Kozintseva 2001: 257). For example:

32 *Aṙanjin*   *ban*   *čka,*   *gluxn*   *ēₑcavum₂,*
   particular   thing   NEG:be:PRES:3SG,   head   ache:PRES:3SG$_{1,2}$,

   kancni   *mi*   *anhangstana*
   COND:pass:FUT:3SG   NEG   worry:IMP:2SG (PROHIB)
   'It's nothing, she's only got a headache, it'll pass. Don't worry (PROHIB).'

The different uses of preventive and prohibitive markers may be summed up as follows. While the basic use of the preventive is with uncontrollable actions, it is also used to advise caution about actions that may be controllable, and also to make more emphatic prohibitions. The prohibitive is usually used to forbid controllable actions, but is also used when wishing to improve the listener's currently adverse emotional state, and in strong prescriptions to keep the situation under control, even when the action may be strictly uncontrollable.

The above description of the different meanings of preventive and prohibitive markers demonstrates that it is difficult to clearly differentiate the two spheres of meaning, even in languages where it is certain from a formal point of view that there are two separate constructions. This is further confirmed by studying translations between two languages where the distinction is grammaticalised. Golovko has shown that in translations between Russian and Aleut, the prohibitive marker in Russian is sometimes translated by the preventive marker in Aleut, as for example in the following Aleut translation from a Russian Bible (Golovko 2001: 311):

33 *Tx̂idix̂ iĝatnas. Taĝa hamaan ngiin tunux-taqangis:*
 Iĝatu-uĝana-xtxichix
 be afraid:PREV:2PL
 'They were amazed. And he said to them, "Do not be amazed (PREV)..."'   (Mark 16:5, 6)

A study of an Armenian translation of a Russian text has shown that the categories are not equivalent in those languages either (Kozintseva 2001: 259). Since we have seen that the choice between preventive and prohibitive forms can arise from the speaker's desire to present an action in a particular way, it is perhaps unsurprising that the distinction may be different in each language. But it shows that the choice between the two markers is largely subjective, and open to disagreement. It should also be pointed out that the difference between prohibitive and preventive meaning is not always grammatically expressed. For example, Japanese has only one marker which is used with both prohibitive and preventive meanings (Alpatov 2001: 119). Both types are of course translated by the simple 'do not' construction in English, which shows that the same holds there.

4.4.5 Homeric analysis

The traditional explanation for the use of two moods in the negative directive construction is not sufficient, and the evidence from other languages has shown that it is possible to distinguish two different types of negative directive construction. These two findings suggest that the Homeric data should be reconsidered. In this section I will argue that the aorist subjunctive could indeed be described as a preventive marker in this construction, on the basis both of its meaning and its distribution. I must however acknowledge that these arguments largely stem from a necessarily subjective reading both of the Homeric evidence and the distinction as seen in the other languages.

Describing the subjunctive as a preventive marker is particularly attractive in the case of the 'non-hortative' meaning of the first-person subjunctive, examples of which we considered in section 4.3.3:

24.53   μὴ ἀγαθῶι περ ἐόντι <u>νεμεσσηθέωμέν</u> οἱ ἡμεῖς·

Let him take care, or we gods will become angry with him, however brave he is!

8.95   μή τίς τοι φεύγοντι μεταφρένωι ἐν δόρυ <u>πήξηι</u>·

Take care, or a spear may hit you in your back as you flee.

In these sentences the subjunctive is not being used to advise a particular course of action to the subject. Rather, just as in the sentence 'don't wake the baby' the speaker is suggesting that the event will happen unless the addressee takes care. A preventive meaning for the subjunctive would also explain its use in the more 'developed' fear and negative purpose constructions. It is exactly uncontrollable actions that we fear, which is why a preventive marker could develop into subordinate clauses, while a prohibitive marker could not.

But the focus of our investigations here is the second-person construction, where the subjunctive appears most clearly to be 'filling a gap' in the imperative paradigm. There are unfortunately very few examples: in this construction there are only eleven aorist subjunctives in the *Iliad* and the *Odyssey*, compared with sixty-eight present imperatives in the *Iliad* alone.[38] Any claim for the meaning of the subjunctive in this construction must therefore acknowledge the possibility that, were there more examples, they could contradict the suggested meanings. But it is at least interesting to note that

---

[38] There is some difficulty in the classification of this construction, since the borderline between independent directive sentences and subordinate 'lest' clauses is unclear. Here I have only considered examples of the μή + subjunctive construction which are not preceded by another directive sentence, since in this context it is possible to describe the latter construction as dependent on the first, though I acknowledge that this is not an entirely satisfactory solution.

all eleven of the examples of the subjunctive could be described as preventive.

There are four examples of the subjunctive which relate to the emotions of the speaker. For example:[39]

9.33 Ἀτρείδη, σοὶ πρῶτα μαχήσομαι ἀφραδέοντι,
      ἦ θέμις ἐστὶν, ἄναξ, ἀγορῆι· σὺ δὲ μή τι <u>χολωθῆις.</u>

Son of Atreus, I will first oppose you in your folly, as is fitting, in the agora, king, and do not be annoyed.

Emotions are just the kind of uncontrollable actions that we expect to be forbidden by a preventive rather than a prohibitive marker.

Other examples of the aorist subjunctive concern verbs that are controllable. However, as we saw above, preventive markers are used with controllable verbs in other languages too. In these Homeric examples there are again reasons to suggest that the subjunctive was used to express preventive meaning. For example:

24.568 τῶ νῦν μή μοι μᾶλλον ἐν ἄλγεσι θυμὸν <u>ὀρίνηις,</u>
        μή σε, γέρον, οὐδ᾽ αὐτὸν ἐνὶ κλισίηισιν ἐάσω
        καὶ ἱκέτην περ ἐόντα, Διὸς δ᾽ ἀλίτωμαι ἐφετμάς.

Don't stir up my heart to more anger, old man, or I will not let you back to the tents, and will transgress against the laws of Zeus, even though you are a suppliant.

Just as in the 'don't fall over' example we considered above, Achilles is here not really prohibiting Priam from making him angry, but rather asking him not to provoke him any more, in order that he doesn't become angry. Indeed, he says as much at 24.560:

24.560 μηκέτι νῦν μ᾽ <u>ἐρέθιζε</u> γέρον.

Don't provoke me any longer old man!

So 24.568 too could be interpreted 'beware lest you stir up my heart'.

We have already seen that 23.428 could be interpreted as a warning against undesirable consequences rather than a 'normal' prohibition (4.4.3):[40]

---

[39] Also 15.115; 24.779; O3.55.   [40] Also 23.407.

23.428   στεινωπὸς γὰρ ὁδός, τάχα δ' εὐρυτέρη παρελάσσαι -
μή πως ἀμφοτέρους <u>δηλήσεαι</u> ἅρματι κύρσας.

The road is narrow here – soon it will be wider. Don't harm us both by crashing
the chariot.

This too corresponds well to the definition of preventive markers
given above.

9.522 and O11.251 appear to be straightforward prohibitions
from doing something. But the suggestion that the action would be
harmful could serve to strengthen their force:

9.522   τῶν μὴ σύ γε μῦθον <u>ἐλέγξῃς</u>
μηδὲ πόδας·

Do not treat either their story nor their journey here with contempt.

O   νῦν δ' ἔρχευ πρὸς δῶμα, καὶ ἴσχεο μηδ' <u>ὀνομήνῃς</u>·
11.251   αὐτὰρ ἐγώ τοί εἰμι Ποσειδάων ἐνοσίχθων.

Go home now, and restrain yourself and don't name me. But, for you, I am
Poseidon, the Earth-Shaker.

By taking the subjunctive as preventive here, the power of the
injunction is increased, since it would imply that naming the god
or questioning the story would be harmful in some way.

There is one final group of lines that will perhaps provide the
most convincing evidence for the true meaning of the moods in this
construction: examples where the same verb is found in both the
present imperative and aorist subjunctive. Elsewhere it would be
possible that the semantics of the particular verb in question would
interfere with the interpretation of the moods. When the verb is the
same, this element is removed from the enquiry. I will argue that
in these cases too, it is attractive to analyse the subjunctive as
a preventive marker and the present imperative as a prohibitive
marker.

We may first take the case of νεμεσάω:

10.145   διογενὲς Λαερτιάδη πολυμήχαν' Ὀδυσσεῦ,
μὴ <u>νεμέσα</u>· τοῖον γὰρ ἄχος βεβίηκεν Ἀχαιούς.

Cunning Odysseus, Zeus-born son of Laërtes, don't be angry. Such is the grief
that has overwhelmed the Achaeans.

16.22   ὦ Ἀχιλεῦ, Πηλῆος υἱέ, μέγα φέρτατ' Ἀχαιῶν,
         μὴ <u>νεμέσα·</u> τοῖον γὰρ ἄχος βεβήκεν Ἀχαιούς.

Achilles, son of Peleus, greatest of the Achaeans, don't be angry. Such is the grief that has overwhelmed the Achaeans.

15.115   μὴ νῦν μοι <u>νεμεσήσετ',</u> Ὀλύμπια δώματ' ἔχοντες,
         τείσασθαι φόνον υἷος ἰόντ' ἐπὶ νῆας Ἀχαιῶν,

Now, dwellers of Olympus, do not be enraged if I avenge the death of my son and set out against the ships of the Achaeans,

Since becoming angry is an uncontrollable emotion, the use of a prohibitive marker in 16.22 and 10.145 might be considered to be surprising. But we saw above that prohibitive markers *are* used with emotions, when the speaker is asking the addressee to improve his currently adverse state (4.4.4, example 32). This is just the situation in 16.22 and 10.145. In 15.115, on the other hand, the speaker is asking the listeners not to become angry in the future, in reaction to the speaker's action, so a preventive marker is expected.

A similar argument may be made for δέδοικα:

24.779   ἄξετε νῦν, Τρῶες, ξύλα ἄστυδε. μηδέ τι θυμῶι
         δείσητ' Ἀργείων πυκινὸν λόχον·

Men of Troy, now bring me wood to the city, and don't have any fear of an Argive ambush:

20.366   Τρῶες ὑπέρθυμοι, μὴ <u>δείδιτε</u> Πηλείωνα.

Courageous Trojans – don't fear the son of Peleus.

Becoming frightened is another essentially uncontrollable action on the part of the listener, and so again a prohibitive marker is less expected. But there is a significant difference between the contexts of the two sentences. In 24.779, Priam is ordering his men to go and get some wood. It would be a reasonable reaction for them to fear the Greeks at this stage as Hector has just been brutally killed. But Priam tells them there is no need as Achilles has promised that no one will be hurt. The subjunctive therefore refers to a possible event that the speaker considers to be negative and likely to happen. On the other hand in 20.366, Hector is encouraging his men in reaction to the words of Achilles who had been rousing his fighters with

SUBJUNCTIVE

terrifying words. Hector is therefore telling his men to correct a presently adverse emotion.

There is a rather more complicated case to be made for κεύθω:

1.363 ἐξαύδα, μὴ κεῦθε νόωι, ἵνα εἴδομεν ἄμφω.

Tell me, don't hide it within your heart, so we can both know.

Ο λίσσομ' ὑπὲρ θυέων καὶ δαίμονος, αὐτὰρ ἔπειτα
15.263 σῆς τ' αὐτοῦ κεφαλῆς καὶ ἑταίρων, οἵ τοι ἔπονται,
εἰπέ μοι εἰρομένῳ νημερτέα μηδ' ἐπικεύσῃς·

I beg you by these offerings and by fate, and then by your life and that of all the men that follow you, tell me truthfully the answer to my question, and don't hide it away:

The main difference between these two lines is the time to which the verb refers: in 1.363, Achilles has called on his mother and claimed that Zeus has dishonoured him without giving the exact reason. When Thetis appeals to him not to keep silent, she is therefore referring to something that is already happening. In O15.263, on the other hand, Theoclymenus has just approached Telemachus. He starts his address to him with this prayer to answer him fully. This therefore refers to a possible action in the future. Cross-linguistically, preventive markers are most commonly (though not always) found with actions that will occur in the future (Birjulin and Xrakovskij 2001: 37). We can also perhaps discern a difference in the discourse context of these two lines: while in 1.363 a mother addresses a son, with no need for conventionalised formulae, in O15.263 a stranger approaches a stranger and begs him by the gods not to keep silent. Such an expression seems to be very conventionalised, and it would perhaps not be strange for the speaker to present the potential silence of the addressee as a harmful act.

Where the verb ἐάω is found in negative directives, the difference again could be described as a difference between a prohibitive and a preventive construction:

5.684 Πριαμίδη, μὴ δή με ἕλωρ Δαναοῖσιν ἐάσῃς
κεῖσθαι, ἀλλ' ἐπάμυνον.

Son of Priam, don't leave me as prey for the Danaans, but protect me!

22.339 λίσσομ' ὑπὲρ ψυχῆς καὶ γούνων σῶν τε τοκήων,
μή με ἔα παρὰ νηυσὶ κύνας καταδάψαι Ἀχαιῶν,

I beg you by your life, by your knees and your parents' knees, don't leave me by the Achaean ships for the dogs to devour,

8.399 βάσκ' ἴθι Ἴρι ταχεῖα, πάλιν τρέπε μηδ' ἔα ἄντην
       ἔρχεσθ'·

Get up and go, swift Iris. Turn them back and don't let them come face-to-face with me:

In 5.684, Sarpedon is asking Hector, his own leader, to help him up off the floor. The Trojans are beating back the Greeks, and Sarpedon fears that Hector might leave him there in his eagerness to get on with the fight. This turns out to be a justified fear – Hector does leave him and Sarpedon is left to be picked up by Hector's minions. In 22.339 on the other hand, it is a straight request from Hector to Achilles not to do something which he has threatened to do. Hector knows he is going to be killed, he just asks him not to be so brutal as to leave his corpse to be picked apart by animals, but instead to give his body over to his family for burial. Similarly, in 8.399 Zeus knows that Athena and Hera want to come to him, but sends Iris to prevent them. Again, then, the difference of temporal reference and discourse context could suggest that the subjunctive was a preventive and the imperative a prohibitive marker.

A close reading of the relevant lines has shown some support for the suggestion that the Homeric subjunctive could be described as a preventive marker, while the imperative could be described as a prohibitive marker. This is further supported by the relative distribution of the two moods. In those languages where the distinction between preventive and prohibitive meaning is acknowledged to be grammaticalised, prohibitives are found much more regularly than preventives. For example, one Russian novel (Goncharov's *Oblomov*) had 126 negative directives, of which 114 (90 per cent) were prohibitive and only 12 preventive (10 per cent) (Kozintseva 2001: 259). In a selection of Armenian texts, the percentages were 79 per cent prohibitive vs 21 per cent preventive (Kozintseva 2001: 258).[41] This corresponds well with the relative distribution of the subjunctive and imperative in this construction in Greek: Stephens

[41] The Armenian database was 165 negative directive sentences taken from texts by Zaryan, Petrosyan, K'alaphyan, K'alart'aryan, Khanzadyan, and Sahniyan.

(1983: 69, fn. 2) has claimed that for Homeric Greek the aorist subjunctive is found in only 8.22 per cent of second-person negative directive constructions.

4.4.6 *The Indo-European perspective*

Before we conclude the analysis of this construction it is important to note that the term 'preventive' has already been used in the analysis of these constructions in other Indo-European languages. For example, Hoffman (1967: 44), in a study of the injunctive in the Veda, divides negative directive sentences into three types and calls them preventive, inhibitive and corrective. In this model, preventive sentences are used to forbid an event that is expected to happen (*rege dich nicht auf über das, was ich dir jetzt mitteilen werde*), inhibitive sentences are used to stop an event that is already happening (*weine nicht*), while corrective sentences are used to correct an event that has just happened (*sag dies doch nicht*). Meid (1962: 155) claims that the important distinction lies between preventive and inhibitive sentences, since corrective sentences may fall into either one class or another, depending on whether the prohibition is made for the present or for the future. Meid (1962: 157) claims that in Indo-European, the aorist injunctive would generally have been used to express preventive meaning, while the present injunctive would have been used to express the inhibitive (see also Meid 1963 and 1968). These aspects of the injunctive would then have been replaced in Greek by the aorist subjunctive and present imperative.

However, Louw (1959: 46), in his analysis of Greek prohibitions, explicitly denies the connection between the aorist subjunctive and future time and the present imperative and present time. He takes as the basis for these claims the explanations made by Appollonius Dyscolus for the aspectual difference in positive commands, and shows how the same may be said for negative commands. In terms of the classical Greek data, his arguments and examples are convincing. Particularly problematic for the view that the aorist subjunctive only refers to events in the future are those examples with adverbs referring to the present time, like πέρα, πλέον, μηκέτι (Louw 1959: 48–9). For example:

παῦε, μὴ λέξῃς πέρα.

Stop, do not speak any more.

Sophocles *Philoctetes*: 1275

Conversely, he also gives examples of the present imperative referring to events which have not happened yet (Louw 1959: 53–4).
For example:

καὶ μὴ πρόκαμνε. τόνδε βουκολούμενος
πόνον·

Do not grow weary too soon, by brooding on your trial.

Aeschylus *Eumenides:* 78

But this analysis of the classical Greek sentences does not entirely
contradict the analysis of Homeric sentences I suggested above.
Firstly, while Louw finds persuasive examples of the aorist subjunctive referring to the present in classical Greek, all the examples
in Homer refer to a future event. This suggests that by the time
of the classical language the aorist subjunctive should indeed be
described as the perfective equivalent of the present imperative. But
it also allows the possibility that in the earlier language the subjunctive did express a subtly different meaning. Secondly, the definition of preventive sentences proposed above on the basis of
the cross-linguistic evidence is more sophisticated than the definition proposed in the Indo-European studies. The difference is
not purely temporal, and thus prohibitive markers are not excluded
from prohibiting events that will happen in the future, although it is
acknowledged that preventive markers usually refer to future events
(Birjulin and Xrakovskij 2001: 37). Finally, it must be remembered
that my proposal is not intended to explain the *aspect* of the subjunctive in this construction, but rather the use of the mood *per
se*. Louw's arguments against the temporal understanding of the
different moods in this construction could well stem from a wish
to correct misconceptions about the meanings of the present and
aorist aspects which are still ingrained in some descriptions of
Greek. But I believe that the evidence presented here shows that
the aspect of the two moods is not the most important difference to
take into consideration in the analysis of this construction, at least
at the Homeric stage of the language.

4.4.7 Conclusion

Previous explanations of the negative directive construction have assumed that the difference between the subjunctive and imperative was merely aspectual, and therefore describe the subjunctive as 'filling the gap' in the imperative paradigm. This account must explain why the aorist imperative was not used instead, but in section 4.4.2 I showed that previous attempts at an explanation are unconvincing. Furthermore, there are clear syntactic and semantic differences between the two moods which suggest that they do not only differ aspectually: the subjunctive develops a subordinate use, unlike the imperative, and the subjunctive appears to express the meaning 'beware lest' as well as the more 'straightforward' negative directives. The metrical evidence also suggests that the subjunctive and imperative were introduced at different times. It is thus attractive to explain the use of two different moods as reflecting a distinction between two different types of construction.

In this context it is therefore very interesting to note that in other languages two different types of negative directive construction have indeed been grammaticalised. However, because the choice between a prohibitive or preventive marker generally appears to be a rather subjective one, it is difficult to clearly delimit the distinction. I have shown that the Homeric evidence could be interpreted in such a way that allows the imperative to be described as a prohibitive marker and the subjunctive as a preventive marker, but acknowledge that in certain places my interpretation could be seen as imposing a reading on the data to fit the theory, particularly when we consider the subjunctive used in the 'strong warnings' at 9.522 and O 11.251.

Nonetheless, the claim that the subjunctive was a preventive marker and the imperative a prohibitive marker has clear advantages over the previous models. First, it provides a reason for the preponderance of present imperatives in negative constructions in Greek. In other languages too, prohibitive meaning is far more common than the preventive meaning, perhaps because of the greater specificity of the preventive meaning. Secondly, it explains the use of the subjunctive in the 'related' constructions in the first and third person and the subordinate fear clauses. Perhaps most importantly, it offers an explanation for using a different form from the aorist imperative. Finally, a preventive meaning of the subjunctive ties in well with the meaning of the subjunctive we have seen in other constructions: a form that elsewhere expresses a future meaning is perfect for the meaning of the preventive. Indeed, in Armenian, it is the future subjunctive with a negative particle which is used (Kozintseva 2001: 256).

The claim that there are two different types of negative construction in Homeric Greek does however raise its own questions. Firstly we need to explain why there is no aspectual contrast in the two constructions. The cross-linguistic evidence shows that paradigms of positive and negative directives are independent entities (Birjulin and Xrakovskij 2001: 36–7). We should not therefore necessarily expect an aspectual contrast in the negative directive constructions merely because there is one in the positive paradigm. But given the thoroughgoing nature of aspect in Greek, perhaps a more relevant observation is that the difference between prohibitive and preventive markers appears to be connected to aspect in other languages as well: in Russian prohibitive meaning is expressed by the imperfective imperative, while preventive meaning is expressed by the perfective imperative (Golovko 2001: 308–9). Perhaps it is also relevant to note that in similar constructions in the first and third person both aspects *are* found (Goodwin: §261; Monro: §278). For example:[42]

O   Ὣ μοι ἐγώ, μή τίς μοι <u>ὑφαίνῃσιν</u> δόλον αὖτε
5.356   ἀθανάτων,

Help! I fear another immortal is weaving a trap for me,

O   εἰ ἐτεόν γ᾽ ἐμός ἐσσι καὶ αἵματος ἡμετέροιο,
16.301 μή τις ἔπειτ᾽ Ὀδυσῆος <u>ἀκουσάτω</u> ἔνδον ἐόντος,

If you really are my son, and a blood-relation, let no one know that Odysseus is inside,

It would therefore be possible to suggest that the lack of aorist imperative and present subjunctive is pure coincidence in the second-person construction. The lack of present subjunctives is

---

[42] Also 16.128; O15.19 (present subjunctives) and 16.200 (aorist imperative).

particularly easy to explain given the overall rarity of the preventive construction, and we could perhaps explain the lack of aorist imperatives with reference to the 'obscure' nature of its origin. The 'rule' that we see in the data could therefore perhaps have developed from what is an explicable tendency, which would also then explain why the subjunctive was reanalysed as the perfective equivalent of the present imperative in the later language.

Another question relates to the exact nature of the original system which the Greek system replaced. As we showed above, the metrical evidence suggests that the aorist subjunctive 'replaced' the aorist injunctive during the composition of the Homeric poems, later than the replacement of the present injunctive by the present imperative. This suggests that the distinction between prohibitive and preventive meaning was originally marked by the different aspects of the injunctive. But if that was the case it is difficult to explain why the injunctive was not replaced by a single paradigm of forms: if the distinction in meaning was marked by a difference in aspect in the original system, why not also in Greek? To resolve this question will require more investigation into the nature of the injunctive or its descendants in other languages.

In spite of these unresolved questions, there is enough evidence at least to argue that the 'system' of negative directives is in a state of some flux in Homeric Greek. I have claimed elsewhere that the subjunctive was originally some kind of future marker. The connection to future time and therefore preventive meaning of the aorist subjunctive originally at least would thus be predicted. By the Attic period, however, the subjunctive appears to have been reanalysed as the perfective equivalent of the present imperative. In the Homeric language, it is thus unsurprising to find examples of the aorist subjunctive which may easily be described as preventive alongside those (such as 9.522 and O11.251) which appear to fit better with the later system.

4.5 Summary and conclusions

In this chapter I have analysed the evidence given for the epistemic, hortative and negative directive constructions, and shown that traditional accounts are unsatisfactory, both in terms of the way they describe the meanings that they do distinguish, and because there are more distinctions to be made. I hope to have finally put to rest the notion that the field of modality may be neatly divided into two types, and to have shown that any description of the subjunctive which attempts to do so will fail to account for the rich variety of its meanings and the interrelationships between them.

In section 4.2, I showed that the crucial question to answer with regards to the epistemic meaning of the subjunctive is how it differs from the future indicative. I showed that the distinction is difficult, both on formal and functional grounds, but argued that the traditional description, according to which the subjunctive is more irrealis than the indicative, could be confirmed if the subjunctive marks the potential reality of the speaker and the future indicative the projected reality. However, in all contexts I showed that such a distinction may not be made. The only distinction is one of distribution, and while the future indicative is arguably restricted to more 'realis' contexts, the lack of clear-cut 'rules' which would explain the choice of mood in any context, coupled with the meaning of the subjunctive in the contexts in which it is found suggests that the difference is not one of irrealis level. While it is true that the subjunctive is developing more 'modal' uses, they could all be derived from an original future meaning, and merely suggest that the subjunctive was more 'mature' than the future indicative.

In section 4.3, I considered the evidence given for the hortative construction. Some examples had been correctly interpreted as performative utterances, expressing the invitation and occasionally the auto-prescription of the speaker. I argued that these could have developed from the combination of a future marker with the category of first person. I argued that other examples reveal that the subjunctive had true deontic meaning, as well as the epistemic and speaker-oriented meanings already considered. While this conclusion is entirely unsurprising, given the analysis of the mood as a future marker, it adds complexity to the map of the subjunctive and shows that the boundaries between two different meanings may be fuzzy and dependent on other categories, here the category of person.

In section 4.4, I considered the second-person performative construction in negative directives. The subjunctive in this construction has previously been explained as the perfective equivalent of the imperative, but I showed various reasons to doubt this explanation, and suggested instead that we are dealing with two different constructions. Two different types of negative directive construction have been distinguished in other languages and I argued that the Homeric types could be explained in the same terms. While this way of interpretation is necessarily subjective and does not answer all the questions surrounding the construction, I argued that it explained more of the aspects of the construction than previous accounts.

The complex nature of subjunctive, caused perhaps by the nature of future reference, which has both epistemic and deontic meanings, makes it extremely difficult and rather unnecessary to categorise it in any one simple way. The question of whether it is a future tense or a mood is thus largely irrelevant. Instead we may conclude that, just as expected from the theory of grammaticalisation, the subjunctive has a wide range of different meanings which are connected to each other by various diachronic paths. The conclusion about the nature of the subjunctive bears on our understanding of the field of modality more generally. The way in which the different meanings have been argued to relate to each other, as well as their diversity, confirms the claim made in chapter 2 that the field should not be seen as divisible into neat boxes, but rather as a web, where different core areas of meaning are related to each other along various different axes.

5

OPTATIVE

5.1 Introduction

Traditional accounts of the optative describe it as more 'remote' than the subjunctive, both in main and conditional clauses where it appears to express 'remote possibility', and in wishes, where it is described as a weaker form of the imperative.[1] The optative is thus positioned at the irrealis end of Greenberg's irrealis continuum (see 2.2.2).

As mentioned in section 2.2.2, the claim for the meaning of the optative is supposed to have morphological foundation: the optative is associated with secondary endings, distinct from the primary endings found on the subjunctive.[2] In section 5.2 I will examine this morphological evidence, and show it to be unconvincing. Even if the optative was associated with secondary endings, we may not assume a connection to greater remoteness. I thus argue that any claims for the meaning of the optative should be based on the semantic analysis alone. It is this analysis which is carried out in the remainder of the chapter. I will claim that the semantic evidence too casts doubt on the traditional account. This is perhaps unsurprising: now that I have redefined the subjunctive, it is to be expected that the optative, so often defined only in relation to the subjunctive, will also need to be redefined. But I will show that the optative has been misunderstood even on its own terms.

I will first consider the two meanings of the optative discussed in the traditional accounts: the meaning found in conditionals and the speaker-oriented meaning found in wishes. I will argue that the traditional descriptions of both of these meanings need some revision. Perhaps even more importantly, in section 5.5 I will argue

---

[1] Delbrück 1871: 13; 1879: 117; Wackernagel 1926: 230–8; Goodwin: §12; Chantraine: §314; Hahn: §16; Vairel 1979: 579.
[2] Benveniste 1951: 16; Hahn: §8; Whitney 1892: 294; Monro: §317c; Shields 1988: 552.

that there are several examples of the optative which do not fit into either of these categories. I illustrate two further types of modality which are expressed with the mood, and will therefore argue that the semantic map of the optative needs to be significantly redrawn.

5.2 Morphological argument

The use of secondary endings on the optative seems to prove the traditional claims about the meaning of the mood and its relation to the subjunctive. Secondary endings are elsewhere found on past tenses of the indicative, which suggests that the optative is the 'past-time variant' of the subjunctive (Palmer[2]: 205, also Lightfoot 1975: 135). The relationship between the subjunctive and the optative is thus compared to the relationship between the present and past tenses of modal verbs in English (Palmer[2]: 204ff.). It is a commonplace that past time is often connected with greater 'remoteness': we may consider for example the use of the English past tense in 'unreal' conditional sentences and the use of the imperfect indicative in 'unreal' conditional clauses in later Greek.[3] The secondary endings on the optative in Greek have thus been taken as morphological confirmation of the claim that the optative expresses 'remote' possibility and 'remote' imperatives. However, when we consider the evidence more closely we can see that the confirmation is not secure.

Firstly, it is not even universally agreed that the subjunctive and optative would originally have been formed with primary and secondary endings respectively. Wathelet (1997: 253), for example, claims that the subjunctive was originally formed with secondary endings, which were only later replaced with primary endings, 'de par la nature même du mode'. In the *Rig Veda* both primary and secondary endings are found on the subjunctive.[4] Hahn (8, fn. 17) apparently solves this problem by claiming that any secondary

---

[3] Horrocks 1995: 163; Lyons 1977: 809–23; Palmer[2]: 207; Comrie 1985: 19–21. Dahl 1997 attributes the hypothesis first to Joos 1964. For cross-linguistic descriptions see Steele 1975 and James 1982.

[4] Hahn: §8; Shields 1988: 552; Sihler 1995: §334; Basset 1989: 136 fn. 11.

endings on 'subjunctive' forms in daughter languages in fact derive from original optative forms. The evidence shows that the reconstruction of just primary endings on the PIE subjunctive is at best uncertain.

Even if the optative was originally associated with secondary endings, this implies no affinity between the mood and past tense. What are now called secondary endings appear to have been the original endings, neutral with respect to time, while primary endings were a later 'invention' to mark the *hic et nunc*.[5] Secondary endings are not reserved for past tenses, but are also used, for example, for the second-person middle imperative –σο (Basset 1989: 136).

Of course, in historic Greek there *is* a certain connection between the optative and the past-tense endings. It may be argued that this was felt to be significant, whatever the original situation in PIE, and whatever the other uses of secondary endings. However, the use of the primary ending in the first person (λέγοιμι) suggests that even in historic Greek the connection was not absolute.

Finally, it has been argued that, in spite of the cross-linguistic patterning between past time and remoteness there is not a straightforward connection. Bybee (1995: 514) argues that in all cases it is not the past tense alone which contributes to the meaning, but rather it is the past tense 'in combination with a modal verb, a subjunctive mood, a hypothetical marker (such as *if*), or, in some cases, the imperfective aspect'. It thus follows that the connection between the optative and past tense in Greek would not be sufficient to explain its remoteness.

The diachronically unproven and synchronically inconsistent nature of the link between the optative and secondary endings, together with uncertainty about what that link would mean if it did exist, suggest that the morphological evidence should not be used as the basis for any argument about the meaning of the optative. Therefore the analysis to be carried out here will be based on the semantic evidence alone.

---

[5] Sihler 1995: §538; Gonda: 47, with references to further literature.

5.3 Conditionals

5.3.1 Introduction

In this section I will consider the evidence for the 'epistemic' meaning of the optative. Traditional accounts describe this as the meaning of 'remote possibility'. This meaning is most often found in the protasis and apodosis of conditional clauses, where the optative is used to express what have been termed 'unreal' conditionals.[6] For example:

1.255 ἦ κεν <u>γηθήσαι</u> Πρίαμος Πριάμοιό τε παῖδες,
      ἄλλοί τε Τρῶες μέγα κεν <u>κεχαροίατο</u> θυμῶι,
      εἰ σφῶϊν τάδε πάντα <u>πυθοίατο</u> μαρναμένοιιν,

Priam and Priam's sons and all the Trojans would exult and rejoice in their hearts, if they heard the two of you battling like this,

As well as in unreal conditionals, the optative is also occasionally found with this meaning in independent main clauses. However, even in these clauses a sense of a conditional is generally 'understood'. For example, the use of the optative in the second of these two sentences may be best understood with reference to the previous sentence (Kirk et al. ad loc.):

4.95 τλαίης κεν Μενελάωι ἔπι προέμεν ταχὺν ἰόν;
      πᾶσι δέ κε Τρώεσσι χάριν καὶ κῦδος <u>ἄροιο</u>,

Would you dare to shoot off an arrow at Menelaus? Then you'd win glory and fame in the eyes of all the Trojans,

We might gloss this as 'Would you dare to shoot? [If you did], then you would dare to shoot an arrow etc.'

As already discussed in 2.3.3, the conditional context of this meaning means that it is unsatisfactory to describe this modality as epistemic as traditionally defined. In this section I will also argue that the traditional description of the meaning ('remote possibility') is mistaken.

'Unreal' conditionals are one of two types of future-referring conditionals, opposed to 'real' conditionals (see 3.2.3). According to traditional accounts, in real conditionals the speaker considers

---

[6] Abbott and Mansfield: 46–8; Smyth: 256; Goodwin: §392.

that there is a real possibility that the event described in the protasis will happen. This type of future-referring conditional is usually expressed by the subjunctive or future indicative in Homeric Greek, and has been considered in 4.2. In unreal conditionals, on the other hand, it is said that rather less-likely possibilities are entertained, in order to speculate on what might happen. (For this definition of real and unreal conditionals, see e.g. Comrie 1986b: 88 ff.; Podlesskaya 2001: 998.) The two types may be exemplified by the following English examples:

34 Real: If Tom gets home in time, I'll take him to the station.
35 Unreal: If I won the lottery, I'd go abroad (or 'If I were to win . . .').

The difference between the two types may be seen by considering how the speaker would express the possibility of the event in the protasis. Sentence 34 would appear to equate to sentence 36, and sentence 35 to sentence 37:

36 Tom may get home in time
37 I might win the lottery

The use of the optative in unreal conditionals in Homeric Greek would therefore appear to confirm its traditional description as expressing 'remote possibility'. But in this section I will give two reasons to doubt the claim. The first is that the optative is not only found in conditionals where the possibility is unlikely. The second, more theoretical argument, is that we need not explain even 'classic' examples of unreal conditionals as expressing the speaker's belief that the possibility is unlikely. The definition that I will suggest here brings the optative into line with the definition of the indicative proposed in chapter 3, aligning it with that rather than the subjunctive, and also has ramifications for our theoretical understanding of 'unreal' conditionals in general.

5.3.2 Analysis

The problem for the traditional description of the optative is that there are many examples of the mood which do not seem to describe particularly remote possibilities.

In some cases, the 'offending' examples may be explained away as non-epistemic. For example:

4.18 εἰ δ' αὖ πως τόδε πᾶσι φίλον καὶ ἡδὺ <u>γένοιτο</u>,
   ἤτοι μὲν οἰκέοιτο πόλις Πριάμοιο ἄνακτος,
   αὖτις δ' Ἀργείην Ἑλένην Μενέλαος ἄγοιτο.

If everyone thought it was a good idea, Priam's city might remain inhabited, and Menelaus might take the Argive Helen back home.

Here the speaker clearly does not want to suggest that it was only a 'remote' possibility that everyone thought the idea was good. But in this case the mood could be explained as an optative of wish, and it has indeed been taken in this way in various translations. For example, Fagles: 'Ah if only it might prove well and good to all, to every immortal god, men might still live on in royal Priam's citadel.'

More troubling for the traditional account are several examples of the optative which are clearly epistemic but which are used in a strong affirmation or denial. For example:[7]

3.220 <u>φαίης</u> κε ζάκοτόν τέ τιν' ἔμμεναι ἄφρονά τ' αὔτως.

You'd call him a sullen fellow or just a plain fool.

6.141 οὐδ' ἂν ἐγὼ μακάρεσσι θεοῖς <u>ἐθέλοιμι</u> μάχεσθαι.

I would not like to fight the blessed immortals.

In 3.220, the optative does not correspond to an English 'you might call' expressing remote possibility. Rather, it is used to express the belief that, given the unreal situation where you did see Odysseus talking, then you would *surely* say that he was an idiot. This is not a one-off: Kirk et al. (ad loc.) note that it is a frequently occurring rhetorical phrase. Similarly, 6.141 could be translated 'you won't catch me fighting gods'. Diomedes is not presenting the likelihood of this event as small, rather he is saying that he would certainly never do it, whatever the condition. Indeed, the same may be said for all apodoses of unreal conditionals: however unlikely the event in the protasis, in all apodoses the optative expresses the belief of the speaker that the event is a *certain* consequence of the protasis being fulfilled.

[7] Also cf. O7.333; O14.155; O17.546; O22.350.

It could be argued that it is the context of an 'unreal conditional' which enables the use of the optative in the apodosis. That is, because of the unlikeliness of the event of the protasis, the event in the apodosis is equally unlikely. Thus examples from apodoses may not be used on their own to criticise the belief that the optative expresses 'more remote' possibilities. But there are also examples of the optative in the protasis of conditionals which do not express any idea of 'remoteness'. For example:

5.273   εἰ τούτω κε <u>λάβοιμεν</u>, ἀροίμεθά κε κλέος ἐσθλόν.

If we took them both we'd win ourselves great fame.

It does not seem reasonable to claim that the event in the protasis in this context is unlikely. After all, the speaker is actually trying to urge Sthenelos on to take the horses.

The optative is also found occasionally in threats, where the likelihood of the event is obviously being emphasised rather than mimimised:[8]

20.426   ἐγγὺς ἀνὴρ ὃς ἐμόν γε μάλιστ' ἐσεμάσσατο θυμόν,
            ὅς μοι ἑταῖρον ἔπεφνε τετιμένον· οὐδ' ἂν ἔτι δὴν
            ἀλλήλους <u>πτώσσοιμεν</u> ἀνὰ πτολέμοιο γεφύρας.

Here's the man who's most hurt my heart, who killed my cherished comrade! We won't shrink from each other for long on the battle-field!

In various different contexts, then, the optative often does not express the 'least likely' proposition.

This behaviour of the optative has been noted by previous analysts of the language, and it led Goodwin to conclude (§239) that the optative 'may express every grade of potentiality'. He claims instead that, rather than expressing a certain type of possibility, it is the speaker presentation of the event which is important, that the difference between the moods lies not in the different likelihood of the proposition but rather in the degree of 'vividness' with which the speaker wants to present the proposition (Goodwin 1876: 91–107). This definition enables him to preserve the relationship which is meant to hold between the subjunctive and optative, describing the subjunctive as 'more vivid' and the optative as 'less vivid'.

---

[8] Also cf. O18.27; O22.325.

However, while the term 'vivid' is useful in that it emphasises the role of the speaker, it has been misunderstood. For example, Hahn (§113) explicitly links a 'more vivid' presentation to an event which is more likely to happen. Even without these misunderstandings, the term is not significantly more successful than the term 'remote' when it comes to explaining the use of the optative in the 'less imaginary' protases and threats considered above. For example we may consider 5.273 again:

5.273 εἰ τούτω κε λάβοιμεν, ἀροίμεθά κε κλέος ἐσθλόν.

If we took them both we'd win ourselves great fame.

I have already claimed that the speaker would not present the event he is urging as 'unlikely', and given its pressing nature, it seems just as unsuccessful to describe the event as 'less vivid'.

A successful definition of the optative must be able to account for its use in such a range of different contexts, that is, by finding what it is that all those contexts share. I believe that this shared feature is the speaker's belief that the occurrence of the event is *unreal*, that is, that the event is *not* in line with their view of the world. This provides a more satisfactory explanation of the use of the optative in 5.273: by describing the event as 'unreal' the speaker can imply that the addressees will need to put in some effort before the event is achieved. This would therefore explain why this utterance has the force of urging the addressee on. Of course, pragmatically, an 'unreal' meaning will often mean that the speaker believes that the fulfilment of the possibility is unlikely. Thus this new definition may not appear to be radically different from the traditional one. However, this definition is more successful than the traditional one, as it also accounts for lines in which the likelihood of the event is rather high.

If this analysis of the optative is correct, it would mean that it was the direct opposite of the indicative as I defined it in chapter 3. Using the same terms as were introduced there, the optative may thus be defined as expressing the 'negative epistemic stance' of the speaker. This term has in fact already been used to describe a mood in another language: Mortelmans (2000: 197) uses it to describe the past subjunctive in German, and demonstrates that, when using the 'Konjunktiv II', the speaker assumes that the proposition is not true, or 'has her doubts about its truth value'.

Seeing the optative as the direct opposite of the indicative rather than in parallel to the subjunctive will help to explain further a context in which the two moods are both found: that is, in counterfactual conditionals. As stated in my discussion on the use of the indicative in these constructions (3.2.4), the two moods were previously described as interchangeable in this context, and the indicative was described as 'modal' because it appeared to be a modal environment. But I argued that the indicative retains its meaning of positive epistemic stance in this context. I used the indicative in 2.156 to make this claim:

2.156   ἔνθά κεν Ἀργείοισιν ὑπέρμορα νόστος ἐτύχθη,
         εἰ μὴ Ἀθηναίην Ἥρη πρὸς μῦθον ἔειπεν·

And now the Argives would have won their journey home, beyond what was ordained by fate, if Hera had not alerted Athena:

Here the speaker suggests that the event *nearly* happened, apart from the intervention of the events in the protasis: the world in which the event happened is therefore in line with the speaker's view of the real world. This may be contrasted with a counterfactual in which an optative is used. To repeat the example I considered in chapter 3, 5.311 appears to describe an event which the 'speaker' does not want to acknowledge *could* have really happened:

5.311   καί νύ κεν ἔνθ᾽ ἀπόλοιτο ἄναξ ἀνδρῶν Αἰνείας,
         εἰ μὴ ἄρ᾽ ὀξὺ νόησε Διὸς θυγάτηρ Ἀφροδίτη,

And then Aeneas, the captain of men, would have died, if Zeus's daughter Aphrodite had not been quick to notice him,

The choice of the optative of 'negative epistemic stance' is entirely expected.

It is true that the examples I have considered so far are not the 'core' of the uses of the optative in conditional clauses. It could be argued that these may be slightly different, but that their definition should not detract from the analysis of the optative as used in classic unreal conditionals. After all, there the analysis of the optative as expressing remote possibility corresponds entirely with the usual theoretical definition of unreal conditionals in general. However, modern work on conditional sentences has analysed unreal conditionals in a way which supports the definition I have proposed for the optative in more unusual contexts. Wierzbicka (1997: 35–6) has shown that unreal conditionals in English too are not exclusively used when the speaker considers their fulfilment less probable. For example, she points out that the sentence 'If I were you, I would go,' does *not* mean 'I think that it is very improbable that I am you,' but rather 'In the situation of being you (which is unreal), I would go.' She therefore argues that the only important semantic feature of an 'unreal' conditional is the 'unreality' of that proposition. It should of course again be admitted that in many, if not most, unreal conditionals the event *is* unlikely to happen (or the speaker at least views it in this way). Such, for example, are the 'purely imaginary' conditionals of the type 'If I won the lottery'. But the existence of 'unreal' conditionals where the likelihood of the event is not an issue, such as the 'if I were you' example, shows that there is no causal link between small likelihood and unreal conditionals. It is thus just coincidental that 'unreal' events will often be ones with a smaller likelihood of happening than real ones. These two analyses, of the optative in Homeric Greek and of unreal conditionals in general thus mutually reinforce each other.

For the sake of completeness we must finally address the claim made by Hahn (83), that the optative, just as the subjunctive and future indicative, was a future marker. It is true that the optative usually has reference to future time. And the use of the optative to refer to rather more 'likely' events than we would expect given its traditional description sometimes leads to it appearing rather interchangeable with the future. For example:

O   ταῦτα δ' ἅ μ' εἰρωτᾷς καὶ λίσσεαι, οὐκ ἂν ἐγώ γε
17.139 ἄλλα παρὲξ εἴποιμι παρακλιδὸν οὐδ' ἀπατήσω,

As for the things which you are asking and begging, I will not avoid the subject and talk of other things, and neither will I deceive you,

Critically for her claim, Hahn admits that the optative is generally used to express events in the future which are 'more vague' than those expressed by the future indicative or subjunctive. In chapter 4, I defined a way to distinguish between future forms and more irrealis forms, namely that markers which describe the projected reality of the speaker should be described as future markers, while markers of the speaker's potential reality are more irrealis (4.2). The 'more vague' possibilities expressed by the optative in Hahn's definition, ('unreal' possibilities in my definition) would appear to be more potential than projected. It therefore seems unwarranted to lump the optative together with the future indicative.

A further problem for Hahn's claim is that the optative is not only used to refer to the speaker's future but also to contingent events in the speaker's present and past.[9] For example:

2.81[10]   εἰ μέν τις τὸν ὄνειρον Ἀχαιῶν ἄλλος ἔνισπεν,
          ψεῦδός κεν <u>φαῖμεν</u> καὶ <u>νοσφιζοίμεθα</u> μᾶλλον·

If any other Achaean had told us of this dream we would have called it a lie and turned our backs on it.

13.343   μάλα κεν θρασυκάρδιος <u>εἴη</u>,
          ὃς τότε <u>γηθήσειεν</u> ἰδὼν πόνον οὐδ' <u>ἀκάχοιτο</u>.

He would have had to be very strong at heart, whoever would have rejoiced at the sight of that battle and not grieved.

This timelessness appears to be important for its subsequent development, as I will show in chapter 6. It is therefore implausible to describe it as a future marker.

5.3.3 Summary

In this section I argued that both of the previous descriptions of the optative are flawed. Hahn's claim that the optative was a future marker is contradicted by the use of the optative to refer to potential rather than projected reality as well as its possible reference to past and present time. Unlike the subjunctive we thus appear here to be dealing with a 'real mood'.

The more traditional and widely held belief is that the optative expresses 'remote possibility'. This appears to equate it with the English epistemic modal 'might'. However, there are several examples of the optative which do not fit this definition or equation. The

---

[9] Monro §300c; Sideri 1996: 206. For optatives with past or present reference Monro cites 3.220; 4.223; 4.429; 4.539; 5.85; 5.311; 5.388; 12.58; 13.127; 13.343; 15.697; 17.70; 17.366; 17.398; O7.293; O13.86. Also cf 11.467 (past) and 11.791 (present).

[10] This 'past counterfactual' from Horrocks (1995: 161–2) and Chantraine: §325.

optative is used to describe events with a variety of different levels of likelihood: what appears to be important is that the event is viewed as 'unreal'. With its range of different meanings, it would be attractive to describe the optative in similar terms to the indicative in chapter 3, i.e. as expressing 'negative epistemic stance'. This definition confirms the reanalysis of unreal conditionals in general that was made by Wierzbicka (1997: 35–6). She argued that these encode the speaker's belief not that the event is unlikely, but that it is merely unreal.

The conclusions about the indicative and optative suggest the following model should replace the irrealis continuum drawn up by Greenberg:

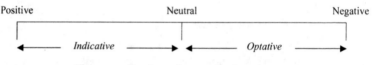

Figure 5.1 Greek continuum of epistemic stance

5.4 Wish

5.4.1 Introduction

The wish construction is found in all persons, both singular and plural, and in both positive and negative forms. For example:

2.418 πολέες δ᾽ ἀμφ᾽ αὐτὸν ἑταῖροι
   πρηνέες ἐν κονίῃσιν ὀδὰξ <u>λαζοίατο</u> γαῖαν.

and may many comrades fall head-first round him in the dust and gnaw the earth!

2.260 μηδ᾽ ἔτι Τηλεμάχοιο πατὴρ κεκλημένος <u>εἴην</u>,

may I no longer be called the father of Telemachus

Given the frequency of prayers to the gods in the Homeric epics, it is a particularly common construction, and its correct analysis is important not only for linguists but for those interested in the poems from a literary perspective.

In the traditional accounts, the optative is seen as an 'attenuated' version of the subjunctive in this construction just as in

the epistemic constructions we considered in the previous section. The wish optative is considered as a weaker form of the
imperative, while the subjunctive is thought of as its equivalent
(Goodwin: §12–13). However, it is clear from its distribution that
this speaker-oriented meaning of the optative is rather different
from the speaker-oriented meaning of the subjunctive. The optative
is found without restriction while the subjunctive in the hortative
and negative directive constructions is restricted to the first person
or constructions with μή respectively, as we saw in chapter 4.

In this section I will consider the meaning of the optative in the
wish construction in more detail, comparing similar sentences with
the imperative, and will show that the optative expresses a different
kind of performative illocutionary force. I will also examine the
claim made by Justus that the optative is replacing the imperative
in Greek and show it to be unfounded. I conclude by making some
suggestions for the correct interpretation for the mood.

5.4.2 The relationship between the optative and imperative

On first considering the relationship between wishes and imperatives in Homeric Greek, it is easy to understand why the former
has been seen as a weaker version of the latter. For example:

1.1   Μῆνιν ἄειδε, θεά, Πηληϊάδεω Ἀχιλῆος
       οὐλομένην, ἣ μυρί᾽ Ἀχαιοῖς ἄλγε᾽ ἔθηκεν,

Sing, Muse, the rage of Peleus' son Achilles, the doomed rage, which brought
the Achaeans countless sorrows,

1.20   παῖδα δ᾽ ἐμοὶ λύσαιτε φίλην, τὰ δ᾽ ἄποινα δέχεσθαι,

Release my darling child, and accept this ransom,

In 1.1, the imperative is addressed to the second-person subject of
the verb, and is an order for that person to fulfil the state of affairs
referred to, and to become the agent of the action. The use of the
imperative suggests that the speaker has some control or influence
over the addressee and that the addressee is capable of carrying
out the order. In 1.20, the second-person optative is used to urge
the subject to do something and thus the subject of the optative is

again asked to be the agent of an action.[11] The use of the optative rather than an imperative in this context has been said to arise from the speaker's wish to be more polite (Monro: §299b).

However, this comparison is rather unjustified as the optative example is not really characteristic of the category. Typically, the subject of the optative is *not* the addressee or the agent of the action (Scholz 1987). For example:

1.42   <u>τείσειαν</u> Δαναοὶ ἐμὰ δάκρυα σοῖσι βέλεσσιν.

may the Danaans suffer your arrows as payment for my tears.

The wish is addressed to the second person, Apollo, rather than the third-person subject of the verb. The speaker does not consider that the Danaans will be the agents of the wished-for state of affairs, but rather hopes that the god will bring the wish about. The presence of an addressee is not even necessary in wishes: often, they have no clear addressee at all. For example:

22.304   μὴ μὰν ἀσπουδί γε καὶ ἀκλειῶς <u>ἀπολοίμην</u>,

May I not die without a struggle, and without glory,

This wish is spoken by Hector, alone, as he realises that death is upon him. He does not have a specific agent in mind, but is just wishing for the fulfilment of a certain event.

It thus appears that prototypical wishes may be semantically differentiated from prototypical directives: in directives the agent of the action is addressed, while in wishes he is not; in directives the speaker has some control over the addressee or agent, while in wishes he again does not.

Third-person directives might appear to contradict this distinction. These by their nature do not directly address the agent of the action, so that they appear to be more like wishes. Indeed, for

---

[11] It should be noted that there is textual confusion here (Leaf ad loc.): MSS are divided between λύσαιτε and the imperative λύσατε. The word division is also not clear: there is very little difference between λύσαιτε and λῦσαί τε, the reading of Apio and Herodoros adopted by Wolf. Whatever the reality, the sentence with the optative may be used to represent traditional views of the meaning of wishes and their difference from sentences with the imperative. Mention will not be made here on the use of the infinitive to express directives. On the difference between infinitives and imperatives see further Neuberger-Donath 1980.

this reason Lyons (1977: 747) claimed that third-person imperatives are not true imperatives at all. However, Xrakovskij (2001a: 1029) has argued that the directive paradigm may have a true third-person exponent, where the third person is the performer of the prescribed action. And we may see that the third-person directives in Homeric Greek may be differentiated from wishes in the same way as second-person directives.

Most of the Homeric third-person imperatives are used to transmit an order to a third person who is either present but unspecified or entirely absent from the communicative act. Thus although the agent is not directly addressed, the relationship between speaker and (eventual) addressee is the same as in second-person directives. For example:

4.304   μηδέ τις ἱπποσύνηι τε καὶ ἠνορέηφι πεποιθώς
         οἶος πρόσθ' ἄλλων <u>μεμάτω</u> Τρώεσσι μάχεσθαι,

Let no man, so sure of his horsemanship and soldier's prowess dare to fight it out alone with the Trojans,

7.286   'Ιδαῖ', Ἕκτορι ταῦτα κελεύετε μυθήσασθαι·
         αὐτὸς γὰρ χάρμηι προκαλέσσατο πάντας ἀρίστους. <u>ἀρχέτω</u>.

Idaeus, tell Hector to call the truce. He challenged all our bravest, mad for a fight. Let him start.

Although these imperatives are not directly addressed to the agent of the action, these examples may still be easily differentiated from prototypical uses of the optative as seen in 1.42 above. The third-person subject of the imperative is the agent of the action and the speaker has power over the actions of that agent. The distinction between wishes and directives as drawn above can thus also apply to the third-person directives.

It must be admitted that both directives and wishes have less prototypical examples, in which the distinction between them is harder to draw. But I think that all of these types may be explained in terms of the prototypical definition.

One less prototypical type of directive sentence is where the third-person imperative is used when the subject will in all likelihood never actually hear the order that is being uttered. These could be termed 'hypothetical directives'. For example:[12]

5.411   τὼ νῦν Τυδείδης, εἰ καὶ μάλα καρτερός ἐστιν,
<u>φραζέσθω</u>, μή τίς οἱ ἀμείνων σεῖο μάχηται,

Diomedes should be careful, however powerful he is, that someone better than you fight against him,

Here Dione is tending Aphrodite who has been wounded in battle by Diomedes. Dione says that Diomedes should beware fighting against any god stronger than Aphrodite. Dione is not therefore ordering Diomedes to behave in a certain way as we would expect according to the definition of the prototypical imperative given above. This is a peripheral use of the imperative: although the protagonist will never hear this order, by uttering it Dione suggests that she *would* order him if he were able to hear it. This use is however still distinguishable from the wishes described above, since the subject of the imperative is still the would-be agent of the action, even if that subject cannot know he is being ordered.

Another more wish-like use of the imperative is when its subject is inanimate. Here the subject has by definition no control over the fulfilment of the action, and will thus not be the true 'agent' of the action. For example:[13]

8.181   ἀλλ' ὅτε κεν δὴ νηυσὶν ἔπι γλαφυρῆισι γένωμαι,
μνημοσύνη τις ἔπειτα πυρὸς δηΐοιο <u>γενέσθω</u>,

But as soon as I reach their hollow ships, let it be remembered that there should be lethal fire,

The impersonal construction ('let there be memory') is used to order the second-person addressee to remember the fire. While it has the illocutionary force of a directive, the agent of the action is not directly asked to carry out a particular action, just as in a wish. But again there is still a difference between these types of utterance and wishes. The second-person agent does have clear control over the fulfilment of the verbs in the imperative, even if he is not

[12] Also cf. 3.160; 8.431; 9.337; 21.467.
[13] Also cf. 16.494; 18.178; 19.178; 20.122; 24.181.

directly addressed. They could all be turned into normal imperative sentences. For example σέβας δέ σε θυμὸν ἱκέσθω (18.178: 'let awe come upon your soul') could be translated 'be amazed', while μὴ δέ τί τοι θάνατος μελέτω φρεσὶ μηδέ τι τάρβος (24.181: 'Let not death be in your thoughts, nor any fear') could be translated 'do not think about death'. The choice of the third-person imperative rather than the second-person imperative would seem not to depend on any difference in 'directness', but rather in the focus of the sentence. By making 'death' or 'awe' the subject of the sentence that word is highlighted to a greater extent than it would be in the equivalent second-person directive sentence.

Closely related to this use are two examples of the third-person imperative with animate subjects:

15.231   σοὶ δ' αὐτῶι μελέτω, Ἑκατηβόλε, φαίδιμος Ἕκτωρ·

Glorious Hector should be your main concern, far-shooting god.

21.339   σὺ δὲ Ξάνθοιο παρ' ὄχθας
δένδρεα καῖ' ἐν δ' αὐτὸν ἵει πυρί· μηδέ σε πάμπαν
μειλιχίοις ἐπέεσσιν ἀποτρεπέτω καὶ ἀρειῆι·

You, burn the trees by the banks of the Xanthus, hurl the stream itself into conflagration, and do not let him turn you back with honeyed words and threats.

Just as with the inanimate type considered above, it is the second-person addressee who is being ordered to do something. Again, it is just the focus of the sentence which is changed by this choice in construction: the actors in the situation remain the same.

Although these more peripheral uses of the imperative share more features with wishes than their prototypical counterparts, they are still distinguishable from prototypical wishes. The third-person imperative is *never* used when there is no specific agent of the action. This difference may be clearly seen in the following sentence where the third-person imperative and optative are used in parallel:

3.160   ἀλλὰ καὶ ὧς, τοίη περ ἐοῦσ', ἐν νηυσὶ νεέσθω,
μηδ' ἡμῖν τεκέεσσί τ' ὀπίσσω πῆμα λίποιτο.

Still, however ravishing she is, let her sail home, and not be left behind as a bane for us and our children after us.

Here the third-person imperative may be used with νεέσθω, since the subject of the verb is also the agent of the action. With the passive λίποιτο on the other hand the 'agent' of the action is unclear, so that the imperative may not be used.

We must now return to the example I quoted earlier where the optative is very similar to the imperative. According to my definitions, this must be a peripheral use of the optative, since, unlike in prototypical wishes, the agent *is* specified:[14]

1.20   παῖδα δ' ἐμοὶ <u>λύσαιτε</u> φίλην, τὰ δ' ἄποινα δέχεσθαι,

Release my darling child, and accept this ransom,

The definitions of the optative and imperative proposed above therefore do not provide a rule which can predict the choice of mood in any situation. Nevertheless, I believe that the distinction has some explanatory power here too. Previously, the perceived 'politeness' of the speaker in this sentence has been accounted for by the greater 'weakness' of the optative as compared with the imperative (Monro: §299b). But the definition I have proposed above would also predict that the optative would be more 'polite'. Since optatives are generally not addressed directly to the agent of the action they are therefore clearly more indirect expressions than imperatives. Thus even when the agent *is* specified as in 1.20, the use of the optative rather than the imperative enables the speaker to avoid directly asking the addressee to do something, instead he just wishes that something could be accomplished.

Of course, indirect forms are not necessarily more polite than their direct equivalents (Palmer[1]: 29). For example, the expression 'come in' may be considered *more* polite than 'you may come in', because in the second the granting of permission (and the subsequent implications about relative status of speaker and addressee) is made explicit. But it seems clear that in the case of sentences like 1.20, use of the optative will involve less 'loss of face' if the addressee decides not to obey them.[15] We might compare the English 'if only you would practise your scales today' rather than the imperative 'practise your scales today'. This suggests that it

[14] Also cf. O4.735; O24.491.
[15] Brown and Levinson 1987: 13, see also Sadock and Zwicky 1985: 193.

is possible to explain the optative as more polite because of its greater indirectness, and thus to claim that the semantic distinction between wishes and directives that I have proposed above holds even for the more peripheral examples of both types of sentence.

5.4.3 A replacement for the imperative?

The claim I have made above would appear to contradict a theory recently proposed by Justus, that the optative is 'replacing' the third-person imperative in Greek (Justus 1993: 142). If her theory is correct we would expect the two categories to overlap in use, and for the semantic distinction I have proposed to have some exceptions. In this section I will show that Justus' theory is unjustified.

Justus points to the use in Hittite of an imperative form in third-person prayer petitions, contexts in which we would expect to find the optative in Greek. For example:

38 {INA KUR ᵘʳᵘHatti =ma **māu** **sesdu** [...]
   in land (city) Hatti =ptc grow-3S-IMP sleep-3S-IMP

   nu KUR ᵘʳᵘHatti karuiliatt =a **kisaru**}
   ptc land (city) Hatti earlier =ptc become-3S-IMP
   'Let the Hatti land grow and sleep, (and) let the Hatti land become as before.' (Mursili to the Sungoddess)

39 {n=at ANA ᵈUTU ᵘʳᵘArinna kattawatar namma **kisaru**
   ptc-it to Sungoddess city-A. vengeance again become-3S-IMP
   'Let it again become a matter of revenge for the Sungoddess of Arinna.' (Mursili to the Sungoddess of Arinna)

It is certainly true that the optative is used in very similar situations in Greek, as we have already seen above. For example:

3.300 ὥδέ σφ' ἐγκέφαλος χαμάδις ῥέοι ὡς ὅδε οἶνος,

may their brains be thus poured forth upon the ground as this wine,

Justus (1993: 144) regards the one example of a third-person imperative in Greek prayer petitions as a frozen archaism, a relic of a time when Greek too would have only used imperative forms in prayer petitions:

10.329 ἴστω νῦν Ζεὺς αὐτός,

Now Zeus be my witness,

However, there are various reasons to think that we should analyse this data in a rather different way. Firstly, we may consider the later development of Greek: third-person imperatives where humans are the agent of requests are still flourishing as late as the New Testament (Moulton 1908: §84). For example, James I: 4–8 has four examples in as many verses. If the optative was indeed replacing the imperative, this would be rather surprising. Secondly, the claim that the optative is replacing the third-person imperative requires us to analyse the Greek and Hittite sentences in the same way. That is, we must analyse both the imperative sentences in Hittite and the sentences which resemble them in Greek as directive sentences. But this would appear to be unwarranted: Myhill (1998) has discussed the need to analyse speech acts differently in different languages (see also Bartsch 1994). More specifically, it has been shown that the discourse context of prayers changes from Indo-European to Latin.[16] The earlier construction is grounded in the second person as expressed by imperatives. The later construction is to use the first-person subject 'I pray that . . .' We could see the wish construction found in Greek prayer petitions as a mid-way point between these two states, no longer directly addressing the gods, but not yet grounding the prayer in a first-person form. That is, rather than claiming that the optative replaced imperatives in prayer petitions, we could claim that the wish construction replaced the directive construction. To put this another way, we could claim that Hittite speakers accorded their gods a greater level of agency than Greek speakers, and that in their eyes, sentences such as 38 and 39 above (p. 131) were seen as more like orders, so that sentences where the agent of the action was a god were conceived in the same way as sentences with a human agent were perceived in Greek. Thus, while it is true that the third-person imperative in Hittite has a wider range than the equivalent Greek form, we should not see the Greek optative as 'encroaching' on meanings that would originally have been expressed with a third-person imperative.

It is significant in this respect that the one example of the third-person imperative in prayer petitions in 10.329 has a clear agent,

---

[16] Traugott and Dasher 2002: 196, with reference to Benveniste 1973.

a particular god, and is really an 'indirect order' rather than a true wish. It is therefore unnecessary to describe it as a frozen archaism: certainly in sychronic terms it is found in just the situation we expect to find an imperative.

The conclusion that the Greek categories are rather different from the Hittite is confirmed by a consideration of the morphological form of Greek third-person imperatives. The one ancient marker (-τω) seems originally to have been a deictic marker added to the second-singular form, meaning 'from this point', 'then', perhaps the ablative singular of the pronoun *to-.[17] The Hittite forms continue instead the original marker of the third-person imperative. The ancient system may well have more resembled the Hittite system, with the third-person imperative used with what we have called here both directive and wish-like meanings. But both the third-person imperative and the optative forms in Greek are later developments, and we may not therefore claim that the form that expresses the third-person imperative in Greek would originally have had the wider meaning expressed by the Hittite third-person imperative form.

5.4.4 A new description

Above I have shown how previous accounts of the optative are unsuccessful, and have argued that the wish optative should not be defined in terms of the imperative: it is neither weaker than the imperative, nor replacing it. But I have yet to offer a more attractive explanation. In this section I will make some tentative suggestions, but acknowledge that there are more answers still to be found.

It is firstly necessary to describe this use of the optative in terms of the model of modality proposed in chapter 2. Wishes are clearly performative, and so this use should be described as 'speaker oriented'. But wishes are not so clearly linked to deontic modality as the hortative and negative directive constructions: one of the defining features of deontic modality is that there should be an agent to carry out the obliged event (Heine 1995a: 32). Palmer has in fact

---

[17] Buck 1933: 303; Szemerényi 1954: 12, with references, though note a problem with the etymology at Sihler 1995: §548.

argued that the modality of wishes could be described as epistemic since they indicate 'attitudes to propositions rather than unrealized events' (Palmer[2]: 134). But elsewhere he claims that wishes are 'partly deontic, partly epistemic' (Palmer[2]: 13).

This difficulty of description mirrors the difficulty of describing wishes in the speech act literature. In preliminary explanations of the theory, wishes were described as separate illocutionary acts from directives. For example, Searle (1965: 132) contrasts the wish 'Would that John left the room' with the question 'Will John leave the room?', the statement 'John will leave the room', and the 'directive' 'John, leave the room!' His claim that wishes are one way of expressing indirect directives confirms the theory that he originally considered the two to have different illocutionary forces (Searle 1975: 171). But his later taxonomy of speech acts divides all speech acts into four basic categories, differentiating between assertives, directives, commissives, and expressives (Searle 1979: 147–9). Subsequent scholars have assigned wishes to either the directive or the expressive category.[18] The problem is that wishes do not fit neatly into one or the other of these categories. By uttering wishes, the speaker hopes to be able to change the world: they are thus 'world-changing' just as directives are (Haverkate 2002: 34). But they are not 'attempts . . . by the speaker to get the hearer to do something', as Searle (1979: 147) defined directives. They therefore share some elements with expressives, since they express the psychological state of the speaker (Searle 1979: 148). Because they may not easily be categorised as either directive or expressive, some scholars have been led to invent an entirely new category. For example, Risselada (1993: 41) argues that wishes constitute a transitional type between the two categories. Similarly, the modality of wishes may be described in a 'transitional' way, recognising it as 'speaker oriented' while acknowledging that there is not as close a connection with deontic modality as with the hortative and negative directive constructions.

As far as the definition of the optative in terms of the irrealis continuum is concerned, the wish construction provides further

---

[18] Hancher 1979: 4; Sadock and Zwicky 1985: 164; Vanderveken 1990: 15; Skerrett 1971: 162; Melo 2001: 109–10.

evidence to query the claim that the optative lies at the most remote, irrealis end. In theoretical discussions it has been argued that wishes have more and less irrealis sub-types. For example, Haverkate (2002: 32) has shown that wishes in Spanish are expressed by more or less irrealis markers according to whether they are realisable or non-realisable. The distinction between these two types of wishes stems back to Jespersen (1924: 320) who called the former optative and the latter desiderative (Palmer[1]: 117):

40 May he still be alive!
41 Would that he were still alive!

If the subjunctive and optative did express different parts of the irrealis continuum we might expect the subjunctive to express realisable wishes, and the optative to express non-realisable wishes. But instead the optative is found with both meanings.[19] For example:[20]

7.132   αἲ γάρ, Ζεῦ τε πάτερ καὶ Ἀθηναίη καὶ Ἄπολλον,
        ἡβῶιμ᾽ ὡς ὅτ᾽ ἐπ᾽ ὠκυρόωι Κελάδοντι μάχοντο

If only, Father Zeus, Athena and Apollo, if only I were as young as when they fought by Celadon's rapids

1.17   Ἀτρεῖδαί τε καὶ ἄλλοι ἐϋκνήμιδες Ἀχαιοί,
       ὑμῖν μὲν θεοὶ δοῖεν Ὀλύμπια δώματ᾽ ἔχοντες
       ἐκπέρσαι Πριάμοιο πόλιν, εὖ δ᾽ οἴκαδ᾽ ἱκέσθαι·

Sons of Atreus and well-greaved Achaeans, may the gods who dwell on Olympus give you Priam's city to plunder, and a safe passage home.

Chantraine (§318) has claimed that 'la question de savoir s'il est réalisable ou non ne se pose pas'.

A complete understanding of this use of the optative requires relating it to the other use of the optative. Unfortunately, this still remains unclear, although there seem to be clear similarities between the two. After all, conditional sentences, usually taken to express epistemic modality, are also used with the optative to express wishes. For example:

---

[19] Goodwin: §739; Gonda: 51–2; Wakker 1994: 212, fn. 171; Sideri 1996: 206.
[20] Also cf. 7.157; 11.670; 23.629; O14.468; O14.503 (future); 8.538 (present).

4.289 αἲ γάρ, Ζεῦ τε πάτερ καὶ Ἀθηναίη καὶ Ἄπολλον,
τοῖος πᾶσιν θυμὸς ἐνὶ στήθεσσι <u>γένοιτο·</u>

Father Zeus, Athena and Apollo! If only everyone had the same spirit in their breasts.

Indeed, in this context it is often difficult to distinguish whether the optative should be interpreted as epistemic or wish. For example:

O   αἲ γὰρ τοῦτο <u>γένοιτο</u>, ἄναξ ἑκατηβόλ᾽ Ἄπολλον·
8.340 δεσμοὶ μὲν τρὶς τόσσοι ἀπείρονες ἀμφὶς ἔχοιεν,
ὑμεῖς δ᾽ εἰσορόῳτε θεοὶ πᾶσαί τε θέαιναι,
αὐτὰρ ἐγὼν <u>εὕδοιμι</u> παρὰ χρυσέῃ Ἀφροδίτῃ.

If this came to pass, lord Apollo, the far-shooter, then three times as many bonds would hold me, inextricable, and you gods and all the goddesses might be looking on, but I would sleep alongside golden Aphrodite.
OR
If only this could come to pass! Bonds might hold me, but I would sleep by Aphrodite.

However, the mechanism for the development of one meaning from another is less clear. In chapter 4 I argued that the speaker-oriented meanings of the subjunctive develop in particular constructions from the future meaning of the mood in main clauses, through conventionalisation of implicature. Some examples of the wish optative would appear to be explicable in the same way. For example:[21]

4.93 ἦ ῥά νύ μοί τι <u>πίθοιο</u>, Λυκάονος υἱὲ δαΐφρον;

Would you obey me, glorious son of Lycaon?

The particle ῥα supports the editorial interpretation of this sentence as a question (Denniston 1954: 284; also Leaf ad loc.). In that case the 'wish' meaning could be seen as an indirect illocutionary force, a 'conversational implicature' of the meaning of 'negative epistemic stance'.

However, given that the agent is specified in this example, this is not what I have described as the prototypical use of the optative, and a similar explanation for the more prototypical types is not so plausible. Unlike the subjunctive, which is found with hortative

---

[21] Also 7.48; 14.190; O4.193. The same combination of particles is found in two of the three lines.

meaning only in the first person and in the negative construction, the optative is found without restriction, so that, even if this meaning did develop through conventionalisation of an implicature in the second person, that meaning has subsequently been generalised. We may not therefore be sure of the path by which the use of the optative in wishes developed, or whether it should be described as the 'primary' or 'secondary' use of the mood. Because of the small number of 'grams' in BPP's survey which express optative notions, they are not able to describe cross-linguistically common paths of development which might be tested here (BPP: 211). It is perhaps worth noting that the name 'optative' (from Latin *optare* 'to desire', translating the Greek εὐκτική) suggests that, at least for early grammarians, it is this use which was seen as primary (Goodwin: §720; Chantraine: §320). But unfortunately, there is no evidence to support or refute that belief.

5.4.5 Summary

In this section I have argued that a reanalysis of the wish construction reveals that its traditional description as 'weaker' than the imperative is wrong: rather there is a semantic difference between wishes and directives. While directives involve an agent, over whom the speaker has control, wishes do not have to. This distinction holds even in the more peripheral examples, and explains why the optative may be used as a 'polite form' of the imperative. The claim that the optative may be semantically distinguished from the imperative argues against Justus' theory that the former is replacing the latter, and indeed I have shown further reasons to doubt this theory in section 5.4.3.

The positive explanation of the optative in this construction remains, however, somewhat more elusive. I have argued that, just as in the epistemic construction, the optative does not express the most irrealis meaning, since it is used in both realisable and unrealisable wishes. The status of this type of modality and its relationship to other types has not widely been discussed. I argue that, while it is clearly speaker oriented, it is not as closely related to deontic modality as other speaker-oriented modality, and would thus perhaps best be described as 'performative desire'. In terms of drawing the map of the different meanings of the optative in Homeric Greek, its development remains unclear. Although some peripheral types could be derived through a conventionalisation of implicature from its meaning of 'negative epistemic stance', the meaning has become very generalised, and it is not clear that this is the path by which the more prototypical uses have developed.

5.5 Other meanings

5.5.1 Introduction

The conviction that the optative is a 'remoter' version of the subjunctive has meant that the uses of the mood in conditional clauses and in wishes have received most attention, since it is these uses which are (apparently) most similar to uses of the subjunctive. But in this chapter I have argued that the parallelism with the subjunctive in these uses is illusory, just as we would expect given the findings from the theory of grammaticalisation. In this section I will support this argument by describing meanings of the optative which have no corresponding meaning in the subjunctive.

Grammarians have long recognised that there are other meanings of the optative which do not fit so easily into the traditional model, but have not considered them in any great detail.[22] Now that the traditional model has been shown to be flawed in other ways, these other uses of the optative may be looked at in a new light.

5.5.2 Dynamic

The first group of optatives which fit uneasily into the traditional bipartite model are most successfully translated by the English modal verb 'can' or 'could', rather than 'might' or 'would'. For example:[23]

---

[22] Goodwin §13, Chantraine §321, Monro §300.

[23] Also cf 1.100; 1.272; 1.301; 2.012; 2.029; 2.066; 3.066; 3.223; 3.235; 4.539; 5.192; 6.522; 8.451; 9.077; 9.304; 10.243; 11.803; 12.059; 12.382; 12.448; 12.465; 14.054; 14.058; 14.245; 14.335; 14.344; 17.260; 17.327; 17.399; 17.711; 19.218; 19.321; 19.415; 20.247; 20.359; 20.367; 24.149; 24.566; O1.402; O3.114; O4.064; O4.078; O4.649; O6.300; O7.213; O8.177; O8.195; O8.280; O9.242; O9.351; O10.384; O10.574; O11.375; O12.077; O12.084; O12.102; O12.107; O2.287; O13.087; O14.123; O14.197; O15.321; O16.196; O17.268; O18.031; O19.108; O19.286; O20.212; O22.138; O23.126; O23.188.

3.223 ἀλλ' ὅτε δὴ ὄπα τε μεγάλην ἐκ στήθεος <u>εἴη</u>
κ αὶ ἔπεα νιφάδεσσιν ἐοικότα χειμερίῃσιν,
οὐκ ἂν ἔπειτ' Ὀδυσῆϊ γ' ἐρίσσειε βροτὸς ἄλλος·

But whenever he let loose his great voice from his chest, and words like a winter blizzard, then no other mortal <u>could</u> rival Odysseus.

12.448 Ἕκτωρ δ' ἀρπάξας λᾶαν φέρεν, ὅς ῥα πυλάων
ἑστήκει πρόσθε πρυμνὸς παχύς, αὐτὰρ ὕπερθεν
ὀξὺς ἔην· τὸν δ' οὔ κε δύ' ἀνέρε δήμου ἀρίστω
ῥηϊδίως ἐπ' ἄμαξαν ἀπ' οὔδεος <u>ὀχλίσσειαν,</u>
οἷοι νῦν βροτοί εἰσ'· ὁ δέ μιν ῥέα πάλλε καὶ οἷος.

And Hector seized and lifted a rock that lay before the gates – it was thick at the base, but sharp at the point. Two men, the best of the lot, <u>could</u> not easily lift it from the ground to the chariot, as mortals now are, but Hector wielded it easily even on his own.

This meaning is apparently recognised for the optative by Goodwin – he translates 3.223 with 'could' (§442). However, he groups the line with examples of the optative which he translates with 'would' or 'might', and describes the whole group of examples as belonging 'to the borderland between past and future conclusions'. He thus does not distinguish a different type in the same way as I propose here. In a similar fashion, Smyth (§1824) claims that the optative may sometimes be translated by 'can' as well as by 'may' or 'might'. However, he describes these as just one sub-type of the category 'potential optative', which would suggest that the modality of these lines expressed the same type of modality as found in conditional clauses. The formal marking supports this argument: the presence of the modal particle suggests that these uses should be considered together (2.2.3). I have argued however, that the formal marking is not as clear cut as the traditional accounts would have us believe (2.2.3 and appendix 1). Furthermore, there is a clear *semantic* difference between these examples and the examples from conditional sentences considered above (5.3). In 12.448 the speaker is not claiming that there is no *possibility* that two men *would* lift the stone. Rather he is claiming that they would not be *able* to lift it, despite being 'the best of the lot'. A description of the type of people involved is often found in the examples of this meaning which I have distinguished. For example:

139

O   οὐδέ κεν ἀμβαίη βροτὸς ἀνὴρ οὐδ' ἐπιβαίη,
12.77   οὐδ' εἴ οἱ χεῖρές τε ἐείκοσι καὶ πόδες εἶεν·

No mortal man could climb it or set foot upon the top, not even if he had twenty hands and feet.

If the optative is used to describe the ability of the subject, we must conclude that the map of meanings expressed by the optative is more complicated than the bipartite model suggested in the traditional account, a conclusion which was expected from modern theoretical studies in modality (see 2.3). The expression of the ability of the subject has been recognised as a distinct type of modality by theoreticians, and termed 'dynamic' (Palmer[2]: 9; BPP: 177). Dynamic modality has the same 'axis' of possibility and necessity that is found in deontic and epistemic modality (2.2.3), as illustrated by the following examples (from van der Auwera and Plungian 1998: 80):

42 Boris can get by with sleeping five hours a night.
43 Boris needs to sleep ten hours every night for him to function properly.

Unfortunately, the status of this type of modality and its relationship to the other types is disputed. In the first edition of *Mood and Modality*, Palmer (1986: 12) claims that dynamic modality does not have the same status as deontic and epistemic modality. It is certainly the case that dynamic modality appears to have important differences from the other types of modality, particularly that it is often apparently 'factive' in meaning (Coates 1983: 91). For example:

44 I can see clearly now the rain has gone.

In this sentence the speaker *does* see clearly. A further important difference: dynamic modality is related to characteristics inherent to the subject of the verb, rather than attitudes of the speaker. However, this does not mean that it should be excluded from descriptions of modality. In their 'semantic map', van der Auwera and Plungian (1998: 81) describe this type of modality as 'participant-internal', which is distinguished from both 'participant-external' (which includes the traditional deontic domain), and epistemic modality. Most modern studies of modality include it as a separate type of modality, and in the second edition of *Mood and Modality*, Palmer himself includes it (2000: 9).

It may of course be questioned whether it is really necessary to distinguish this meaning for the optative in Homeric Greek. Certainly, expression of this notion is not restricted to the optative. The idea of ability is more often expressed lexically (e.g. with δύναμαι), but also seems to be carried by the indicative and subjunctive of certain verbs. For example:

22.47   καὶ γὰρ νῦν δύο παῖδε Λυκάονα καὶ Πολύδωρον
οὐ δύναμαι ἰδέειν Τρώων εἰς ἄστυ ἀλέντων,

Even now I cannot see my two sons, Lycaon and Polydorus, in the group of Trojans gathered in the city,

5.893   μητρός τοι μένος ἐστὶν ἀάσχετον, οὐκ ἐπιεικτόν,
Ἥρης· τὴν μὲν ἐγὼ σπουδῆι δάμνημ' ἐπέεσσιν·

You have your mother Hera's uncontrollable, unceasing rage. I can hardly control her with my tongue.

2.488   πληθὺν δ' οὐκ ἂν ἐγὼ μυθήσομαι οὐδ' ὀνομήνω,
οὐδ' εἴ μοι δέκα μὲν γλῶσσαι, δέκα δὲ στόματ' εἶεν,

I would not be able to count the masses or name them, not even if I had ten tongues, or ten mouths,

The existence of these examples suggests that the 'meaning' of dynamic modality is really a rather subtle semantic nuance, expressed by many different grammatical categories. However, the use of the optative with this meaning is rather more wide-spread than that of the indicative and subjunctive. The meaning is found much more frequently in the optative (I have classed seventy-one Homeric optatives as dynamic).[24] Furthermore, while the indicative and subjunctive examples are always in the first person the optative has the value in the third person too. For example:

4.539   ἔνθά κεν οὐκέτι ἔργον ἀνὴρ ὀνόσαιτο μετελθών,
ὅς τις ἔτ' ἄβλητος καὶ ἀνούτατος ὀξέϊ χαλκῶι
δινεύοι κατὰ μέσσον,

Then no man who entered into that task was able to scorn it any longer, whoever whirled into the crowd, still untouched and unharmed by sharp bronze,

---

[24] See appendix 2.

This is significant since in the first person the subject and speaker overlap. The indicative and subjunctive are not therefore clearly discussing the subject as separate from the speaker. The dynamic use is thus more stable and widespread for the optative than for the indicative and subjunctive, where we should perhaps explain the sense of ability as more of a pragmatic inference from the context. On these grounds it seems justified at least to consider the possibility that, in the case of the optative, dynamic meaning should be described as a separate meaning.

For those who still wish to deny the existence or importance of this further meaning, it may be felt significant that, unlike the English modal verb 'can', the optative most frequently expresses potential or 'unreal' abilities or possibilities. Most of the examples are also negated. For example:

O   αὐτὰρ ἔπειτ' ἐπέθηκε θυρεὸν μέγαν ὑψόσ' ἀείρας,
9.242   ὄβριμον· οὐκ ἂν τόν γε δύω καὶ εἴκοσ' ἄμαξαι
        ἐσθλαὶ τετράκυκλοι ἀπ' οὔδεος ὀχλίσσειαν·

And then he lifted overhead a great door-stone, a huge one. Not even twenty-two fine four-wheeled chariots could move that from the ground.

Since these dynamic sentences share the semantic feature of 'potentiality' with the conditional meaning described above, it could again be argued that the examples discussed here should be described as a sub-type of the other category. However, as I argued in chapter 2, in order to account for the different meanings which are expressed by a certain form, it is not sufficient to show that they share some abstract feature: it is still interesting that it is these two types of potentiality which are expressed rather than any other type. Indeed, studies of modality suggest that modal forms develop their web of meaning gradually. It is therefore entirely to be expected that the different meanings expressed by a single modal form will share a particular feature, and that there will be examples which may not be clearly categorised as expressing one type of modality rather than another.

In this regard it is particularly interesting to note that just like the meaning of the modal verb 'can' in English (cf. Coates 1983: chapter 5), the 'dynamic' meaning of the optative is not a simple domain. Coates distinguishes the following three sub-meanings:

45 Ability: I can only type very slowly as I am quite a beginner.
46 Permission: You can start the revels now.
47 Root possibility: I think there is a place where I can get a cheap kettle.

The three meanings have been related to each other through two different gradients. Meanings can be defined as expressing ability when they refer to properties inherent to the actor, whereas they will be defined as root possibility when they relate to characteristics of the external circumstances: thus these meanings are related on the gradient of 'inherency'. The meaning of permission will be used when human laws and rules are in force, whereas the meaning of root possibility indicates that only natural law is acting: permission is more restricted than root possibility and thus these two meanings are related on the gradient of 'restriction' (Coates 1983: 93. See also van der Auwera 1986).

The Greek optative appears to be used with the same three meanings as the English modal verb. As well as the 'basic' ability meaning exemplified above, there are a few examples where the optative appears to express 'permission':[25]

2.29   νῦν γάρ κεν ἕλοις πόλιν εὐρυάγυιαν
        Τρώων·

now you may take the broad streets of the Trojans!

Other examples are ambiguous between an ability sense and a sense of 'root possibility'. For example:[26]

14.335   πῶς κ᾽ ἔοι, εἴ τις νῶϊ θεῶν αἰειγενετάων
         εὕδοντ᾽ ἀθρήσειε, θεοῖσι δὲ πᾶσι μετελθὼν
         πεφράδοι; οὐκ ἂν ἔγω γε τεὸν πρὸς δῶμα νεοίμην
         ἐξ εὐνῆς ἀνστᾶσα· νεμεσσητὸν δέ κεν εἴη.

How would it be, if one of the eternal gods spied us sleeping, and went to the other gods and told them? I would not be able to rise from your bed and dwell in your home: it would be too awful.

Here it is unclear whether the speaker is implying that she would not have the ability to show herself again or whether it would not be possible for her to do so. It is interesting that this example is found in the context of a conditional sentence: this is perhaps the locus from which the more clearly differentiated examples such as 3.223 developed.

Just as with the meaning of wish, it remains unclear exactly how the dynamic meanings are related to the other meanings of the optative. The lines connecting up the different meanings in this map must therefore remain speculative. But this is no reason to ignore this group of meanings. Semantically, they are clearly distinguishable.

5.5.3 Objective deontic

A further meaning which I wish to distinguish for the Homeric optative is an objective deontic meaning. In chapter 2 I briefly described the distinction between subjective and objective types of modality (2.3.3). The following sentences (from Lyons 1977: 797 and Verstraete 2001: 1508) illustrate these different meanings for deontic modality:

48 Subjective deontic: You must not include me in your plan of action.
49 Objective deontic: To reach orbit, an object must accelerate to a speed of about 17,500 miles per hour.

In the subjective example the speaker is clearly 'involved' in the utterance, imposing his own will, whereas in the objective version the speaker is not involved. Instead, an immutable law of physics is being invoked. More recently, it has been argued that the difference between these types of modality is a question of illocutionary force, so that Sweetser describes them as 'performative' and 'constative' respectively (Sweetser 1990: 65–8, also see Verstraete 2001: 1517).

The evidence for the claim that the optative may express objective deontic modality is more restricted than for the claim in support of dynamic modality made above. The claim is primarily based on some sentences in which an unexpected negator is used, although I believe that there may be more examples of the type. Again, though, it is difficult to categorise a particular example as objective deontic rather than exemplifying another meaning, which is just as we would expect given the usual way in which modal forms gain their meaning.

In section 2.2.3 I noted the claim made in traditional accounts that the meaning of the mood is marked by the choice of negator. For example, Chantraine (§306) claims that the 'subjonctif d'éventualité' (the epistemic meaning) is negated by οὐ whereas the 'subjonctif de volonté' (the speaker-oriented meaning) is negated with μή. However, there are some sentences in which the choice of negator is rather surprising. For example:

2.250   τὼ οὐκ ἂν βασιλῆας ἀνὰ στόμ᾿ ἔχων <u>ἀγορεύοις</u>
       καί σφιν ὀνείδεά τε <u>προφέροις</u>, νόστόν τε <u>φυλάσσοις</u>.

You must stop taking the names of kings in vain, insulting them, all the time looking for a chance to get home.

14.127   τὼ οὐκ ἄν με γένος γε κακὸν καὶ ἀνάλκιδα φάντες
        μῦθον <u>ἀτιμήσαιτε</u> πεφασμένον, ὅν κ᾿ εὖ εἴπω.

So you should not disregard the advice I give by claiming that my birth is low and cowardly, advice which is well meant.

O 20.135   οὐκ ἄν μιν νῦν, τέκνον, ἀναίτιον <u>αἰτιόῳο</u>.

Child, you shouldn't hold her responsible this time.

These lines have often been analysed as epistemic, but with circular reasoning: because οὐ is found in the prototypical epistemic constructions all lines with οὐ are described as epistemic (Leaf ad loc.; Monro: §300dβ).[27] But in all these sentences the speaker is not expressing a particular belief but is rather stating how he thinks the hearer should behave. For example, in 2.250 the speaker is not suggesting epistemically that the addressee is not mentioning the names of kings, rather he is suggesting that it would be a good idea if he did not. Goodwin (§237) describes this line as an example of the potential optative being used in the second person to express a 'mild command'. Were it not for the formal marking, it would probably have been explained as a 'quasi-imperative' use of the optative. However, it is clearly rather different from the meaning of the optative as found in the wish construction examined above (5.4). While wishes are performative impositions of will, these are constative reports of the existence of an obligation. Thus it appears

---

[27] See appendix 1 for further discussion of these sentences in respect to the meaning of the negators.

that the optative is used to express another meaning in addition to the epistemic and speaker-oriented ones distinguished in the traditional accounts. I believe that this meaning should be described as objective deontic.

If we accept that the optative may express objective deontic modality it is possible to reconsider many examples that have previously been assigned to one of the two 'traditional' categories. For example:

6.163 τεθναίης, ὦ Προῖτ᾽, ἢ κάκτανε Βελλεροφόντην,

You should die, Proetus, or kill Bellerophon,

Anteia is here trying to persuade her husband that he should kill Bellerophon, and that, if he is not successful, it is his duty to die trying. The presence of the imperative has led commentators to align the optative with the imperative here, as in the wish construction, and to suggest such translations as 'Die, Proetus' or 'May you die' (Goodwin: 383, 725). Monro describes it as a 'rhetorical wish' (§299c), implying that the optative was again chosen from a desire to be more polite. But as the speaker uses the imperative only four words later this implication is implausible. Clearly, wives are 'allowed' to address their husbands with imperative forms in Homeric Greek without being considered impolite. We could explain the two different forms in this sentence in terms of 'politeness' by pointing to the greater unpleasantness the wife may have felt uttering the first order. But imperatives are found elsewhere in situations where the speaker does not really want the ordered actions to take place (Monro: §298). For example:

4.29 ἔρδ᾽· ἀτὰρ οὔ τοι πάντες ἐπαινέομεν θεοὶ ἄλλοι.

Do it. But we other gods will not praise you.

Describing the optative in 6.163 as expressing objective deontic modality allows us to explain the choice of moods in a more sophisticated way. Anteia is ordering her husband to kill Bellerophon and thus uses the imperative, but she is not ordering him to die, rather she is just pointing out to him that it is his duty to die, if he does not first kill his wife's alleged abuser. The optative is thus being used to report the existence of an obligation rather than performatively impose it on the addressee.

Many other examples of so-called 'polite optatives' could also be explained in terms of the objective deontic meaning of the mood. I argued earlier that the greater politeness could be explained by describing these as examples of the 'wish' meaning of the optative, since the semantics of a wish as opposed to an imperative does not entail that the subject of the verb is the 'agent' of the action. But these uses of the optative could also be explained with reference to its objective meaning. For example:

1.20   παῖδα δ' ἐμοὶ λύσαιτε φίλην, τὰ δ' ἄποινα δέχεσθαι,

Release my darling child, and accept this ransom,

By using the optative rather than the imperative in 1.20, Chryses may imply that there is another, higher source for the obligation, 'you ought to release my child to me'.

A similar difference between optative and imperative may be discerned in 20.121:

20.121   ἀλλ' ἄγεθ', ἡμεῖς πέρ μιν ἀποτρωπῶμεν ὀπίσσω
αὐτόθεν· ἤ τις ἔπειτα καὶ ἡμείων Ἀχιλῆϊ
παρσταίη, δοίη δὲ κράτος μέγα, μηδέ τι θυμῶι
δευέσθω,

Come on, let's turn him back from here. Otherwise one of us should stand by Achilles and give him great strength, and not let his spirit flag.

With the objective meaning of the optative, Athena can distance herself from the obligation. Her ideal is to turn back Achilles from the fight. If the other gods do not choose that option, she is adamant that someone will at least stand by his side.

An objective meaning of the optative would also explain why the mood is used when reporting an imperative uttered by someone else. For example:

24.140   τὴν δ' ἀπαμειβόμενος προσέφη πόδας ὠκὺς Ἀχιλλεύς·
τῇδ' εἴη ὃς ἄποινα φέροι καὶ νεκρὸν ἄγοιτο,
εἰ δὴ πρόφρονι θυμῶι Ὀλύμπιος αὐτὸς ἀνώγει.

Swift-footed Achilles replied: 'So be it. The man who brings the ransom must also take away the body, if Olympian Zeus himself really insists in all earnest.'

Here Achilles is ordering on behalf of Zeus, and the objective deontic meaning of the optative would allow him to avoid being held personally responsible for the order.

This meaning of the optative may also explain its use in 'delayed' imperatives. For example, at O15.14, Athena is addressing Telemachus and telling him to wake up and go home. She uses imperatives for this immediate task, and later uses infinitives to explain how to avoid the waiting party of suitors (O15.33–42).[28] Crucially, at line 24 she gives him advice for the future concerning his choice of wife with the optative:

O   ἀλλὰ σύ γ' ἐλθὼν αὐτὸς <u>ἐπιτρέψειας</u> ἕκαστα
15.24   δμῳάων ἥ τίς τοι ἀρίστη φαίνεται εἶναι,
        εἰς ὅ κέ τοι φήνωσι θεοὶ κυδρὴν παράκοιτιν.

You should go yourself and turn over everything to the servant who seems to you the best, until the gods bring to light a noble bride for you.

The use of the optative here has previously been claimed to arise from Athena's desire to be more polite (e.g. Merry, Riddell and Monro who translate it 'I would have you entrust'). However, I see no need for greater politeness in this context. The difference rather seems to be that this is a piece of advice to be acted on later rather than an order. It makes sense to use a marker of objective deontic modality here: it would express Athena's belief that this is what Telemachus *ought* to do, in order to avoid his mother taking any of his inheritance.

If it is admitted that this meaning of objective deontic modality exists, it must also be explained how it relates to the other uses of the optative. Importantly, this use corresponds to the objective deontic meaning demonstrated for English in example 49 reporting the existence of an obligation. The use of the optative previously described as deontic (the 'wish' meaning), is not the subjective equivalent of this meaning. It has been claimed above that wishes express the desire of the subject; they were described as 'performative desire'. The objective equivalent of this would report the existence of a desire, rather than reporting the existence of

---

[28] For the use of infinitives with imperative force in Homer see Neuberger-Donath 1980.

an obligation. Interestingly, there are a few examples which do appear to express just this meaning of objective desire, which are best translated 'would like to'. For example:[29]

23.151   νῦν δ', ἐπεὶ οὐ νέομαί γε φίλην ἐς πατρίδα γαῖαν,
          Πατρόκλωι ἥρωϊ κόμην <u>ὀπάσαιμι</u> φέρεσθαι.

Now, since I am not going to my dear homeland I would like to give Patroclus this lock of my hair to go with him.

However, it is rather more difficult to distinguish these clearly from the more performative examples. Nevertheless, whether we can distinguish constative from performative expressions of desire in the data, it is clear to me that we should distinguish the objective deontic meaning illustrated above.

To conclude, the meaning of the optative in 2.250, 14.127 and O20.135 is surprising, particularly given the choice of negator. Closer analysis of the meaning of the lines suggests that the optative expresses a meaning which is different from the two discussed previously in this chapter. In these lines the optative appears to be reporting the existence of an obligation on the subject, and thus expressing objective deontic modality. I have argued that, if we accept this meaning for the optative, we may wish to reanalyse other examples, where the optative has previously been described in terms of the traditional model. If this deontic meaning can be said to be distinguished, it is clearly markedly different from the 'wish' meaning that was previously thought of as corresponding most closely to the deontic meaning of the moods in English. This meaning is constative and expresses obligation. The wish meaning is performative and expresses desire.

5.5.4 Conclusion

I have argued in this section that the traditional accounts of the optative are not just wrong in their description of the two 'core' uses of the optative. They also fail to acknowledge the full range of meanings expressed by the mood, which further suggests that the

---

[29] Also 24.664; O4.637; O20.326; O21.113; O22.262; O24.436.

parallelism traditionally argued to exist between the subjunctive and optative is a construct of grammarians rather than a linguistic reality.

I have found seventy-one examples of the optative used to describe the ability of the subject. These have previously been classed in the same way as the modality found in conditional clauses. But there are clear semantic as well as syntactic differences. The modality has been termed 'dynamic', although I have pointed out that this category of dynamic modality does not appear to be unified. Rather, the meanings can be explained as related on a series of gradients to one another, and perhaps to the meaning found in conditional sentences. It is perhaps unsurprising that, as this is the first time that this type of modality has been distinguished for the mood, it is not yet possible to describe how it is related to the other types of modality. The existence of the type seems indisputable.

In certain lines it could also be argued that the optative expresses objective deontic meaning. The clear examples of this are less common than those of the dynamic meaning, but the acknowledgement of this meaning also allows us to reinterpret other examples in an interesting way. The map of the meanings of the optative therefore appears to be even more complicated than traditionally thought.

5.6 Summary and conclusions

In traditional accounts, the optative is described as more 'remote' than the subjunctive or as its 'past-time variant'. This claim is said to be supported by the association of the mood with secondary endings, but it was argued in section 5.2 that this formal argument carries very little weight. Semantically, too, there are many problems with the definition. This is partly caused by the redefinition of the subjunctive made in chapter 4, which suggests that any parallelism between the two 'moods' will only be synchronic. Here the reanalysis of the optative constructions has provided further evidence against the traditional description.

In conditional clauses, the mood is used with a wide variety of meanings as I demonstrated in section 5.3. As well as its 'classic' use in unreal protases where it appears to describe events of low probability, it is also found in apodoses where the speaker describes an event as a certain consequence of the event in the protasis, as well as in other protases expressing rather greater degrees of probability. It is therefore more similar to the indicative, expressing a wide spectrum of attitudes towards the likelihood of the proposition. All the events described by the optative are viewed as 'unreal' by the speaker, and the optative was therefore redefined as expressing 'negative epistemic stance'. This aligns the optative with the indicative, defined in chapter 3 as expressing 'positive epistemic stance'. This conclusion has important consequences for our understanding of the field of modality in general, suggesting that our understanding of unreal conditionals should be changed.

A detailed comparison of several different types of wishes and directive sentences in section 5.4 led to the conclusion that imperatives are used when the agent of the desired action is specified, and the speaker is in control of the subject, while in wishes the agent does not have to be the subject of the verb, and is often not under the control of the speaker. The possibility of semantically distinguishing between directives and wishes suggests that the optative should not be described in terms of the imperative. The meaning of the optative in this construction confirms the conclusions reached in the previous section, that the optative cannot be described as simply more 'irrealis' than the subjunctive, as it is found in both realisable and non-realisable wishes. But it remains unclear how to relate the wish use to the other uses of the moods, and to determine which is the 'primary' meaning out of which the others have developed. Certain examples of the 'wish' construction may be explained as having developed from the epistemic sense of the mood through a conventionalisation of implicature, but this only applies to a small proportion of the whole.

In section 5.5, I outlined evidence to suggest that the range of meanings expressed by the optative is wider than traditionally thought, and described the 'dynamic' and 'objective deontic' groups of meanings. The evidence strongly suggests that the parallelism seen between the optative and subjunctive should be finally laid to rest, and that the map of the meanings of the optative is significantly more complex than that suggested in traditional accounts. In the following chapter I will present more evidence to suggest that the optative is more than just the past-time variant of the subjunctive.

6

SUBORDINATE USES

6.1 Introduction

Certain uses of the subjunctive and optative in subordinate clauses have already been considered in previous chapters. But there are still more meanings attributed to the moods in subordinate clauses which have yet to be discussed, such as the purpose meaning, iterative meaning, and the so-called 'non-specific' meaning found in some relative clauses, as seen in the following examples:

4.300   κακοὺς δ' ἐς μέσσον ἔλασσεν,
         ὄφρα καὶ οὐκ ἐθέλων τις ἀναγκαίηι <u>πολεμίζοι</u>.

but he drove the cowards into the middle, so that each one would have to fight, even if he did not want to.

1.166   ἀτὰρ ἤν ποτε δασμὸς <u>ἵκηται</u>,
         σοὶ τὸ γέρας πολὺ μέζον, ἐγὼ δ' ὀλίγον τε φίλον τε
         ἔρχομ' ἔχων ἐπὶ νῆας, ἐπεί κε <u>κάμω</u> πολεμίζων.

but if it comes to sharing the spoil, your prize is bigger by far, while I take something small but dear back to my ships, when I am worn out from the fight.

5.301   ἀμφὶ δ' ἄρ' αὐτῶι βαῖνε λέων ὣς ἀλκὶ πεποιθώς,
         πρόσθε δέ οἱ δόρυ τ' ἔσχε καὶ ἀσπίδα πάντος ἐΐσην,
         τὸν κτάμεναι μεμαὼς ὅς τις τοῦ γ' ἀντίος <u>ἔλθοι</u>,

he stood round him like a lion, trusting in his strength, and protected him with spear and shield, burning to kill any man who approached him,

These uses are clearly a significant part of the role of the moods in Homeric Greek: the subordinate meaning even led to the name of the subjunctive (ὑποτακτική in Greek).[1] Nonetheless, it is

---

[1] For etymology and first use see LSJ s.v. Also see Palmer[2]: 108; Schwyzer II: 302; Humbert 1945 and also, with a rather different approach, Lakoff 1968 and Lightfoot 1975: 21.

expedient to consider these various uses in a single chapter rather than in the chapters devoted to the particular moods for two reasons. Firstly, it has been suggested that some subordinate uses ought to be explained differently from the uses discussed previously. Jespersen (1924: 313) claims that 'in some cases the choice of mood is determined not by the attitude of the actual speaker, but by the character of the clause itself and its relation to the main nexus on which it is dependent' (see also Palmer[1]: 22; Gonda: 3). In studies of various languages there is general uncertainty over whether forms which mark subordinate clauses carry meaning, or are instead semantically empty, marking only the syntactic clause type.[2] But in this chapter I will show that the uses of the moods in these contexts may be explained in semantic rather than grammatical terms.

The second issue regards the relationship between the two moods, since it is in subordinate clauses where their perceived parallelism has traditionally been argued with most vehemence. In past-time subordinate clauses the optative is described as the 'substitute' for the subjunctive (Smyth: §2176; Chantraine: §330). Goodwin (386) claims that the optative 'represents a dependent subjunctive': the sentence ἦλθεν ἵνα ἴδοι τοῦτο ('he came that he might see (this)') is considered the 'past-time equivalent' of ἔρχεται ἵνα ἴδῃ τοῦτο ('he comes that he may see (this)'). The distribution of moods in subordinate clauses in Greek is thus often compared to the 'sequence of tense' rule in English where the tense of the verb in the subordinate clause is apparently dependent on the tense of the main verb rather than expressing a semantic relation to time.[3] Again, I will argue that the traditional accounts are wrong, and that, once the detail of their distribution is considered from a diachronic perspective, it is unhelpful to describe the two moods as parallel.

---

[2] Bybee 1985: 186; BPP: 213; Rijksbaron 1986: 32–3; Wakker 1994: 218.

[3] Quirk et al. 1985: 14.31; Gildersleeve 1906: 202. It should be pointed out that the exact mechanism of that 'dependence' is not agreed on in English – see Comrie 1985: 107–17; 1986; van der Wurff 1993; also Mitchell 1985: 360: 'A mechanical dependence of the tenses of the subordinate sentence upon those of the main sentence does not exist, and . . . the choice of the tense in each sentence depends upon the conception lying at the bottom of it.'

6.2 Purpose

6.2.1 Introduction

The 'purpose meaning' of the moods is found in subordinate purpose clauses: clauses which are generally introduced by the conjunctions ὄφρα, ἵνα, or ὡς. According to the grammar-book rule, subjunctives are found in primary sequence and optatives are found in secondary sequence. For example.[4]

5.227   ἐγὼ δ' ἵππων ἀποβήσομαι, ὄφρα μάχωμαι·

I'll dismount from the car to fight.

5.24   ἀλλ' Ἥφαιστος ἔρυτο, σάωσε δὲ νυκτὶ καλύψας,
        ὡς δή οἱ μὴ πάγχυ γέρων ἀκαχήμενος εἴη.

but Hephaestus guarded him, and saved him, covering him in darkness, so that the old man would not be utterly devastated by grief for him.

The 'irrealis' nature of the environment might suggest that the moods in this construction are used to mark the type of clause. But in section 6.2.2 I will examine the development of the construction and argue that the presence of the moods may in fact be explained in semantic terms. In section 6.2.3 I will claim that the distribution of the moods may be explained in the same way, showing that the grammar-book rule is not strictly supported by the data.

6.2.2 Development

Purpose clauses have previously been described as having arisen from the paratactic association of two clauses, of which the second has the 'jussive' subjunctive.[5] Proponents of this claim point to lines such as the following which have two possible interpretations:

6.340   ἀλλ' ἄγε νῦν ἐπίμεινον, ἀρήϊα τεύχεα δύω·

Stop, wait, let me put on my armour.

---

[4] For useful statistics of purpose clauses and the conjunctions which introduce them, see Gildersleeve 1883 and Knünz 1913. On the meaning of purpose clauses and further statistics related to Homer, see Wakker 1988: 327ff.

[5] Monro: §282, §316; Chantraine: §340; Palmer[1]: 199.

This line may be translated as three consecutive directives as above, but could also be translated as imperatives followed by a purpose clause: 'stop, wait for me to put on my armour'.

It is plausible that negative purpose clauses, which are introduced by μή, have developed in just this way, from prohibitions or wishes. For example:

6.432   ἀλλ' ἄγε νῦν ἐλέαιρε καὶ αὐτοῦ μίμν' ἐπὶ πύργωι,
           μὴ παῖδ' ὀρφανικὸν θήηις χήρην τε γυναῖκα.

Wait, take pity and stay here on the wall, so you don't make an orphan of your child and a widow of your wife.

10.348   εἰ δ' ἄμμε παραφθαίηισι πόδεσσιν,
           αἰεί μιν ποτὶ νῆας ἀπὸ στρατόφι προτιειλεῖν
           ἔγχει ἐπαΐσσων, μή πως προτὶ ἄστυ ἀλύξηι.

If he outruns us, keep pressing him against the ships, away from his forces, and rush at him with your spear so he can't escape back to town.

O   πὰρ δ' αὐτὸς κλισμὸν θέτο ποικίλον, ἔκτοθεν ἄλλων
1.133   μνηστήρων, μὴ ξεῖνος ἀνιηθεὶς ὀρυμαγδῷ
        δείπνῳ ἀδήσειεν, ὑπερφιάλοισι μετελθών,

Beside it he drew up an inlaid chair for himself, away from the other suitors, worried that his guest might shrink from food, offended at their uproar, in the midst of such arrogant men,

6.432 has been translated as containing a purpose clause although the μή clause may be interpreted as an independent imperative clause (see section 4.4.3). But the construction has undergone development: in 10.348, the μή clause is no longer in direct speech, and must be interpreted as a subordinate purpose clause (Chantraine: §397; Schwyzer: 672). O1.133 appears to have developed in a similar way, from the conjunction of an imperative sentence and a negative wish.

But positive purpose clauses may not be explained so simply. As we have seen, most positive purpose clauses are introduced by a conjunction, whose presence is unaccounted for by this 'paratactic' explanation. An analysis of the meaning of the particular conjunctions used in this construction will allow us to trace its true development.

In 4.2.2.3 I considered the development of the conjunction ὄφρα from the simple temporal meaning 'while', to the meanings 'until' and 'so that'. Examples of these different meanings are repeated here for ease of study:

4.220 ὄφρα τοὶ ἀμφεπένοντο βοὴν ἀγαθὸν Μενέλαον,
τόφρα δ' ἐπὶ Τρώων στίχες ἤλυθον ἀσπιστάων·

And while they tended Menelaus, good at the battle-cry, the Trojan ranks reformed with shields.

6.113 ἀνέρες ἔστε θοοὶ καὶ ἀμύνετε ἄστεΐ λώβην,
ὄφρ' ἂν ἐγὼ <u>βείω</u> προτὶ Ἴλιον ἠδὲ γέρουσιν
<u>εἴπω</u> βουλευτῆισι καὶ ἡμετέρηις ἀλόχοισιν
δαίμοσιν ἀρήσασθαι, ὑποσχέσθαι δ' ἑκατόμβας.

Now be swift, and ward off disgrace from the city, while I go to Troy and ask the old counsellors and our wives to pray to the gods, and promise them sacrifices.

1.510 τόφρα δ' ἐπὶ Τρώεσσι τίθει κράτος, ὄφρ' ἂν Ἀχαιοὶ
υἱὸν ἐμὸν τίσωσιν <u>ὀφέλλωσίν</u> τέ ἑ τιμῆι.

Grant the Trojans victory until the Achaeans repay my son, and raise him in honour.

1.515 νημερτὲς μὲν δή μοι ὑπόσχεο καὶ κατάνευσον,
ἢ ἀπόειπ', ἐπεὶ οὔ τοι ἔπι δέος, ὄφρ' εὖ <u>εἴδω</u>
ὅσσον ἐγὼ μετὰ πᾶσιν ἀτιμοτάτη θεός εἰμι.

Promise me truthfully, and bow your head in assent! Or deny me, since you have nothing to fear, so that I can know properly just how much I am the most dishonoured goddess of them all.

It is clear from the meaning of the correlative τόφρα that the temporal meaning was the original meaning. It is also clear that the development to purpose marker is a gradual one, as we can see from the following lines:

2.299 τλῆτε, φίλοι, καὶ μείνατ' ἐπὶ χρόνον, ὄφρα δαῶμεν
ἢ ἐτεὸν Κάλχας μαντεύεται, ἦε καὶ οὐκί.

Courage, friends, and wait a little longer, so we can find out if Calchas divined the truth or not.

Ο   μαῖ', ἄγε δή μοι ἔρυξον ἐνὶ μεγάροισι γυναῖκας,
19.17 ὄφρα κεν ἐς θάλαμον καταθείομαι ἔντεα πατρός.

Nurse, come, shut up the women in their rooms for me, so that I can put my father's weapons away in the store-room.

The translation suggests that these should be read as purpose clauses. But in 2.299, the word χρόνον still allows us to interpret it with a temporal meaning. We could translate it 'hold out a little longer, until we find out if Calchas divined the truth or not'. Similarly, the ὄφρα in O19.17 could be translated as 'while' rather than 'so that'. The existence of these indeterminate examples reveals that the stages of development undergone by the conjunction are gradual.

Similar developments may be traced with the other purpose markers, ἵνα and ὡς. The original meaning of ἵνα appears to be locative, 'where', which is generally found with the indicative (Schwyzer I: 615; Chantraine 1980).[6] Though there are no straight-forward examples of sentences with the subjunctive where the conjunction may be interpreted purely as a locative conjunction, there are some indeterminate examples similar to 2.299 above:

3.130   δεῦρ᾽ ἴθι, νύμφα φίλη, ἵνα θέσκελα ἔργα ἴδηαι

Come here, dear girl, so you can see the wondrous deeds

24.382   ἀλλ᾽ ἄγε μοι τόδε εἰπὲ καὶ ἀτρεκέως κατάλεξον,
ἠέ πηι ἐκπέμπεις κειμήλια πολλὰ καὶ ἐσθλὰ
ἄνδρας ἐς ἀλλοδαποὺς, ἵνα τοι τάδε περ σόα μίμνηι,

Come now, tell me this, and tell me frankly: are you taking these many good treasures somewhere, to outsiders, so that they can be safe for you?

O   ἀλλὰ χρήματα μὲν μυχῷ ἄντρου θεσπεσίοιο
13.364   θείμεν αὐτίκα νῦν, ἵνα περ τάδε τοι σόα μίμνῃ·

Come, let us put your belongings inside the incomparable cave, so that they will be safe for you:

All lines may be translated in a way which highlights the locatival origin of the conjunction: 'come here, where you may see'; 'are you taking these treasures to somewhere ... where they can remain safe?'; 'let us put your belongings in the cave where they will be safe'.

---

[6] In the *Iliad*, ἵνα is found as a locative ten times, seven of which are with the indicative (2.558; 5.360; 8.456; 9.441; 10.127; 11.806; 20.478), and three of which are with a noun (2.604; 8.479; 22.325).

As for ὡς, Schwyzer (662ff.) and Chantraine (1980: s.v.) derive it from *yō, the instrumental of the relative stem. The most basic sense appears to have been 'as', but it has also developed the meanings 'that', 'how', 'when' according to context.[7] The purpose meaning with the subjunctive appears to have developed out of the 'manner' meaning of the conjunction, as we may see in the following example:

7.294   νὺξ δ' ἤδη τελέθει· ἀγαθὸν καὶ νυκτὶ πιθέσθαι,
ὡς σύ τ' εὐφρήνῃς πάντας παρὰ νηυσὶν Ἀχαιούς
σούς τε μάλιστα ἔτας καὶ ἑταίρους, οἵ τοι ἔασιν·

Night has fallen already, and it's best to yield to night, so that you will cheer all the Achaeans at their ships, and most of all your own men and the comrades who you command.

Again, the sentence is indeterminate between the manner meaning and the purpose meaning. If we interpret the conjunction as a manner adverbial we might translate it 'in such a way/so as you will make the Achaeans glad'. French 'de façon que' has the same double meaning (Chantraine: §394–6).

The use of the subjunctive in purpose clauses thus appears to have arisen through a gradual development of meaning originating from the future meaning of the mood in combination with certain conjunctions. The subjunctive may not therefore be described as 'semantically empty' in this environment.

It is with regards to the optative where the grammarians are most explicit about the 'grammatical requiredness' of the mood (e.g. Goodwin: §14, §307). But although the optative is found less frequently with the original meanings of the conjunctions, it is possible to show that it developed the purpose meaning in the same way as the subjunctive.

There is one example of ὄφρα with the optative which is again 'indeterminate' between the temporal and purpose meaning of the conjunction:

---

[7] Chantraine 1980: s.v.; Neuberger-Donath, 1982; Biraud, 1985; Cristofaro. An analysis of all subordinate clauses in Homer has revealed 110 examples introduced by ὡς. Of these 110, 49 mean 'as', 19 mean 'when', 1 means 'since', 23 mean 'in order that', 9 mean 'how', 6 are complements. 72 are followed by the indicative, 36 by the subjunctive, 2 by the optative.

10.571 νηΐ δ᾽ ἔνι πρυμνῆι ἔναρα βροτόεντα Δόλωνος
θῆκ᾽ Ὀδυσεύς, ὄφρ᾽ ἱρὸν ἑτοιμασσαίατ᾽ Ἀθήνηι.

Then Odysseus stowed Dolon's gory armour in the stern of his ship, ready for the time when they would make a sacred offering to Athena.

This sentence has been here translated with the temporal meaning of the conjunction. But a purpose meaning is possible too (see Leaf ad loc.): 'they placed the spoils on the ship to make a sacred offering to Athena'.

Similarly with ἵνα, the optative is found with the more original meaning of the conjunctions:[8]

16.576 = O14.71 οἱ δ᾽ ἅμ᾽ Ἀχιλλῆϊ ῥηξήνορι πέμπον ἕπεσθαι
Ἴλιον εἰς εὔπωλον, ἵνα Τρώεσσι μάχοιτο.

and they sent him off with Achilles, breaker of men, to Ilium of the many horses, to fight against the Trojans. OR
they sent him to Ilium, where he might fight with the Trojans.

O   τόν ποτ᾽ ἐγὼν ἐπὶ νηὸς ἐϋσσέλμοιο μελαίνης
17.250 ἄξω τῆλ᾽ Ἰθάκης, ἵνα μοι βίοτον πολὺν ἄλφοι.

One day I'll take him in a black-benched ship far from Ithaca, so he can bring me much wealth. OR
I will take him away, where he might bring me much wealth.[9]

There is a possible example of the optative after ὅππως at 1.344:

1.344 οὐδέ τι οἶδε νοῆσαι ἅμα πρόσσω καὶ ὀπίσσω,
ὅππως οἱ παρὰ νηυσὶ σόοι μαχέοιατ᾽ Ἀχαιοί.

He doesn't know how to think back and think ahead, so the Achaeans can battle safely by the ships. OR
He doesn't know how to think back and think ahead, in such a way that the Achaeans might fight in safety.

The manuscript reading here is μαχέοιντο, which is felt to be not a Homeric form (Leaf ad loc.). Although Bentley conjectured the

---

[8] Also O2.52; O13.401; O23.134; O24.532.
[9] For this interpretation, compare O20.383:

O   τοὺς ξείνους ἐν νηΐ πολυκληΐδι βαλόντες
20.383 ἐς Σικελοὺς πέμψωμεν, ὅθεν κέ τοι ἄξιον ἄλφοι.

let's fling these strangers on board a benched ship, and send them to the Sicilians, from whom they would fetch a fitting price.

alternative optative form adopted by the Teubner edition, the subjunctive μαχέωνται and the future μαχέονται have also been suggested (Kirk et al. ad loc.), so that the use of the optative is not guaranteed here. The parallels with other conjunctions do however suggest that it would have been a possibility for ὅππως to have been used in its original meaning with the optative.

It is important to note that in O17.250 and 1.344, the optative follows a primary rather than a secondary main verb, contradicting the rule laid out in the grammars. We will return to this in more detail in section 6.2.3. For now the point is that the optative appears to have developed its 'purpose meaning' gradually in the same way as the subjunctive.

The gradual nature of the development of these purpose constructions suggests that this is not a construction in which the presence of the mood may be explained as due to its grammatical nature alone. While purpose clauses can be described as an 'irrealis' environment, it is unnecessary to explain the presence of the subjunctive and optative in the construction as dependent on this. Rather, it seems that it is the epistemic meaning of the moods in association with particular conjunctions which has led to the development of the construction.

It is possible to speculate that the development to purpose meaning took place through a process of 'conventionalisation of conversational implicature'. In 'until' sentences, for example, it is often conversationally implied that the event that will result is the reason for the agent to do the preceding activity. For example:

50 Tom will stay at home until he gets his work done.

This sentence may be interpreted purely temporally: Tom will stay at home until the time that he will get his work done. But it is conversationally implied that staying at home will help him to get his work done, and that getting his work done is the reason that he is staying at home. The sentence is thus very close in meaning to:

51 Tom will stay at home in order to get his work done.

We may see that this additional meaning is only a conversational implicature of sentence 50 by the possibility of explicitly stating a different purpose:

52 Tom will stay at home until he gets his work done so that he will meet his deadline.

This sentence shows that getting his work done is not the purpose of him staying at home; the purpose is getting it done *on time*, thus showing that the implicature in sentence 50 is defeasible. However, it would be possible for this meaning to become so frequently associated with this type of sentence that it was considered as part of the meaning of the construction. It would then be unsurprising if the construction extended to contexts in which the temporal reading is not appropriate.

It is likely that the exact mechanism and details of the development of the purpose constructions will remain unclear for lack of evidence. Nevertheless, both the original meaning of the conjunctions which introduce purpose clauses in Homeric Greek and the existence of some transitional examples suggest that the moods developed the purpose meaning gradually. It is thus only from a synchronic point of view that it would be at all useful to describe the moods as marking the nature of the clause and therefore as being used for purely grammatical reasons.

6.2.3 Distribution

Although it seems unnecessary to account for the *presence* of the subjunctive and optative in purpose clauses in grammatical terms, the distribution of the moods in purpose clauses and indeed their precursors suggests that by the time of Homer the *choice* of mood at least was grammatically determined, and that the two moods are in some way parallel. But in this section I will show that neither mood is restricted to the contexts that the grammar-books 'assign' them to. I will argue that the choice of mood can be explained with reference to the meanings that I have proposed for the moods in chapters 4 and 5, and thus that the grammatical context need not be invoked to explain any particular mood.

The trend for using the subjunctive in primary sequence, where the main verb is in the present or future (Goodwin: §21), is entirely unsurprising given the definition of the subjunctive I have proposed in chapter 3. After all, the fulfilment of purposes conceived of in the present and future automatically lies in the *real* future, and we would therefore expect to find some kind of future marker in this context. There is a small development of the subjunctive in this context, as may be exemplified by the following:

3.110   αἰεὶ δ' ὁπλοτέρων ἀνδρῶν φρένες ἠερέθονται·
οἷς δὲ γέρων μετέῃσιν, ἅμα πρόσσω καὶ ὀπίσσω
λεύσσει, ὅπως ὄχ' ἄριστα μετ' ἀμφοτέροισι <u>γένηται</u>.

the hearts of the young are always unstable, but whatever an old man takes part in, he knows how to look back and to look ahead, so that things will turn out for the best for both armies.

Here the primary main verb refers to an event which happens frequently, so that the subjunctive in the purpose clause does not refer to a particular future time. However, the event in the purpose clause is still in the future with respect to the event in the main clause: the development can be explained with reference to the possibility of using the present tense to refer to general truths as well as the actual present, rather than as an independent development of the subjunctive.

The use of the subjunctive in primary sequence is thus entirely in keeping with the meaning of the mood that I have claimed in chapter 4. The preference for the optative after past-time main verbs is also in line with the semantics of the mood as described in chapter 5. As we have seen in conditional clauses, the optative is intrinsically timeless (5.3.2), which means that it can be used in more contexts than the future-referring subjunctive. Furthermore, an 'unreal' marker is also itself appropriate to past-time purpose clauses, since the fulfilment of the event is not asserted. For example, the following constitutes a classic example of a past-time purpose clause:

53 Tom went to Cambridge to sing.

This sentence may be followed by either of the two following consequences, showing that the question of the fulfilment of the purpose is not part of the meaning of the sentence:

54 ... and so he really enjoyed his time there (because he did sing).
55 ... but discovered instead a love for rowing (he didn't sing).

The usual distribution of the subjunctive and optative may thus be explained in semantic terms.

A yet more compelling reason to claim that the choice of mood is not grammatically determined in this context is that there are exceptions to the 'sequence' rule. The use of the subjunctive after secondary main verbs, described as the 'vivid construction' has received much attention and I will discuss it later (p. 166), but I believe it is the use of the optative in primary sequence which holds the real key to the explanation of the choice of moods in this construction. For example:[10]

O   αὐτὰρ θεῖος ἀοιδὸς ἔχων φόρμιγγα λίγειαν
23.135 ἡμῖν ἡγείσθω φιλοπαίγμονος ὀρχηθμοῖο,
        ὥς κέν τις <u>φαίη</u> γάμον ἔμμεναι ἐκτὸς ἀκούων,
        ἢ ἀν' ὁδὸν στείχων ἢ οἳ περιναιετάουσι·

And let the divine bard take up the shrill lyre for us and lead off a playful dance, so that anyone who heard it outside would say that a wedding-feast was under way, whether he was a passerby or a neighbour.

Goodwin (§322) has explained away the examples of the optative after a primary main verb in purpose clauses as irregular exceptions to the grammatical rule: 'Most of these are emended by various editors; and no good reason for the anomaly appears in any of them.' However, the examples in question are rather 'conditional'. For example:

O   τόν ποτ' ἐγὼν ἐπὶ νηὸς ἐϋσσέλμοιο μελαίνης
17.250 ἄξω τῆλ' Ἰθάκης, ἵνα μοι βίοτον πολὺν <u>ἄλφοι</u>.

One day I'll take him in a black-benched ship far from Ithaca, so he can bring me much wealth.

Jebb (1885, commentary to Sophocles *Oedipus Coloneus*, line 11) explains the use of the optative in O17.250 in the following way: 'him some day I will take far from Ithaca, – so that (if I should do so) he might bring me large gain'. Similarly, we could translate

---

[10] See also Monro: §306b; Goodwin: §329 1a. Also 1.344; 7.340; 19.332; O2.53; O2.54; O12.157; O16. 297; O17.250; O23.135.

O23.135 (above): 'let the minstrel lead us so that, if anyone heard us, they would think that it was a wedding feast'.[11]

The comparison with conditional clauses suggests that the choice between subjunctive and optative in purpose clauses in primary time depends on the same factors as found in conditional clauses, and that purpose clauses too may be divided into 'real' and 'unreal' types. This then, would the reason for the 'anomalous' use of the optative: in purpose clauses in primary time where the event is seen as a natural consequence of the event, the subjunctive is used. When the speaker wants to stress that the event is only a possible and conditional consequence of the main clause, he may use the 'unreal' optative.

If, as I suggest, the presence of the optative in primary time may be explained in semantic terms, it is also possible to reinterpret another group of examples: purpose clauses with the optative which depend on an optative of wish in the main clause. The optative in these contexts has previously been explained in terms of 'assimilation' (Smyth: §2186). But the optative in these contexts may be explained in the same terms as those in primary sequence above: wishes too are rather like 'unreal' conditionals. For example:[12]

O   νῦν δ' ὥρη δόρποιο· τάχιστά μοι ἔνδον ἑταῖροι
14.408 εἶεν, ἵν' ἐν κλισίῃ λαρὸν τετυκοίμεθα δόρπον.

But it is now time for supper: may my comrades soon be here, so that we can prepare a savoury meal in the hut.

It could be argued that if the subjunctive and optative really were semantically motivated in this construction, we would expect to find more examples of the optative after primary main verbs. But even the *preference* for the subjunctive rather than the optative after primary main verbs may be explained semantically. The subjunctive is most commonly found after imperatives.[13] The use of the subjunctive rather than an optative in this context is unsurprising,

---

[11] It might be thought that the presence of κε in O23.134 and the absence of the modal particle in O17.250 is somehow significant. The statistics suggest that the use of the particle is directly connected to the particular conjunction which introduces the purpose clause, as I will show in Appendix 1 p. 203.

[12] Also O15.537; O15.538; O17.165; O18.369; O19.311.

[13] Monro: § 316. In the first six books of the *Iliad* there are 68 purpose clauses with the subjunctive, of which 49 are introduced by imperatives.

as it is much more likely that the speaker will present the consequence of action as an achievable purpose rather than merely a potential eventuality. For example:

1.32   ἀλλ' ἴθι, μή μ' ἐρέθιζε, σαώτερος ὥς κε <u>νέηαι</u>.

Now go, don't aggravate me, so you can leave in safety.

In 1.32 there is good reason for the speaker to suggest that the addressee 'leaving in safety' follows on directly from not aggravating him, as it heightens the power of the threat.

Another reason for the preference for the subjunctive after primary main verbs could be the person addressed. Most of the subjunctive examples are in the first or second person, while all but three of the optatives in primary time are in the third person.[14] This again fits in with the semantics of the subjunctive and optative: while the speaker may have control over himself and to some extent a second person, the purposes of a third person are rather more unsure and uncontrollable. This would appear to explain the use of the optative in O23.135 above – while the speaker has the lyre-player in his control, he can only hope that he will have the desired effect on the passers-by.

While the existence of 'rule-breaking' optatives in primary sequence supports my argument that the choice of mood is semantically governed, the use of the 'future' subjunctive in past time would appear to be more difficult to explain. This construction has previously been termed the 'vivid' construction, and is said to result from the desire to present the purpose from the point of view of the speaker when he conceived it (Goodwin: §318–21). For example:

9.495   ἀλλὰ σὲ παῖδα, θεοῖς ἐπιείκελ' Ἀχιλλεῦ,
        ποιεόμην, ἵνα μοί ποτ' ἀεικέα λοιγὸν <u>ἀμύνῃς</u>.

But I made you my son, god-like Achilles, so you could one day ward off terrible ruin from me.

When Phoenix made Achilles his son, he would have said, 'Now I will have someone to save me.' By 'retaining' the subjunctive, we

---

[14] The exceptions are 19.332 (second person), O12.156 (first person plural) and O16.297 (first person plural).

therefore remain closer to the speaker's original words. The use of the future-referring subjunctive in these contexts is therefore described in the same way as the use of the 'historic present' in languages such as English: a shift in deictic centre can bring the event 'alive'.[15]

But many of the examples of the subjunctive in secondary sequence may be explained in exactly the same way as those in primary sequence, that is, they refer to an event that will take place in an actual future moment. These examples occur in direct speech, where a purpose conceived of in the past has two possible times of fulfilment. It may be a 'logical' future, only future with respect to the past time, or it may be an 'absolute' future with respect to the time of speaking. We may understand these two different possibilities by considering the following time-line:

If t_0 is the time of speaking and t_{-2} is the past time of the main verb, the purpose may be relegated to the past, that is, presented as taking place at t_{-1} (a 'logical' future). (Of course, purpose clauses do not strictly assert whether the event happened or not. In this sense the event cannot be placed on a time-line. The point is, that in most past-time purpose clauses, the *possibility* of it happening lies before the moment of speaking). However, in direct speech, the fulfilment of the purpose may also lie in the speaker's future, at t_{+1} (an 'absolute' future). For example:

56 Tom has gone to town, to have dinner with a friend this evening.

The presence of the deictic 'this evening' could imply that the purpose is still in the future (if e.g. the sentence was spoken at 3pm). This type may be called the type of 'continuing validity',

---

[15] Goodwin: §318; Quirk et al. 1985: 4.8. See also Kiparsky 1968: 30. It should be pointed out that this explanation only works for Homeric Greek: in Attic Greek the future meaning of the subjunctive is rare outside subordinate clauses, so that the 'reported speech' explanation would only work if the future indicative was found.

and it is in this way that most of the so-called 'vivid' subjunctives should actually be explained (Monro: §298). For example:[16]

5.127　ἀχλὺν αὖ τοι ἀπ' ὀφθαλμῶν ἕλον, ἣ πρὶν ἐπῆεν,
　　　 ὄφρ' εὖ <u>γιγνώσκῃς</u> ἠμὲν θεὸν ἠδὲ καὶ ἄνδρα.

I've taken away the mist that previously lay on your eyes, so that you will be able to discern easily between god and man.

Here, Athena is addressing Diomedes, and saying that Diomedes will have to recognise who is a god and who is a man *after* the point at which Athena tells him that she has removed the mist (also see Leaf ad loc.). Similarly, in 9.495 considered above, Achilles has yet to help Phoenix (p. 166).

The Spanish indirect speech construction may be explained in the same way. There it is usual to find the present subjunctive after non-past main verbs and the past subjunctive after past main verbs. But there are also occasional examples of the present subjunctive after past main verbs which were previously also described as 'vivid'. Comrie (1985: 106–7) has shown that all the examples in fact have 'continuing validity' like the sentences above. For example:

57 *dije que Juan se fuese mañana.*
　　'I told Juan to leave tomorrow.'

Similarly, Quirk et al. (1985: 14.31) note that 'backshifting' of tense in English is optional if the event is still relevant today. For example,

58 Socrates said that the sun is round.

Back-shifting would be grammatically permitted here (so we would have 'Socrates said that the sun *was* round'), but because the sentence has continuing validity the present tense has been retained.

The construction with the subjunctive in past time may be compared to the following example of the 'regular' construction in which the optative is found. This example, too, occurs in direct

---

[16] See also 1.158; 6.358; 7.270; 9.99; 9.495; 9.691; 12.356; 17.445; 20.126; 20.185; 22.282; O3.15; O4.713; O4.749; O6.173; O8.580; O9.13; O13.303; O13.304; O13.306; O13.418; O16.234.

speech, and so a 'future moment' does exist. But the use of the optative relegates the possible fulfilment of the purpose to the past (with respect to time of utterance):

15.470   νευρὴν δ' ἐξέρρηξε νεόστροφον, ἣν ἐνέδησα
        πρώϊον, ὄφρ' <u>ἀνέχοιτο</u> θαμὰ θρώϊσκοντας ὀϊστούς.

He's snapped the freshly tied string, which I tied at dawn, to bear the many springing arrows.

The purpose of 'bearing the arrows' can no longer be fulfilled, since the string has been broken. We may see the difference between them in the translation: the past event in 5.127 has present relevance, and is thus translated with a perfect (I've taken), while the past event in 15.470 is relegated to the past and is thus translated with a simple past (I tied).

In most of the examples of the subjunctive in purpose clauses after secondary main verbs we thus have no reason to invoke the 'vivid' explanation. Indeed, Monro claims that the 'vivid' subjunctive in purpose clauses is not Homeric (§322). However, to substantiate his claim he must 'correct' several of the subjunctives in the text to optatives (Monro: §298). In these cases, the subjunctive is not in direct speech, and so may not be argued to have continuing validity. I have already argued that correcting the text to make it fit in with a particular theory is unattractive (2.2.3 p. 20). Here I will claim that the subjunctives in this context may be explained in semantic terms, with no need to return to the 'vivid' argument.

One of the subjunctives that is not in direct speech can be explained by considering in more detail the nature of the 'past tense' in the main clause:

4.486   τὴν μέν θ' ἁρματοπηγὸς ἀνὴρ αἴθωνι σιδήρωι
        ἐξέταμ', ὄφρα ἴτυν <u>κάμψηι</u> περικαλλέϊ δίφρωι·

A chariot-maker fells it with shining iron axe to bend for the rim of some handsome chariot wheels.

Here the aorist is gnomic, as suggested by the 'epic τε' (Ruijgh 1971: §419), and therefore the subjunctive here is in primary sequence. 4.486 may be compared to 21.38, where the same event occurs after an imperfect:

21.38 ὃ δ᾽ ἐρινεὸν ὀξέϊ χαλκῶι
τάμνε νέους ὄρπηκας, ἵν᾽ ἅρματος ἄντυγες εἶεν·

he was cutting the young branches of a fig with sharp bronze, so they could make chariot-rails.

As expected, the optative is used in this sentence, as the cutting actually took place in a past time, as did its purpose. The imperfect, focusing on the 'internal temporal structure' of the action, relegates the purpose to the past (Comrie 1976: 24).

The five remaining examples of the so-called 'vivid subjunctive' construction are undoubtedly in secondary sequence:

13.649 ἂψ δ᾽ ἑτάρων εἰς ἔθνος ἐχάζετο κῆρ᾽ ἀλεείνων,
πάντοσε παπταίνων, μή τις χρόα χαλκῶι ἐπαύρηι.

and back he shrank into the throng of his comrades, avoiding fate, glancing warily on every side, lest some man should wound his flesh with the bronze.

19.354 ἣ δ᾽ Ἀχιλῆϊ
νέκταρ ἐνὶ στήθεσσι καὶ ἀμβροσίην ἐρατεινὴν
στάξ᾽, ἵνα μή μιν λιμὸς ἀτερπὴς γούναθ᾽ ἵκηται·

into the breast of Achilles she shed nectar and pleasant ambrosia that grievous hunger-pangs should not come upon his limbs;

O   αὐτὴ γὰρ ἐνὶ φρεσὶ θάρσος Ἀθήνη
3.78 θῆχ᾽, ἵνα μιν περὶ πατρὸς ἀποιχομένοιο ἔροιτο
ἠδ᾽ ἵνα μιν κλέος ἐσθλὸν ἐν ἀνθρώποισιν ἔχησιν.

for Athena herself put courage in his heart, that he might ask about his father who was gone, and that good report might be his among men.

O   νηὶ δ᾽ ἐνὶ γλαφυρῆ κατέδει μέρμιθι φαεινῆ
10.24[17] ἀργυρέη, ἵνα μή τι παραπνεύσῃ ὀλίγον περ·

And in my hollow ship he bound it fast with a bright cord of silver, that not a breath might escape, not even a slight one.

O   ἅμα δ᾽ ἠελίῳ καταδύντι
16.369 οὔ ποτ᾽ ἐπ᾽ ἠπείρου νύκτ᾽ ἄσαμεν, ἀλλ᾽ ἐνὶ πόντῳ
νηΐ θοῇ πλείοντες ἐμίμνομεν Ἠῶ δῖαν,
Τηλέμαχον λοχόωντες, ἵνα φθίσωμεν ἑλόντες αὐτόν·

and at set of sun we never spent a night upon the shore, but sailing over the deep in our swift ship we waited for the bright Dawn, lying in wait for Telemachus, that we might take him and slay the man himself.

---

[17] Bekker proposed replacing παραπνεύσῃ with the optative παραπνεύσει' (Chantraine §398).

In these lines the subjunctive cannot be explained in terms of 'continuing validity'. Rather they appear to be like 'normal' past-time purpose clauses. If they are to be accepted as genuine readings, they show that the subjunctive *has* developed in meaning from a marker that only refers to the future literally. However, I believe that the model I have proposed for the meaning of the subjunctive and optative in primary time allows us to interpret them in a rather different way than the 'vivid' explanation.

I have argued above (p. 165) that the choice between subjunctive and optative in primary time depends on the possibility in question, just as in conditional clauses: the subjunctive is found when 'real possibilities' or natural consequences are being described, while the optative is used to express the 'unreality' of the purpose. If such a distinction is accepted, it is likely that the same distinction would be desirable in the past. While the optative is the expected or default marker of purpose clauses in the past because of the future meaning of the subjunctive, the optative would thus still carry the overtones of the 'unreal' possibilities, used both in unreal conditional clauses and in less immediate purpose clauses in primary time. The subjunctive could therefore occasionally have been used to highlight the belief of the subject or speaker that the purpose was a natural consequence of the main verb. In all of the four examples above, the subjects are certainly very keen that the purposes come to fruition. Indeed, it is this which has led previous commentators to describe them as 'vivid'. I believe it is more helpful to term them 'real', thereby avoiding any reference to the original words of the speaker. O3.78 is a particularly interesting example in this respect, as it has a purpose clause with the (expected) optative in just the previous line. The choice of mood in the second purpose clause is therefore even more significant, and suggests that the main reason that Athena put courage into his heart was so that he would gain a good reputation among his men; the courage to ask a question of Nestor was only secondary (after all, Nestor has no useful information for Telemachus).

It could be argued that the purpose clause in O16.369 may not be described as 'real': after all the purpose (slaying Telemachus) did not actually occur. However, the speaker was very sure that their actions would result in the desired consequence, explaining his conviction that his continued survival was owed to the gods' intervention. The speaker therefore has good reason to choose the 'real' subjunctive of natural consequence.

The conclusion that the subjunctive may be found in purpose clauses if the purpose is a real possibility has consequences for the editing of the text. In three of the 'vivid' purpose clauses noted by Monro (§298: 19.354; 24.586; O22.467), the manuscripts show evidence for both subjunctive and optative forms, but the optative has often been preferred by editors. The explanation for the 'guaranteed' subjunctives in the examples above allows a reconsideration of these lines. This is not the place to consider the individual lines in depth, but possible justification for printing the subjunctive is merely noted.

This account of the use of the subjunctive in purpose clauses also appears to be useful in explaining the use of the mood in other constructions in secondary time. The following subjunctives could be explained as having continuing validity:

24.781   ἦ γὰρ Ἀχιλλεύς
πέμπων μ᾽ ὧδ᾽ ἐπέτελλε μελαινάων ἀπὸ νηῶν,
μὴ πρὶν πημανέειν, πρὶν δωδεκάτη <u>μόληι</u> ἠώς.

For Achilles vowed, when he sent me out from the black ships, that they [the Achaeans] would not harm us until the twelfth day arrive.

O   ἐπεὶ μάλα πολλὰ βροτῶν ἐπὶ ἄστε᾽ ἄνωγεν
23.269   ἐλθεῖν, ἐν χείρεσσιν ἔχοντ᾽ εὐῆρες ἐρετμόν,
εἰς ὅ κε τοὺς <u>ἀφίκωμαι</u> οἳ οὐ ἴσασι θάλασσαν
ἀνέρες, οὐδέ θ᾽ ἅλεσσι μεμιγμένον εἶδαρ ἔδουσιν·

He ordered me to go to many cities of men, carrying a well-balanced oar in my hands, until I come to men who do not know of the sea, and who eat food which is not mixed with salt.

The following examples are more like the 'real' subjunctives I have noted in purpose clauses above:

15.23   ὃν δὲ λάβοιμι,
ῥίπτασκον τεταγὼν ἀπὸ βηλοῦ, ὄφρ᾽ ἂν <u>ἵκηται</u>
γῆν ὀλιγηπελέων·

Whoever I caught I would seize them and throw him from the threshold until he reached the earth with little strength left.

O   αὐτὰρ τοὺς ἄλλους κελόμην ἐρίηρας ἑταίρους
9.102 σπερχομένους νηῶν ἐπιβαινέμεν ὠκειάων,
      μή πώς τις λωτοῖο φαγὼν νόστοιο λάθηται.

But I ordered my other trusty comrades to quickly embark on the swift ships so
that no-one would eat a lotus and forget his homecoming.

The evidence thus suggests that, both in purpose clauses and in subordinate clauses expressing future meaning, the subjunctive is not
merely 'grammatically required' by the primary nature of the main
verb. Rather, its use there is fully in line with its future meaning.
The few examples of the subjunctive after secondary main verbs
can be explained in a variety of different ways. The majority refer
to an event which has continuing validity. There are also a few uses
after secondary main verbs where the subjunctive does refer to an
event which has passed, but where the choice of the subjunctive
rather than the optative could be explained as stemming from the
use of the subjunctive in primary time, to distinguish 'real' possibilities from 'unreal' ones. Importantly, all of these uses may again
be explained with reference to the future meaning of the subjunctive. In all cases, then, I would argue that the choice of mood can
be semantically rather than grammatically explained.

6.2.4 Summary

A consideration of the origins of the purpose construction has
suggested that in Homeric Greek the moods are not used in this
context for purely grammatical reasons. The conjunctions which
introduce the construction (ὄφρα, ὡς, and ἵνα) all had other, temporal or locative, meanings before they developed their purpose use
and were regularly found with the subjunctive referring to future
time and, rather less frequently, with the optative expressing an
'unreal' eventuality. It appears that these 'prospective' sentences
developed gradually into purpose clauses.

The distribution of the moods may also be semantically
explained. The use of the subjunctive after primary main verbs
is perfectly understandable in the light of its future meaning. Even
the so-called 'vivid' subjunctives mostly refer to an event that is
in the speaker's future, that has continuing validity at the moment

of speaking. There appears to be some development of the meaning of the subjunctive as it is also used with some more gnomic sentences, referring to a more 'general' future, and also in a few examples where the purpose appears to be relegated to the past. But both these developments can be explained as extensions from the future meaning of the mood.

The timeless optative, on the other hand, could well express a purpose in any time, though its 'unreal' nature suggests that the purposes will be more loosely connected to the main clause. The examples of the optative after primary as well as secondary main verbs confirm that its use is semantically rather than grammatically governed. Even the rarity of the mood in primary time may be explained: the majority of primary purpose clauses follow an imperative, in which context it would be pragmatically surprising to find the 'unreal' optative, and are in the first or second person, over whom the speaker is more likely to have control.

The rarity of the optative after primary main verbs, which becomes even more marked in later Greek (Goodwin: §329), suggests that the distribution of the moods is becoming more grammatically determined. A synchronic description of the optative in Attic Greek might therefore be right to describe it as the 'past-time variant' of the subjunctive in these specific contexts. But in Homeric Greek, and from a diachronic perspective, such a description ignores some of the interesting uses of the moods.

6.3 Iterative

6.3.1 Introduction

The claim that the subjunctive and optative express iterative meaning provides another reason to claim that the moods have developed 'grammatical' uses. The meaning is certainly rather different from the meanings we have examined so far, and the two moods again appear to be parallel, with the subjunctive referring to events which generally happen several times, and the optative referring to events in the past which happened several times. The context is apparently 'irrealis' because of the 'intensional' or 'indefinite' nature of the reference of the verb.[18] We may compare Armenian, Sorbian, Serbo-Croatian and Macedonian, where an 'unreal' mood is used to mark these contexts (Xrakovskij 1997: 54). But in this section I will argue that this meaning may be explained as dependent on the use of the moods in specific conditional clauses. The grammatical context is thus indeed crucial to understand the meaning, but I will show that the moods are not used in parallel, marking the nature of the clause. The use of the moods with this meaning in relative clauses, where the meaning cannot be attributed to the construction itself does suggest that both moods have developed in meaning. But it is more helpful to explain this use as a development from the conditional construction rather than seeing the moods as grammatical markers of any irrealis contexts.

6.3.2 Analysis

The difference between particular and iterative conditionals in Greek was first recognised by Bäumlein in 1846 (Gildersleeve 1882: 436). In the tables subsequent grammarians have drawn up of the different types of conditional clauses, iterative types generally have their own section.[19] In Homeric Greek, two combinations of mood are said to be marked as iterative: subjunctive in the protasis followed by a present indicative in the apodosis, and optative in the protasis followed by a past indicative in the apodosis. The same combinations of mood and tenses also express iterative meaning in temporal clauses. For example:

1.166   ἀτὰρ ἤν ποτε δασμὸς ἵκηται,
         σοὶ τὸ γέρας πολὺ μέζον, ἐγὼ δ᾽ ὀλίγον τε φίλον τε
         ἔρχομ᾽ ἔχων ἐπὶ νῆας, ἐπεί κε κάμω πολεμίζων.

but if it comes to sharing the spoil, your prize is bigger by far, while I take something small but dear back to my ships, whenever I wear myself out in the fight.

---

[18] Givón 1994: 270; Fleischman 1982: 522; Bakker 1988a: 34, 72.
[19] Abbott and Mansfield: §173 II; Bakker 1988b: 5; Greenberg 1986: 255. For a description of iterative conditionals in general, see Podlesskaya 2001: 1000; Langacker 1997; ter Meulen 1986 and Athanasiadou and Dirven 1996.

24.768[20]   ἀλλ' εἴ τίς με καὶ ἄλλος ἐνὶ μεγάροισιν <u>ἐνίπτοι</u>

. . .

ἀλλὰ σὺ τὸν ἐπέεσσι παραιφάμενος κατέρυκες

But if someone else would curse me in the royal halls, [. . .] you'd restrain them, persuading them with words

3.216   ἀλλ' ὅτε δὴ πολύμητις <u>ἀναΐξειεν</u> Ὀδυσσεύς,
σταΰκεν, ὑπαὶ δὲ ἴδεσκε κατὰ χθονὸς ὄμματα πήξας,

But whenever wily Odysseus sprang up, he would stand there, staring down, with his eyes fixed on the ground,

Scholars have argued that there is a difference in meaning between temporal and conditional contexts: in temporal sentences the event is presupposed to have happened, while in conditional clauses it is strictly not (Zycha 1885: 86ff.; Wakker 1994: 197). However, this claim is not uncontroversial (Comrie 1986a: 83). Anyway, the possible difference in meaning is said to lie in the different meanings of the conjunctions, and thus has little relevance for our discussion here.

A preliminary point should be made about the modal particle in this construction. In Attic, iterative conditional clauses are marked by the compulsory use of the particle in the protasis (Goodwin: §532). It might therefore be considered necessary to accompany a discussion of iterative meaning with a discussion of the meaning of the modal particle. But in Homeric Greek, fourteen of the nineteen iterative conditional clauses appear without the modal particle. For example:

4.262   εἴ περ γάρ τ' ἄλλοί γε κάρη κομόωντες Ἀχαιοὶ
δαιτρὸν <u>πίνωσιν</u>, σὸν δὲ πλεῖον δέπας αἰεί
ἕστηχ' ὥς περ ἐμοί, πιέειν ὅτε θυμὸς ἀνώγοι.

Even if the other long-haired Achaeans drink their share, yours stays always full, just as mine does, to drink whenever your heart stirs you.

Since the moods are able to express the meaning without the particle, the absence or presence of the particle in examples of this construction will not be considered further. For more discussion of the modal particle, see Appendix 1.

---

[20] 24.768 is actually the only conditional protasis with past habitual meaning (Monro: §311).

Although iterative sentences are formally marked as being different from specific sentences, it would appear unjustified to entirely separate the two types from each other. Horrocks (1995: 159) has demonstrated that all future-referring conditional and temporal sentences are indeterminate between a specific and an iterative meaning. For example, the following (real) conditional has two possible interpretations, as made explicit in versions (a) and (b) below:

59 If Mary goes out, Bill will go to the pub.
    (a) If Mary goes out (at some unspecified time in the future), Bill will (then) go to the pub.
    (b) If Mary (ever) goes out, Bill will (always) go to the pub.

The same indeterminacy may also be found in 'unreal' conditionals (Horrocks 1995: 160). For example:

60 If Mary went out, Bill would go to the pub.

Wakker (1994: 106) has shown that in fact *all* conditional and temporal clauses can be indeterminate between the two meanings. The following sentences are examples of such indeterminate conditional sentences with present and past reference:

61 If those people do not have identity cards, they'll land in trouble.
62 If those people did not have identity cards, they landed in trouble.

If the expression 'those people' is taken to refer to a particular group of people who are just passing through customs, or who passed through customs on a particular day, these sentences have a specific interpretation: if the protasis is true, then they are in trouble now, or they got in trouble then. But 'those people' may also refer to a certain type of people. In that case, the sentences will have a general interpretation: on each occasion that it is (was) found out that exponents of that type are found to have no identity cards, they will *always* be (were always) landing in trouble (Wakker 1994: 108).

    Since all conditional clauses can express both specific and iterative meaning, the use of the subjunctive and optative with iterative meaning in this context is entirely predictable, if not inevitable, given their use in specific conditional clauses. It is certainly an expected development, and may not be used to argue that they mark the grammatical nature of the clause, or to show that they are somehow parallel.

This conclusion is confirmed by the recognition that iterative meaning is not restricted to the subjunctive and optative. In classical Greek the use of the indicative in iterative conditional clauses is widely acknowledged.[21] For example (Wakker 1994: 109):

Thucydides 2.8.3   εἴ τέ τι ἄλλο τοιουτό τροπον <u>ξυνέβη</u> γενέσθαι, πάντα ἀνεζητεῖτο.

if anything else of that nature happened to occur, it was always questioned.

Thucydides 7.10
τοῦ δ' ἐπιγιγνομένου χειμῶνος ἥκοντες ἐς τὰς Ἀθήνας οἱ
παρὰ τοῦ Νικίου ὅσα τε ἀπὸ γλώσσης εἴρητο
αὐτοῖς εἶπον, καὶ εἴ τίς τι <u>ἐπηρώτα</u> ἀπεκρίνοντο,
καὶ τὴν ἐπιστολὴν ἀπέδοσαν.

The next winter, on arrival at Athens, the people Nicias had sent gave the verbal messages which had been entrusted to them, and if any questions were asked of them they answered them, and delivered the letter.

The indefinite use of the indicative is usually accompanied by εἴ τις or εἴ τι (Smyth: §2342). This could suggest that the 'indefinite' meaning of the construction resides in the indefinite pronoun rather than the mood of the verb. Certainly, it shows that the indicative in this context does not necessarily refer to a specific event.

There are a few examples of the indicative in Homeric Greek being used in the same way. There is one example of the 'gnomic aorist' in a protasis in a present-referring conditional sentence of an iterative type:

4.160   εἴ περ γάρ τε καὶ αὐτίκ' Ὀλύμπιος οὐκ <u>ἐτέλεσσεν</u>,
ἔκ τε καὶ ὀψὲ τελεῖ, σύν τε μεγάλωι ἀπέτεισαν,
σὺν σφῆισιν κεφαλῆισι γυναιξί τε καὶ τεκέεσσιν.

Even if the Olympian doesn't exact punishment straight away, he'll exact it later, and demand more, on their own heads, and those of their wives and children.

This may be compared with 1.81 where the iterative subjunctive is found in a very similar context:

---

[21] Smyth: §2336; Goodwin: §467; Gildersleeve 1882: 435.

1.81 εἴ περ γάρ τε χόλον γε καὶ αὐτῆμαρ <u>καταπέψηι</u>,
  ἀλλά τε καὶ μετόπισθεν ἔχει κότον, ὄφρα τελέσσηι,

Even if he keeps his wrath down on the day, he cherishes the burning within him, until he fulfills it,

In temporal clauses there are rather more examples of the indicative being used with an iterative meaning where we might expect the subjunctive. For example:[22]

2.471 ἠΰτε μυιάων ἀδινάων ἔθνεα πολλά,
  αἵ τε κατὰ σταθμὸν ποιμνήϊον ἠλάσκουσιν
  ὥρηι ἐν εἰαρινῆι ὅτε τε γλάγος ἄγγεα <u>δεύει</u>,
  τόσσοι ἐπὶ Τρώεσσι κάρη κομόωντες Ἀχαιοί
  ἐν πεδίωι ἵσταντο, διαρραῖσαι μεμαῶτες.

Just like the many tribes of swarming flies that buzz about through the shepherd's stalls in the springtime, when the milk floods the pails, that many long-haired Achaeans stood on the plain facing the Trojans, burning to destroy them.

There are also (rather fewer) instances of the imperfect indicative being used in past-time temporal clauses where we would expect the optative according to the pattern observed above. For example:

5.788 ὄφρα μὲν ἐς πόλεμον <u>πωλέσκετο</u> δῖος Ἀχιλλεύς,
  οὐδέποτε Τρῶες πρὸ πυλάων Δαρδανιάων
  οἴχνεσκον·

As long as god-like Achilles went into battle, no Trojan would ever venture beyond the Dardan Gates.

In 5.788, the imperfect πωλέσκετο is found in the subordinate clause introduced by ὄφρα. We could argue that the sense is not necessarily indefinite; however, the imperfect οἴχνεσκον in the main clause, together with the indefinite marker ποτε, suggests that there were a number of different occasions when the Trojans would not 'venture'.

The indicative is certainly often found in similes, which of course do not refer to a specific incident. For example:[23]

---

[22] Also 10.83 = 10.386; O18.367 = O22.301; 8.556; 10.7; 14.397; 18.219; 12.279; 11.87 (Chantraine: §353 Rem III).
[23] Also 3.23; 3.33; 8.555; 11.492; 13.389; 20.490 (Goodwin: §548).

11.415   ὁ δέ τ' εἶσι βαθείης ἐκ ξυλόχοιο
θήγων λευκὸν ὀδόντα μετὰ γναμπτῆισι γένυσσιν,
ἀμφὶ δέ τ' ἀΐσσονται, ὑπαὶ δέ τε κόμπος ὀδόντων γίνεται,

He comes out from the deep thicket, whetting his white tusks in his curving jaws,
and they charge upon him on either side, and the sound of the gnashing of tusks
fills the air.

The use of the indicative with iterative meaning suggests that the
iterative meaning of the subjunctive and optative should not be
considered as a separate meaning. Rather this meaning appears to
develop in all moods, perhaps because of the particular contexts in
which they are found.

The claim that iterative meaning is not really a separate meaning
for the subjunctive and optative is confirmed by the observation
that the iterative meaning of conditional sentences is provided by
the meaning of the apodosis rather than the protasis alone. For
example:

1.610   Ζεὺς δὲ πρὸς ὃν λέχος ἤϊ' Ὀλύμπιος ἀστεροπητής,
ἔνθα πάρος κοιμᾶθ', ὅτε μιν γλυκὺς ὕπνος ἱκάνοι·

and Zeus, the Olympian, lord of the lightning, went to his couch, where he took
his rest, whenever sweet sleep came upon him.

When explaining these sentences to students, teachers might claim
that they are iterative because of the presence of the subjunctive or
optative in the protasis. But the criterion for interpreting these
sentences as iterative is the presence in the main clause of a
verb in the present or imperfect referring to an event which frequently occurs (Smyth: §2340a). We could therefore say that,
in the absence of a specific temporal adverbial, the protasis is
unmarked or neutral with regards to the frequency of the event.
That is, the subjunctive and optative are not iterative *per se,* rather
it is the context that leads to a particular interpretation (Wakker
1994: 218).

However, there are problems for the view that the iterative meanings of the subjunctive and optative are entirely explained by their
use in specific conditional clauses. The meaning of the subjunctive and optative appears to be rather different in iterative contexts.

After all, in specific conditional clauses, both moods usually refer to the future. In iterative clauses, on the other hand, the subjunctive appears to refer to a 'general present', and the optative refers to several events which happened in the past. This appears to confirm that the two meanings may after all be separated.

But the evidence suggests that the change in time-reference is not as significant as might be thought. This is particularly the case with the optative. In 5.3.2 I argued that it was not a future marker but was really timeless. Occasional examples where the optative is used with reference to events that always happen show that the mood is used in the same way in iterative conditional clauses. For example:[24]

O   οὔτ᾽ οὖν ἀγγελίη ἔτι πείθομαι, εἴ ποθεν ἔλθοι,
1.414   οὔτε θεοπροπίης ἐμπάζομαι, ἥν τινα μήτηρ
         ἐς μέγαρον καλέσασα θεοπρόπον ἐξερέηται.

I no longer trust in messages, if they come from somewhere, nor worry about prophecies, if my mother calls some prophet to the palace and asks him questions.

This example is interesting as, because both subjunctive and optative are found in close proximity, it suggests that the choice between them could at least originally have been made on semantic grounds. The subjunctive here is used to describe the regular behaviour of the speaker's mother, asking advice of seers (who may after all be resident in the palace), while the optative describes the rather more sporadic and unexpected arrival of messages from abroad. This is just the same meaning as expressed by the moods in specific clauses: the subjunctive refers to events that are in line with the speaker's view of the world, that is 'normal' events, while the optative refers to events that are rather more unusual and beyond the control of the subject (Monro: §316). Allen (1902: 125) similarly argues that the choice of the moods in this context may be explained on semantic grounds.

---

[24] See Smyth: §2360; Goodwin: §501; Monro: §311. Also cf. 9.318; O5.484; O7.51; O8.138; O14.56. Also perhaps 4.262, though this use of the optative could be due to 'formulaic corruption' of which we may see the more 'correct' form in 8.189 and O8.70. See also in the classical language: Herodotus 7.49.5; Thucydides 1.120.3; Sophocles *OT* 917; *Aj.* 520; *Aj.* 1344; *Ant.* 666.

To return to the question of the time-reference of the moods, it is more difficult to explain the subjunctive. Previous accounts have acknowledged the difficulty of reconciling the two meanings: Goodwin pronounced *aporia* (374), while others describe the subjunctive as a 'future-indefinite entity' (Lightfoot 1975: 13; see also Bakker 1988b). Hahn (§10) claims that the use of a future marker in this context is entirely expected, since future markers have a large span of temporal reference, which makes them appropriate for markers of something which is *always* true. This explanation seems rather arbitrary, since the future time span is not significantly or obviously 'larger' than the past or present time span, and since present tenses are often apparently used for the same purpose, as in English. Nonetheless, it has been shown that the use of a future marker to describe something which is 'gnomically' true, or customarily repeated, is cross-linguistically common.[25] However, for a full understanding of the subjunctive in particular, it would be helpful to trace the development.

It seems plausible to argue that the general reference of the subjunctive originated in the nature of the conditional clause. Indeed there are some examples with future reference but more iterative sense:

5.129   τῷ νῦν, αἴ κε θεὸς πειρώμενος ἐνθάδ' ἵκηται,
μή τι σύ γ' ἀθανάτοισι θεοῖς ἀντικρὺ μάχεσθαι
τοῖς ἄλλοις·

So now, if a god approaches to test you, don't fight any of the other immortal gods head-to-head.

In this sentence, ἵκηται could have iterative reference ('if any god approaches') to an event in the future. The change in time-reference is also explicable in the context of conditional clauses. I have argued above that it is the apodosis which determines whether conditional sentences are iterative or specific. And it could be argued that it is the tense of the apodosis in subjunctive conditionals

---

[25] See Ulkan 1978: 87. Future tense used as 'gnomic tense' in French, classical Greek, Tongan and Dakota, as well as in English on occasion (Ultan 1978: 87). Future tense used as habitual marker in Hausa, Lithuanian, Russian, Rotuman, and Tagalog (Ultan 1978: 102).

which determines the time-reference. In 5.129, the imperative in the apodosis suggests a future interpretation. In the more 'normal' subjunctive iterative clauses, a present tense in the apodosis reveals the correct interpretation.

However, it must be admitted that the subjunctive has developed in meaning, since it is found referring to the 'general present' in relative clauses where the meaning may no longer be explained as connected with the construction. For instance:

5.6 δαῖέ οἱ ἐκ κόρυθός τε καὶ ἀσπίδος ἀκάματον πῦρ,
ἀστέρ᾽ ὀπωρινῷ ἐναλίγκιον, ὅς τε μάλιστα
λαμπρὸν παμφαίνῃσι λελουμένος Ὠκεανοῖο·

She set his helmet and shield ablaze with tireless fire, like the dog-star that shines out so brightly, bathed in the Ocean.

It seems most plausible to explain the use of the iterative sub-junctive in relative clauses as having developed from the use of the moods in conditional clauses. This is also suggested by Goodwin's description of these type of relative clauses as 'conditional relative clauses' (Goodwin: 196). But it seems that we must admit that the meaning has been 'abstracted' from the conditional context, so that, even if in conditional clauses it might be true to say that the iterative meaning is not really 'carried by' the moods but rather by the context, that the meaning *has* become associated with the mood. It is perhaps significant in this respect that the independent meaning of the subjunctive is found in similes, which are argued to belong to the latest chronological slice of the Homeric language (Shipp, 1972: *passim*). The meaning of the subjunctive in this context demonstrates once again that the mood is developing in several different directions, but that all the developments can be traced back to an original 'future' meaning.

6.3.3 Summary

In this section I have shown that the meaning of a particular marker may not be described in isolation from the constructions in which it is found. I have argued that it is because conditional and temporal

clauses are typically indeterminate between specific and an iterative meaning that the subjunctive and optative should have iterative as well as specific meanings. Thus the use of the subjunctive
and optative in iterative conditionals does not prove that they are
used for purely grammatical reasons, or that they are somehow
parallel.

The apparent change in time-reference of the two moods in their
iterative as opposed to their specific uses is also explicable. I have
argued that the optative does not really 'shift' to past reference: the
existence of a few examples with 'general present' reference shows
that in this as well as the specific conditionals the optative is really
timeless, with time-reference only marked in the apodosis. The
subjunctive is restricted to future and 'general' situations, and thus
appears to retain some level of the original 'future' meaning, with a
small shift in meaning. The use of the moods with iterative meaning
in relative clauses does suggest that the moods have developed,
and that the meaning has been 'abstracted' from the context of
conditional clauses. Nonetheless, to explain the meaning as purely
'grammatically required' is again to misunderstand the true nature
of the moods and their developments.

6.4 Non-specific

6.4.1 Introduction

In the previous section I showed that the subjunctive and optative are used with iterative meaning in relative clauses. Previously,
the presence of the moods in this context has been described as
dependent on the nature of the antecedent. For example, Abbott
and Mansfield (165, 166) claim that the relative with a definite
(=specific) antecedent takes the indicative, while with an indefinite (=non-specific) antecedent a 'primary' relative uses the subjunctive, and a 'secondary' relative uses the optative:[26]

---

[26] The use of 'specific' and 'non-specific' in the grammars (e.g. Smyth: 564) agrees with
Hawkins' 1978 definition (Hawkins 1978: 215, quoted by Vester 1989: 336): 'a NP is
used specifically if the speaker may know which individual is being referred to, whereas
the hearer does not; a NP is used non-specifically if neither speaker nor hearer has a
particular referent in mind'.

Specific: ἄνδρα ἄγω, ὃν εἶρξαι δεῖ
                               I bring a man whom it is necessary to
                               lock up
Non-specific primary: ὁποῖον ἄν συμβῆ τλήσομαι
                               I will bear whatever happens
Non-specific secondary: εἵποντο ὅποι τις ἡγοῖτο
                               They would follow wherever any one
                               might lead

Mood choice in other languages has certainly been argued to be
dependent on the specificity of the antecedent. For example, in
French (Vester 1989: 331):

63 *je cherche une jeune fille qui sait parler français* (= a particular
girl)
64 *je cherche une jeune fille qui sâche parler français* (= any girl)

If this claim were to be proved correct for the Homeric language
this would be one way in which the moods appear to be used
to mark a syntactic feature of the clause rather than the 'attitude
of the speaker'. But a closer look at the use of both moods in this
construction will reveal that it is not the specificity of the antecedent
which 'requires' the use of the subjunctive or optative in Homeric
Greek. Instead, the use of the moods may always be explained with
reference to a use of the mood in another construction.

6.4.2 Analysis

The claim that the moods are used to mark the nature of the
antecedent in relative clauses must acknowledge that it is not the
only way to explain the presence of the subjunctive and optative in
this context. There are several Homeric examples of the subjunctive
and optative in relative clauses with a specific antecedent. Several
of these could perhaps be 'excused' on the grounds that they are
non-restrictive relative clauses, merely adding a piece of information to the sentence (terminology from Lehmann 1992, see also
Lehmann 1995). For example:

5.303   ὃ δὲ χερμάδιον λάβε χειρί
         Τυδείδης, μέγα ἔργον, ὃ οὐ δύο γ' ἄνδρε <u>φέροιεν</u>,

But the son of Tydeus grasped in his hand a stone – a mighty deed – one that two men could not carry,

Chantraine (§358) has argued that in relative clauses where the connection between antecedent and relative clause is rather loose such as this one, the choice of mood is exactly the same as in main clauses. But even in restrictive relative clauses, specific antecedents are occasionally followed by the subjunctive or optative. For example:

   i. 'Iterative' subjunctive:

3.61   αἰεί τοι κραδίη πέλεκυς ὥς ἐστιν ἀτειρής,
        ὅς τ' εἶσιν διὰ δουρὸς ὑπ' ἀνέρος, ὅς ῥά τε τέχνῃ
        νήϊον <u>ἐκτάμνησιν</u>, ὀφέλλει δ' ἀνδρὸς ἐρωήν·

Your heart is always hard as an axe, that goes through wood in the hands of a man, who cuts out ship-timbers with skill, and the force helps the man.

ii. 'Unreal' optative:

6.453   ἀλλ' οὔ μοι Τρώων τόσσον μέλει ἄλγος ὀπίσσω,
         οὔτ' αὐτῆς Ἑκάβης οὔτε Πριάμοιο ἄνακτος
         οὔτε κασιγνήτων, οἵ κεν πολέες τε καὶ ἐσθλοί
         ἐν κονίῃσι <u>πέσοιεν</u> ὑπ' ἀνδράσι δυσμενέεσσιν,

The coming grief of the Trojans does not move me so much, not Hecabe's grief nor that of king Priam, nor that of my brothers, of whom so many good ones might fall in the dust at the hands of their enemies,

The evidence shows that the subjunctive and optative are certainly not only found with non-specific antecedents. It is clearly not always the case that the choice of mood is determined by the specificity of the antecedent.

And even when the NP *is* non-specific, the use of the subjunctive or optative may be explained in terms of meanings that are found in other contexts. The following examples show the subjunctive and optative in both headed and headless non-specific clauses:

2.361   οὔ τοι ἀπόβλητον ἔπος ἔσσεται, ὅττί κεν <u>εἴπω</u>·

The word I will speak, is not to be tossed aside.

3.71   ὁππότερος δέ κε νικήσηι κρέσσων τε γένηται,
       κτήμαθ᾽ ἑλὼν εὖ πάντα γυναῖκά τε οἴκαδ᾽ ἀγέσθω·

Whichever man wins and proves himself the better man, he'll rightly take the treasures and lead the woman home.

5.301 ἀμφὶ δ᾽ ἄρ᾽ αὐτῶι βαῖνε λέων ὣς ἀλκὶ πεποιθώς,
       πρόσθε δέ οἱ δόρυ τ᾽ ἔσχε καὶ ἀσπίδα πάντος ἐΐσην,
       τὸν κτάμεναι μεμαὼς ὅς τις τοῦ γ᾽ ἀντίος ἔλθοι,

he stood round him like a lion, trusting in his strength, and protected him with spear and shield, burning to kill any man who approached him,

In all examples, the use of the mood in question could be explained as a normal use of the mood rather than dependent on the nature of the antecedent. In both 2.361 and 3.71, the subjunctive refers to a future event, while in 5.301 the optative in the relative clause is unreal.

Perhaps even more troubling for the claim that the reference of the NP determines the mood in the relative clause is the use of the indicative in non-specific relative clauses (Smyth: 564; Bakker 1988a: 33–5). For example:

6.90   Ἕκτορ, ἀτὰρ σὺ πόλινδε μετέρχεο, εἰπὲ δ᾽ ἔπειτα
       μητέρι σῆι καὶ ἐμῆι· ἡ δὲ ξυνάγουσα γεραιάς
       νηὸν Ἀθηναίης γλαυκώπιδος ἐν πόλει ἄκρηι,
       οἴξασα κληῖδι θύρας ἱεροῖο δόμοιο,
       πέπλον, ὅ οἱ δοκέει χαριέστατος ἠδὲ μέγιστος
       εἶναι ἐνὶ μεγάρωι καί οἱ πολὺ φίλτατος αὐτῆι,
       θεῖναι Ἀθηναίης ἐπὶ γούνασιν ἠϋκόμοιο,

But you, Hector, go back to the city, and tell our mother to gather all the old women in the temple to grey-eyed Athena at the top of the city, and to unlock the doors of the sacred chamber, and to take a robe, whichever she thinks is the most beautiful and the most royal in the palace, and which is most dear to her, and to place it at the knees of Athena of the beautiful tresses.

It has sometimes been claimed when the indicative is found that a single exponent of the genre is taken as representative of the whole type (Goodwin: §534). For example:

O   ἐχθρὸς γάρ μοι κεῖνος ὁμῶς Ἀΐδαο πύλησι
14.156   γίγνεται, ὃς πενίη εἴκων ἀπατήλια βάζει.

I hate that man like the Gates of Death, who in his poverty stoops to telling lies.

187

But the subjunctive is found in very similar contexts. For example:

9.312   ἐχθρὸς γάρ μοι κεῖνος ὁμῶς Ἀΐδαο πύληισιν
ὅς χ' ἕτερον μὲν <u>κεύθηι</u> ἐνὶ φρεσίν, ἄλλο δὲ <u>εἴπηι</u>.

I hate that man like the Gates of Death, who hides one thing in his heart, but says another.

The explanation for the indicative is thus rather weak, as it will fail to predict which mood will be used in a particular context.

It could perhaps be argued that the indicative relative clauses in the 'wrong' context are only here for formulaic reasons (cf section 1.2 on the problems of the Homeric language). This point would require further investigation of whether the clauses in question were truly formulaic (see Bakker 1988a: 152ff.). But even if the evidence from indicative relative clauses should be discounted, it seems clear from the other evidence that the subjunctive and optative are not used *only* because the antecedent is non-specific, but because of the inherent meanings of the moods as revealed in other contexts.

This is not to say that there is no connection between non-specific antecedents and the use of the subjunctive and optative. Indeed it is true that the majority of non-specific antecedents take the subjunctive and optative. But that could be explained by the meanings of the subjunctive and optative in other contexts, rather than by any direct link between non-specificity and use of a general 'irrealis' marker. For example, any future-referring (restrictive) relative clauses are inherently non-specific as we may see in 2.361:

2.361   οὔ τοι ἀπόβλητον ἔπος ἔσσεται, ὅττί κεν <u>εἴπω</u>·

The word I will speak, is not to be tossed aside.

Since the word has not been uttered yet, the relative clause *must* be non-specific, but the use of the subjunctive can be explained as marking the future time reference of the verb. Similarly, in 6.521, the 'unreal' nature of the description, which governs the choice of the optative, is surely connected to the fact that the antecedent is not specific:

6.521   δαιμόνι᾽, οὐκ ἄν τίς τοι ἀνήρ, ὃς ἐναίσιμος <u>εἴη</u>,
        ἔργον ἀτιμήσειε μάχης, ἐπεὶ ἄλκιμός ἐσσι·

My friend, no man who is reasonable could slight your work in battle, since you are strong.

6.4.3 Summary

The 'rule' that mood choice in relative clauses depends on the specificity of the antecedent appears to be another reason to claim that the subjunctive and optative are used syntactically, as markers of irrealis modality. But an investigation of the choice of mood in Homeric relative clauses has revealed that all the uses of the moods may be explained with reference to their meaning in other contexts rather than as dependent on the specificity of the antecedent. It is unsurprising that they are found so regularly in non-specific relative clauses, given that their meanings in other contexts all include an element of 'indefiniteness'. But the link between non-specificity and the subjunctive and optative is in essence coincidental, since the use of the moods in this construction is dependent on their core meanings.

6.5 Summary and conclusions

In this chapter I have considered three types of subordinate clauses in which it could be argued that the moods are used for grammatical rather than semantic reasons, and are parallel in usage. In each case I have argued that the meaning of the mood can be seen as a natural extension of their meaning elsewhere and that their parallelism is really illusory.

In purpose clauses, both subjunctive and optative are found with their 'original' meaning in combination with the conjunctions that later develop purpose meaning. It therefore appears most plausible to explain the purpose meaning as having developed organically, because of the particular combination of meanings. The 'rule' by which the subjunctive is found in primary time and the optative in secondary time has been shown to suffer from some exceptions, and the distribution of the moods can again be explained in terms of their original meanings. There is thus no reason to see the moods as grammatically required in this construction, or to see the optative as the past-time variant of the subjunctive.

The iterative meaning of the subjunctive has been seen as the hardest to reconcile with its future meaning. Here I claimed that the iterative meaning of both moods developed first in conditional and temporal clauses which are by nature indeterminate between specific and iterative meaning. The subjunctive and optative are both independently found in specific conditional clauses so that there is no need to see their use in iterative clauses as grammatically determined. The apparent change in time-reference is particularly easy to explain for the optative: it is not changing from a future marker to a past marker, but remains a timeless marker in all contexts. In the case of the subjunctive, the time-reference is usually provided by the context. The use of the moods with the iterative meaning in relative clauses suggests that the perceived meaning of the moods has developed over time.

Finally, the claim that the moods are used to mark the non-specificity of the antecedent in relative clauses was considered. It was shown that, in fact, the moods are also used after specific antecedents, and that even after non-specific antecedents their use may be explained with reference to another meaning. The claim therefore appears to be untrue, at least for Homeric Greek. It was admitted that the indefinite meanings of the moods leads to them being primarily used in non-specific clauses: perhaps this meaning is again 'abstracted' in later periods of the language.

The development of the 'subordinate meanings' of the subjunctive and optative can thus be traced independently, and with reference to their 'core' meanings in main clauses. Neither mood should therefore be described as 'grammatically required' in these constructions, and it is clear that, at an early stage of their development they were not parallel. Nonetheless, the use of the moods in subordinate contexts is leading to a broadening of their uses, and also to a parallelism between them. Both of these developments appear to have had significant consequences for their subsequent development. The use of the subjunctive in ever more subordinate clauses is widening the difference between it and the future indicative. And the growing parallelism between the moods means that it is unsurprising that the optative should have been seen as a 'back-shifted' form of the subjunctive, particularly in later Greek, where the use of the optative after primary verbs becomes ever rarer. It is thus again interesting to note that the optative soon dies out in Greek (Moulton 1908: 118). We may speculate that, at the stage just before its loss it was seen as rather 'redundant', with all its uses grammatically required. But the optative in Homeric Greek has not yet reached this stage.

7

CONCLUSION

7.1 Introduction

Modality, a particularly fascinating semantic domain, is expressed in a particularly interesting way in Homeric Greek. Unlike English, it primarily uses moods rather than modal verbs, and unlike most other European languages, ancient and modern, it has two distinct 'non-indicative' moods – the subjunctive and optative. Traditionally, these moods have been described in structural terms: they are said to be parallel forms, with one more 'remote' than the other, and both are said to express two fundamental meanings, which appear to relate to the two meanings claimed to be fundamental in modern studies of modality. These claims may be represented in figures 7.1 and 7.2:

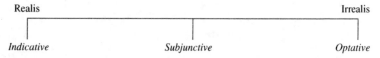

Realis   Irrealis

| | |

Indicative   *Subjunctive*   *Optative*

Figure 7.1 Greenberg's irrealis continuum

	Deontic	**Epistemic**
Less remote	Subjunctive *Want*	Subjunctive *Likely*
More remote	Optative *Wish*	Optative *Unlikely*

Figure 7.2 Meanings of the moods and their interrelationship in traditional accounts

In this book I have considered the range of constructions in which the subjunctive and optative are found, and argued for interpretations which often differ radically from the traditional accounts and which present a picture of the meanings expressed by the moods that is more complicated, but ultimately more informative than the standard view. My conclusions have important ramifications for the understanding of specific constructions, both from a linguistic and a more literary or cultural perspective. They also affect the linguistic understanding of the different categories of the ancient Greek modal system, and the understanding of modal systems in general.

My conclusions about the different moods may be presented in terms of the new 'maps' that I have proposed. The decision to present the meanings of each mood in terms of individual maps rather than attempting to describe them all in terms of a simple table as above was made on methodological grounds. The theory of grammaticalisation has shown that forms gradually accumulate meanings so that any form will have different diachronic layers. It is therefore theoretically implausible that any one form in a language will be satisfactorily described simply as a 'marker of meaning A'. For a start, it is unlikely to have only the one meaning, and anyway, the particular nature of that meaning will be defined by its history. Thus while 'will' in English is often described as a marker of future tense, such a description ignores the variety of its uses and its development from a marker of desire. In order to define a particular form more helpfully, it is necessary to define in more detail the variety of its meanings and the relationships which hold between them. Furthermore, it is also clear from this theory that forms should be described independently from each other, as forms which may appear to express similar meanings at a certain point in time will have had different histories, and different consequent developments. This is particularly important for the description of the subjunctive and optative in Homeric Greek as it shows that the traditional claim that they are parallel is theoretically implausible.

7.2 New map of the indicative

In some basic descriptions of the moods in ancient Greek the indicative is described as non-modal. However, the indicative is just as subjective as other modal forms. Given that subjectivity is crucial to modern definitions of modality, I have argued that an analysis of the indicative is necessary for a description of the modal system of ancient Greek, particularly because the other moods are often defined in relation to it. Furthermore, in Homeric Greek as in many other languages, the indicative is found in conditional clauses. The status of these clauses is unclear in previous descriptions of the domain of modality. The interpretation of the indicative I propose here therefore improves our understanding of the modality of those clauses.

The map I propose for the meaning of the indicative differs from those for the subjunctive and optative because I argue that the indicative expresses fewer meanings than are traditionally assigned to it. I distinguish three different groups of conditional clauses, which I term realis, open and counterfactual, but argue that the same underlying meaning of positive epistemic stance would account for them all. This definition improves on previous accounts as it better explains the mood choice in counterfactual sentences. The use of the indicative in this context has previously been described as a 'modal extension' of meaning, without any explanation of the mechanism by which that extension took place.

This suggests that the modality of conditional clauses should be described in terms of the 'epistemic stance' of the speaker. As the name suggests, this type of modality is epistemic, but different from the epistemic category as usually described in theoretical descriptions of the domain of modality. The failure to describe this type of modality and its relationship to other types in previous accounts has perhaps stemmed from a concentration on the modality of modal verbs, which are the primary way of expressing modality in English. This conclusion thus offers a new perspective on the domain of modality in general.

7.3 New map of the subjunctive

The map I have proposed for the subjunctive is significantly different from the traditional accounts. First, I have argued that the meanings that are traditionally distinguished should be reinterpreted. In its use as a marker of possibility, the subjunctive is described as 'more irrealis' than the indicative. But I show that it is difficult to prove any difference in meaning between it and the future indicative. The domain of future reference is admittedly very murky, leading some scholars to deny the existence of a 'non-modal' future tense. Nonetheless, following Comrie, I believe that it is theoretically possible to make a distinction between a mood and a future marker. The latter should refer to the speaker's 'projected reality' and the former to his 'potential reality'. But the difference between the subjunctive and future indicative in Homeric Greek may not be described in these terms. In fact, the meanings of both markers are rather varied, and often overlap. There is evidently a difference of distribution between the two, with the subjunctive the preferred marker in all subordinate clauses. But while the subjunctive appears to be in the process of accumulating more 'modal' uses, in its basic meaning it is no more 'irrealis' than a realis future marker would be expected to be.

I have also shown that the sense of the subjunctive used with μή cannot merely be the 'aorist equivalent' of the present imperative which is found in what appears to be the same construction. Instead, I have argued that the subjunctive has a certain 'preventive' meaning. This analysis allows a different understanding of the choice of mood in the context of prohibitions, which are often found at emotionally charged situations in the text.

The use of the subjunctive in this construction, as well as the hortative construction, appears at first to suggest that the mood had 'deontic' meaning, as it expresses the wish of the speaker. But because of the performative nature of these utterances I argue that these constructions should be defined as expressing 'speaker-oriented' modality. Ascertaining the true nature of the modality is important for a diachronic description of the mood as, while epistemic modality tends to develop out of deontic modality, speaker-oriented modality tends to develop from other constructions. Indeed, I believe that the restricted nature of the constructions in which these meanings of the subjunctive are found (either in the first person or with the negative particle μή) indicates that these developed later. This again suggests that the modality expressed by moods is rather different from that expressed by modal verbs in English.

I have also argued that it is possible to distinguish more than the three traditional meanings given for this mood. Considering the whole range of examples that are given of the hortative construction I argue that many of them do not in fact have performative illocutionary force, but instead state the intent of the speaker, a true deontic meaning.

As well as redefining the number and type of meanings that should be distinguished, my map offers a different concept of how the relationship between the different meanings should be seen. There are 'fuzzy edges' between the different meanings, which interact with different axes. The meanings of possibility and intent interact with the axis of person: moving from first to third person the likelihood of the possibility interpretation becomes greater. The speaker-oriented meanings appear to be developments from these core meanings. In the first person the mood develops hortative meaning in certain contexts, whereas in conjunction with μή, the aorist subjunctive develops directive meaning. The purpose meaning found in subordinate clauses also appears to be a later development, caused by the interaction in meaning between the mood itself and particular conjunctions. In my interpretation, then, the subjunctive should be mapped with five 'foci' of meanings: possibility, intent, exhortation, prevention and purpose. These foci are not clearly distinguished from each other, but the axes which connect them (person, time) may be drawn, and the conditions under which the developments occur (particular conjunctions) may be specified.

Describing the subjunctive in these terms is not only beneficial for the explanation of the mood in the 'synchronic slice' of the Homeric period but also helps us to understand later developments better. For example, in Attic Greek the 'future' meaning of the subjunctive is only found in subordinate clauses, in which context the future indicative is found even more rarely than in Homeric Greek. This supports the definition presented here: that the subjunctive was essentially a future marker which is taking on more modal meanings in certain contexts. This definition explains the relationship between the two periods more successfully than the traditional accounts, which abstract one common meaning from all the different uses of the mood at various different points in time, and then position the mood at a certain point on an irrealis continuum.

7.4 New map of the optative

My map of the optative is also significantly different from the description given in traditional accounts. Again, the meaning of the mood in wishes should be described as speaker-oriented rather than deontic. Here, however, it is unclear how the speaker-oriented meaning has developed, as it is found with no restriction. But it is apparent that the optative should be described in its own terms rather than as somehow parallel to the subjunctive, just as the theory of grammaticalisation suggests. For example, I believe that wishes may not be interpreted as 'weaker' forms of imperative sentences. Given their uses in prayers to gods, the correct interpretation of the mood here is important for a better understanding of the conception of the relationship between the human and the divine in the ancient world. The evidence from subordinate clauses again confirms that the optative is not parallel to the subjunctive. The distribution of the moods is rather more flexible than the rule-books would have us believe, meaning that every use of the optative can be accounted for with reference to reasons that are semantic rather than purely grammatical.

I argue that the understanding of the meaning of the mood in conditional clauses should also be modified. On the basis of the less 'canonical' examples of such sentences it appears that the optative should be described as a marker of negative epistemic stance, rather than a marker of low probability. Indeed, this seems to be a better way of describing 'unreal' conditionals in general, just as 'positive epistemic stance', the term proposed for the indicative, captures the meaning of 'real' conditional sentences. This conclusion has ramifications for an understanding of not only conditional modality, but also the overall domain of modality, and is therefore of importance for linguists with a more general interest in the domain.

To return to the map of the optative, I have argued that it should again be more complex than traditional descriptions would suggest.

I have distinguished another two 'foci' of meaning which the mood expresses: objective deontic and dynamic. Perhaps the developments which led to these various different layers happened further back in history; certainly the links between these meanings and the more traditional ones are again less clear than for the subjunctive.

7.5 Final thoughts

The moods in ancient Greek have received much attention in previous centuries. But it is clear from this study that there is more work to be done to understand fully their different meanings and the relationships between them. In a study of this size, which has considered a range of different constructions, it is perhaps inevitable that readers will have disagreed with some of the details of the interpretations and the claims that I have put forward. It is also the case that this study has raised many unanswered questions. I have only briefly touched on some of the differences between Homeric Greek and later Greek here: the modal system of later Greek needs to be more completely reassessed in the light of this new analysis of the Homeric system. Similarly, the evidence for the Proto-Indo-European subjunctive from other languages should be considered afresh, given my conclusion that the Greek subjunctive has previously been misunderstood. While it is acknowledged that more work remains to be done, my main purpose in this analysis has been to show that interesting conclusions may be reached by subjecting these familiar constructions to analysis using the findings of modern theoretical and typological research. My hope is that even disagreements with the conclusions reached here will encourage further study and greater understanding of what is a fascinating and highly complex system.

APPENDIX 1: FORMAL MARKERS

A.1 Introduction

In the introduction I briefly introduced the claim made by, among others, Chantraine, that the division between the epistemic and non-epistemic meanings of the moods, considered fundamental in traditional accounts, was supported by formal markers. He claims that the 'subjonctif d'éventualité' is negated by οὐ and is accompanied by the 'modal particle' κε/ἄν, whereas the 'subjonctif de volonté' is associated with the absence of the modal particle and the use of the negator μή (Chantraine: §306). However, I pointed out there that the data do not consistently support those claims. Subsequently I have argued that the division is anyway not a helpful way of understanding the meanings of the moods. I have therefore paid little attention to the formal marking in this study. This may have struck some readers as surprising, given the prominence given particularly to the modal particle in other discussions of the moods.

In this appendix I will further justify my decision to ignore the particle in an assessment of the meaning of the moods in Homer, showing evidence which suggests that it does not modify the sense of the moods in any consistent way. I will here offer a speculative account of the development of the particle which would explain this inconsistent distribution. I will also consider the meaning of the negators, and show that here too, the association with a particular kind of modality is really coincidental.

A.2 Particle

It should first be noted that, for the purposes of this study, the two particles will be treated as having essentially the same meaning.

Ruijgh (1992: 77) claims that they belong to two different dialectal layers of the epic language (κε(ν) = Aeolic, ἄν = Ionic), but there is little evidence for a semantic difference between the two particles. Indeed he argues that the two forms are related, with ἄν arising from a missegmentation of the form οὐ κἄν, where κἄν is the older form of κεν (see also Wathelet 1997: 247). This suggestion is supported by the very rare occurrence of the collocation οὐ κεν rather than οὐκ ἄν (see Chantraine: §503 and Monro: §362 for further discussion).

The claim under investigation here is that the presence of the modal particle indicates an epistemic use of the mood, while its absence indicates the use in prohibitions/wishes. Wathelet (1997: 247) and Ruijgh (1992: 77) have gone so far as to claim that the modal particle was introduced into the language in order to distinguish between the two meanings of the subjunctive.

At first sight the claim looks attractive. Certainly the vast majority of the data follows the expected pattern. But there are various reasons to think that there is no causal link between the type of modality and the presence or absence of the modal particle.

Firstly, the particle is not restricted to the optative and subjunctive where distinguishing between these two uses might be useful, but is also found with past indicative in counterfactual sentences. For example:

18.165   καί νύ κεν εἴρυσσέν τε καὶ ἄσπετον ἤρατο κῦδος,
         εἰ μὴ Πηλείωνι ποδήνεμος ὠκέα Ἶρις
         ἄγγελος ἦλθε θέουσ᾿ ἀπ᾿ Ὀλύμπου θωρήσσεσθαι,

And then he would have dragged it away and won unimaginable glory, except that swift Iris came darting from Olympus, her feet as quick as the wind, with a message for the son of Peleus to prepare for battle,

The particle is also found with the indicative in other contexts. For example:

O   τοῦτο μὲν οὕτω δὴ ἔσται ἔπος, αἴ κεν ἐγώ γε
11.349   ζωὸς Φαιήκεσσι φιληρέτμοισιν ἀνάσσω·

This oath will stand, as sure as I am alive and am lord over the oar-loving Phaeacians.

Chantraine (§359) claims that the particle is also found with the future indicative. For example:

1.175   πὰρ᾽ ἔμοιγε καὶ ἄλλοι
        οἵ κέ με τιμήσουσι, μάλιστα δὲ μητίετα Ζεύς.

With me are others who will honour me, and above all Zeus, the lord of counsel.

However, in all cases it is in fact unclear whether the form is future indicative or a (short-vowel) subjunctive (see further chapter 3).

These examples are perhaps not too problematic for the claim under discussion, since they are clearly 'modal' contexts. Proponents of the traditional explanation could claim that these should be explained as developments from the original meaning. Development certainly seems to have played an important role in the meaning of this marker. What is more problematic for the claim is the existence of the lines given in the introduction, where sentences with epistemic modality are found without particles, and wishes are found with particles.

The inconsistency of the data suggests that, rather than understanding the modal particle as indicative of a certain type of modality, it is more attractive to describe it as having some kind of lexical meaning which would be 'harmonic' with the epistemic meaning of the moods but would not itself be necessary to express epistemic meaning, and which could also be found with non-epistemic meaning. That the particle has some kind of lexical meaning is indeed the general consensus of scholars who have particularly studied the particle. But pinning down what that meaning might be has been found rather difficult (see Gerø 2000 for the history of the question).

Howorth (1955: 76–84) claims that the 'meaning' of the particle was 'futurity'. But the subjunctive refers to the future even when it is not accompanied by the particle and a 'future' meaning would also not explain the use of the particle in the apodosis of counterfactual sentences (Basset 1988: 31–2). Alternatively, it has been claimed that it marks 'modality' alone: Hahn (55) compares Greek to Hittite, where modality was marked solely by particles (see also Gerø 2000: 183–4). But Gonda (133, 135) rejects this claim, given that the particle is used with the indicative as well as the subjunctive and optative. Anyway, it is rather difficult to define exactly what 'modal' means, so that defining the particle as modal is therefore rather too weak and vague. It is certainly not clear what meaning the particle 'adds' to these contexts. Perhaps a more generally accepted suggestion is that the particle had the meaning of 'consecutiveness' or 'contingency' (Gonda: 135; Chantraine: §218, §311; Ruijgh 1992: 78. See also Dionysius Thrax as quoted in Basset 1988: 28). This is more specific than the 'modal' definition, and well explains the frequent association of the particle with future time reference and also in the apodoses of past-time counterfactual clauses. However, even this most successful definition is not able to explain all the uses of the particle. The use with the subjunctive in conditional protases and iterative subordinate clauses is still left unmotivated.

In all studies of the particle this last use has been found particularly hard to explain. Dionysius Thrax defined it separately, calling the particles here παρπληρωματικοὶ σύνδεσμοι ('expletive particles'), without a specific value (Basset 1988: 28). Several authors have been forced to conclude that this use of the particle was introduced secondarily. For example, Howorth (1955: 84ff.) and Brunel (1980: 245–9) argue that the particle could have been transferred from the apodosis by the working of Wackernagel's Law. That is, they claim that the particle would originally have belonged in the apodosis, but would later have been moved to the protasis in order to take up the second position of the sentence. But Basset (1988: 30) argues that it is not clear how this transferral could actually take place. He also points out that many of the 'protases' in Homer are in fact post-posed. Any transferral of the particle from the so-called apodoses in those cases would work *against* Wackernagel's Law, since a particle placed second in a pre-posed apodosis would be in just the position Wackernagel's Law would prescribe. Monro (§362) abandons the idea that the particle expressed contingency and claims instead that the particle was used when it concerned a 'particular case', whereas without the particle the verb would have a 'general' meaning. But Basset (1988: 33) points out that there are too many counter-examples to this claim, and that he must alter many examples of κε to τε in order to prove his point. Basset instead points out that the modal particle in protases may often be translated in the same way as in apodoses; namely as 'in that case'. According to that interpretation, protases with the modal particle are more linked to the context than those without it. However, this argument relies on a very subjective interpretation of conditional protases.

None of the attempts to find one single meaning which the particle consistently adds have been successful, perhaps since a definition which can explain the whole variety of different contexts in which it is found is necessarily too vague. Indeed, the theory of grammaticalisation suggests that the very attempt is misguided. It is entirely expected that one marker will have various different meanings which have accumulated over time, so that trying to find the one feature that they share is an unhelpful way of analysing it.

The evidence from subordinate clauses suggests that this is indeed a particle undergoing grammaticalisation. Firstly, it reveals that particle usage changes over time (see also Monro: §322). I have mentioned elsewhere that in Homer, fourteen of the nineteen iterative conditional clauses appear without the modal particle, while in Attic Greek the particle is required in this construction (Goodwin: §368; Gonda: 141). It would appear that, while the modal particle was originally more independent from the moods, its meaning is already developing in Homer, and its distribution is partly constrained by the nature of the construction. Secondly, the following figures from purpose clauses in the *Odyssey* show that the most important factor in determining whether or not the particle will be found is not the meaning of the clause: after all, they all share the same meaning. Instead, the important determining factor is the conjunction used to introduce the clause:

Conjunction introducing purpose clause	+ particle	− particle
ὄφρα	12	121
ἵνα	3	84
ὡς	29	17

We may also consider the continuing use of the collocation αἴ κε, with the 'older', Aeolic form αἴ, which we would normally expect to have been replaced by εἴ κε, with the 'newer' Ionic εἰ (Buck 1955: 134.1c; Ruijgh 1992: 78). The survival of the older version suggests that it was a collocation that native speakers did not think of as divisible and that therefore κε was seen as part of the construction rather than contributing a separate meaning. (We could compare the later ἐάν from εἰ + ἄν.)

A.2.1 Conclusion

The distribution of the particle in all these contexts suggests that while the particle may originally have had some lexical meaning, most plausibly that of 'contingency', over time it appears to have become more grammaticalised and semantically 'generalised', being associated with particular conjunctions or types of construction rather than contributing any particular meaning itself. This explanation would certainly account for its inconsistent distribution and the difficulty previous scholars have met in trying to explain all its uses in a unified way. It is therefore my belief that, while the presence or absence of a modal particle with a particular use of a mood should not be ignored, an analysis of the meaning of the moods can be carried out independently from that of the modal particle.

A.3 Negator

The claim that the type of modality is marked by the choice of negator is less controversial, as there are fewer examples with the 'wrong' marking. I argued in chapter 5 that three examples which have a rather surprising choice of negator can be explained if we accept that the optative expresses objective deontic modality:

2.250   τῶ οὐκ ἂν βασιλῆας ἀνὰ στόμ' ἔχων ἀγορεύοις,
         καί σφιν ὀνείδεά τε προφέροις, νόστόν τε φυλάσσοις.

You must stop taking the names of kings in vain, insulting them, all the time looking for a chance to get home.

14.126   τῶ οὐκ ἄν με γένος γε κακὸν καὶ ἀνάλκιδα φάντες
         μῦθον ἀτιμήσαιτε πεφασμένον, ὅν κ' εὖ εἴπω.

So you should not disregard the advice I give by claiming that my birth is low and cowardly, advice which is well meant.

O   οὐκ ἄν μιν νῦν, τέκνον, ἀναίτιον αἰτιόῳο.
20.135

Child, you shouldn't hold her responsible this time.

This would suggest that the rule must be modified, but not necessarily abandoned altogether: οὐ is found with epistemic and objective deontic modality, and μή is found with speaker-oriented modality. This modified rule certainly appears to tie in with traditional accounts of the negators in Proto-Indo-European, where scholars reconstruct two different particles, *ne* and *mē*, and claim that one was used to negate statements, while the other was used in prohibitions (Moorhouse 1959: 12; Schwyzer II: 305).

However, this account is not fully explanatory, since it does not answer *why* the different negators are associated with these different kinds of sentence. It also does not exhaustively explain all instances of the negators. For example:

19.261   ἴστω νῦν Ζεὺς πρῶτα, θεῶν ὕπατος καὶ ἄριστος,
        Γῆ τε καὶ Ἠέλιος καὶ Ἐρινύες, αἵ θ' ὑπὸ γαῖαν
        ἀνθρώπους τίνυνται, ὅτις κ' ἐπίορκον ὀμόσσηι,
        μὴ μὲν ἐγὼ κούρηι Βρισηΐδι χεῖρ' ἐπένεικα,

Zeus be my witness first, the highest, best of gods! Then Earth, then Sun, and then the Furies who stalk the world below to wreak revenge on the dead who break their oaths – I swear I never laid a hand on the girl Briseis,

O   ἦ μή τίς σευ μῆλα βροτῶν ἀέκοντος ἐλαύνει;
9.406 ἦ μή τίς σ' αὐτὸν κτείνει δόλῳ ἠὲ βίηφιν;

No one's rustling your flocks against your will, are they? Or trying to kill you by trickery or force?

In 19.261, Agamemnon is not prohibiting himself from having put a hand on Briseis, but is rather asserting strongly his denial. And in O9.406, the other Cyclopes are not prohibiting someone from driving off Polyphemus' flocks. The use of μή in these examples is therefore surprising.

A more explanatory account of the two negators points out the different scope they have. A definition of negators in terms of scope certainly has strong typological support (Jespersen 1917: 42; Moorhouse 1959: 1; Basset 1989: 45). In order to explain the different scopes of the negators it would be useful to have a description of the different 'layers' of the clause over which elements with different scopes may operate. However, there is no general consensus on how many layers there are, or exactly what falls in which layer. For example, Lyons (1977: 770–5) divides the sentence into the neustic, phrastic and tropic, while scholars following Functional Grammar divide the clause into terms, predicates, predications, propositions and clauses (Wakker 1994: 15–17), and many more models have been proposed. Here it is not my purpose to consider in more detail which model is most useful or accurate. Instead we may just work from the widely accepted premise that illocutionary force has scope over the whole sentence.

In performative sentences such as jussive, directive and wish sentences the addition of the negator μή creates a negated exhortation, a negated imperative, a negated wish (Gonda: chapter 10). Thus μή appears to negate the illocutionary force of the proposition rather than an element within the proposition. This may be better understood in diagrammatic form:

μή [X] = NOT ($_{directive}$[X]) *or* NOT ($_{jussive}$[X]) *or* NOT ($_{wish}$[X]).

Thus μή has large scope. In sentences with οὐ, on the other hand, it is an element within the proposition that is negated. For instance, the following sentence is a positive assertion, even though the content of the assertion is negative (from Moorhouse 1959: 1–2):

ὁ Σωκράτης οὐ λέγει 'Socrates does not speak'

Diagrammatically, οὐ [X] = $_{assertive}$ [NOT X]. That is, οὐ produces an assertion of a negative proposition rather than a negated assertion.

This argument will explain the use of οὐ found with the objective deontic meaning of the optative such as 2.250 (above, p. 204). Again, the negator negates the proposition itself, rather than either the illocutionary force or the modality. This suggests the following diagram to explain these sentences: $_{assertive}$\{*deontic*[NOT X]\}.

It is interesting to note that a similar situation appears to pertain in Vedic. Hahn (41) has noticed that prohibitions are sometimes expressed with *na* with the optative, as well as by *mā* + injunctive (*na* is the equivalent of Greek οὐ). But Gonda (197) has pointed out that these are not normal prohibitions, but rather have a more 'general' force. For example:

Taitt. Samh. 2,   *tasyai tad vrataṃ nānṛtaṃ vadet*
5, 5, 6

his (i.e. of any person falling under this head) vow is as follows: he shall not speak untruth.

The general nature of this prohibition means that the speaker does not prohibit any one addressee from acting in a particular way. Rather he states that an obligation exists for various people not to behave in a particular way. The negation therefore does not affect the illocutionary force (which is that of a statement), and *na* appears to be behaving the same way as οὐ in sentences 2.250 etc. above.

The argument that the difference between the two negators is one of scope is confirmed by the occasional use of οὐ in wishes. For example:

O   τῷ κε καὶ οὐκ ἀτελὴς θάνατος μνηστῆρσι γένοιτο
17.546   πᾶσι μάλ', οὐδέ κέ τις θάνατον καὶ κῆρας ἀλύξει.

Let death come down with grim finality on these suitors – one and all – let not a single man escape his fate!

This line is a positive wish: the speaker wishes that death will come to the suitors. The phrase οὐκ ἀτελής lies within the wish and describes the type of death that the speaker wants: 'may a "not unaccomplished" death come to the suitors' (see Merry, Riddell and Monro ad loc.). Unlike in negative wishes, the negator does not negate the illocutionary force but has a smaller scope, only negating the one word ἀτελής.

It must be admitted that not all of the examples of οὐ and μή may be understood so straightforwardly. In particular, I refer to the use of μή in oaths and questions expecting the answer 'no' as found at 19.261 and O9.406, repeated here for ease of reference:

19.261   ἴστω νῦν Ζεὺς πρῶτα, θεῶν ὕπατος καὶ ἄριστος,
            Γῆ τε καὶ Ἠέλιος καὶ Ἐρινύες, αἵ θ' ὑπὸ γαῖαν
            ἀνθρώπους τίνυνται, ὅτις κ' ἐπίορκον ὀμόσσῃ,
            μὴ μὲν ἐγὼ κούρηι Βρισηΐδι χεῖρ' ἐπένεικα,

Zeus be my witness first, the highest, best of gods! Then Earth, then Sun, and then the Furies who stalk the world below to wreak revenge on the dead who break their oaths – I swear I never laid a hand on the girl Briseis,

O   ἦ μή τίς σευ μῆλα βροτῶν ἀέκοντος ἐλαύνει;

9.406   ἦ μή τίς σ' αὐτὸν κτείνει δόλῳ ἠὲ βίηφιν;

No one's rustling your flocks against your will, are they? Or trying to kill you by trickery or force?

But in fact I believe that μή could be argued to have large scope here too, producing negated assertions and negated questions, as described in the following diagrams:

19.261: NOT $_{assert}$[{epistemic}X]

O9.406: NOT$_{question}$[{epistemic}X]

It could be argued that the meaning of 19.261 is little different from an assertion of a negative proposition, in which we would expect οὐ. However an account of this sentence must explain the strength of the denial, and negating the illocutionary force of assertion might have that very effect. Similarly, it would be plausible to explain a question to which a negative response is hoped for as a 'negated question'. It is quite possible that these are extensions from the 'true' meanings of the negator: certainly they are rather marginal and unusual types of sentence. But their very rarity could be explained by the observation that it seems cross-linguistically more unusual to negate the illocutionary force of assertions and questions than that of directives.

While I believe that this analysis of the negators explains their use in main clauses more plausibly than previous accounts, a note of warning must be sounded. Just as with the particle, there are some uses of the negators which are not explained by this definition. This is particularly evident in conditional clauses. Since both negators are used in the context of conditional clauses it seems impossible to describe them as having different scopes. Since conditional protases are generally said to have their illocutionary force suspended (e.g. Dancygier 1988: 18), the general preference for μή is also surprising given the link with illocutionary force suggested above. The use and distribution of negators in conditional clauses is one of the most difficult issues when it comes to defining the use of the negators, and has been widely discussed (e.g. Chantraine 1: §333; Humbert 1943: §625; Tabachovitz 1951; Seiler 1971; Gonda: chapter 10; Basset 1989; Wakker 1994: 287). I do not propose to give a full account, but merely to show that the profusion of different meanings could have originated from the meanings I have suggested for the negators in main clauses above.

Note first that most of the examples of conditional sentences negated by μή may be translated by English 'unless', Latin *nisi* (Kühner and Gerth: 191; Basset 1989: 54). For example:

O   οὐδέ πόλινδε
14.373   ἔρχομαι, εἰ μή πού τι περίφρων Πηνελόπεια
             ἐλθέμεν ὀτρύνῃσιν, ὅτ᾽ ἀγγελίη ποθὲν ἔλθῃ.

I don't go into town, unless wise Penelope asks me to, when a message comes from somewhere or other.

As we may see from the wide variety of proposals summed up in Traugott 1997 to describe 'unless' clauses and their difference from 'normal' conditional clauses, the description of these clauses is not easy. In English, the meaning appears to have developed from the original sense of the conjunction 'of lesse than' (Traugott 1997: 154). But for the purposes of explaining the negator in the Greek sentences, it appears that we may again describe it as having 'wide scope'. For example, O14.373 could be glossed in the following way: 'I (generally) do not go into town, but this (not going into town) is not the case if Penelope asks me.' That is, the negator appears to have scope over the whole apodosis rather than any actual element within the protasis. If this were the only type of conditional sentence in which μή were found, the use of the negator in conditional clauses could then indeed be described in terms of scope.

But it must be admitted that μή is not found only in this particular type of conditional clause. For example:

1.324   εἰ δέ κε μὴ δώῃσιν, ἐγὼ δέ κεν αὐτὸς ἕλωμαι
             ἐλθὼν σὺν πλεόνεσσι, τό οἱ καὶ ῥίγιον ἔσται.

But if he will not give her over, I'll go myself with an army and seize her – that will be even worse for him.

This is a normal negative conditional clause, and the negator has scope only over the proposition in the conditional clause. Basset (1989: 54–5) is thus right to distinguish εἰ μή in Greek from *nisi* in Latin. The use of μή in conditional protases of this type suggests that the meaning of μή is developing from its original use, and is beginning to be attached generally to more 'modal' contexts. This is just the kind of development that studies of grammaticalisation lead us to expect. It is important to note that μή develops this meaning only in this particular construction, which suggests that it is its context of use which is affecting its meaning. This suggests that the behaviour of the negators in conditional clauses should be considered separately from its use in main clauses and need not detract from the conclusion reached there, that μή has wider scope than οὐ.

A.4 Conclusion

The distribution of negators in main clauses suggests that they will most successfully be described as having different scope: οὐ has small scope and μή has large scope. This suggests that the presence of a particular negator is not in itself sufficient reason to categorise a sentence as epistemic or deontic, or performative or constative. The meaning and use of the negator seems to be under-going some development, just like the modal particle. The use of μή in conditional clauses has not been fully explained here, but it is plausible to argue that it originally had the same large scope, and only recently began to develop new uses.

APPENDIX 2: CATALOGUE OF MOOD USES

1 Subjunctive in main clauses

1.1 Future

Iliad

1.150
1.184
1.205
1.262
3.054
3.138
3.417
4.016
6.459
7.087
7.197
7.291
8.354
9.61
9.62
9.619
9.619
9.701
9.702
11.387
11.404
11.433
13.742
13.744
14.129
14.235
15.63
15.350
16.129
16.437
16.650
16.650
17.451
18.188
18.308
22.418
22.505

Odyssey

1.396
3.22
3.22
4.29
4.391
4.692
5.299
5.465
5.465
6.126
6.201
6.275
9.37
10.507

13.215
13.215
14.183
14.184
14.184
15.300
15.509
15.509
15.511
16.74
16.74
16.76
16.138
16.304
16.437
17.418
18.265
19.528
22.167
22.168
23.73
24.337
24.405

1.2 Hortative

Iliad

1.62
1.141

1.142	9.26	15.297
1.143	9.27	15.477
1.144	9.65	16.205
2.139	9.66	17.340
2.140	9.112	17.634
2.236	9.165	17.712
2.236	9.625	18.266
2.435	9.704	18.297
2.436	10.70	18.304
2.440	10.97	19.148
3.94	10.126	19.237
3.283	10.251	20.119
3.441	10.344	20.136
4.14	11.348	20.244
4.62	11.348	20.258
4.418	11.469	20.300
5.34	12.75	21.160
5.34	12.78	21.309
5.249	12.216	21.467
5.469	12.241	22.130
5.718	12.328	22.231
6.70	13.115	22.231
6.226	13.292	22.243
6.230	14.61	22.254
6.340	14.74	22.381
6.526	14.76	22.392
7.29	14.76	22.392
7.38	14.77	22.450
7.290	14.128	23.7
7.299	14.314	23.9
7.333	14.340	23.48
7.336	14.370	23.98
7.337	14.374	23.239
7.339	15.060	23.244
7.341	15.060	23.485
7.351	15.062	23.486
8.502	15.294	23.537
8.503	15.295	23.661

23.661	13.13	*1.3 Prohibitive*
23.893	13.179	*Iliad*
24.208	13.182	
24.356	13.296	1.26
24.601	13.364	2.195
24.618	13.365	4.38
	14.45	5.233
Odyssey	14.168	5.233
1.76	15.219	5.233
1.85	15.399	5.236
1.369	16.348	5.236
1.372	16.349	5.488
2.168	16.371	5.489
2.404	16.383	5.684
2.410	16.384	8.95
3.18	16.389	9.33
3.240	16.402	9.522
4.213	17.190	14.111
4.776	17.194	15.115
6.31	17.274	16.128
8.31	18.420	16.128
8.34	20.246	17.93
8.100	20.271	17.95
8.100	20.383	18.8
8.133	21.135	21.563
8.292	22.73	21.564
8.389	22.75	22.123
8.394	22.139	23.407
10.44	22.429	23.428
10.177	23.83	24.053
10.192	23.117	24.568
10.228	23.254	24.779
10.269	24.358	
10.334	24.432	*Odyssey*
10.549	24.437	2.101
12.213	24.462	3.55
12.291	24.485	5.356
12.321	24.495	5.415

11.251	4.171	10.204
12.301	4.173	10.211
15.19	4.223	10.211
15.90	4.290	10.212
15.91	4.318	10.247
15.263	4.429	10.303
16.381	5.85	10.345
16.381	5.456	10.398
16.382	6.129	10.398
17.24	6.141	10.557
18.334	6.329	11.654
19.81	6.410	11.838
19.121	6.456	12.228
19.122	6.457	12.345
19.143	7.42	12.358
22.213	7.48	13.57
24.133	7.125	13.118
	7.456	13.238
	8.24	13.287

2 Optative in main clauses

	8.26	13.321
	8.26	13.324
	8.143	13.343
2.1 Potential	8.210	13.377
	9.257	13.378
Iliad	9.62	13.741
	9.125	13.815
1.232	9.157	14.79
2.160	9.267	14.108
2.176	9.299	14.191
2.242	9.303	14.247
3.41	9.373	14.248
3.52	9.376	14.333
3.53	9.386	14.336
3.220	9.417	15.45
3.392	9.437	15.70
3.410	9.444	15.197
4.93	9.601	15.697
4.94	10.57	16.16
4.95		

214

16.45	24.463	6.57
16.723	24.565	6.285
17.105	24.619	7.22
17.149	24.664	7.212
17.366	24.665	7.293
17.563	24.665	7.333
17.586	24.666	7.333
17.630	24.733	8.208
18.308		8.336
19.81	*Odyssey*	8.467
19.82	1.65	8.570
19.90	1.228	8.571
19.206	1.266	9.131
19.227	1.390	9.133
20.134	2.74	9.135
20.250	2.77	9.459
20.427	2.86	9.460
21.358	2.145	10.269
21.412	2.185	11.104
21.561	2.334	11.144
22.20	3.124	11.330
22.42	3.232	11.489
22.43	3.365	12.88
22.108	4.223	12.388
22.253	4.348	13.141
22.253	4.443	13.147
22.287	4.547	13.291
23.151	4.595	14.155
24.14	4.596	14.406
24.149	4.637	14.504
24.178	4.644	15.181
24.212	4.651	15.195
24.213	4.692	15.305
24.263	4.753	15.306
24.264	4.789	15.317
24.371	4.790	15.431
24.437	5.74	15.449
24.439	5.74	15.452

15.453	21.116	3.300
15.506	21.162	3.301
15.513	21.196	3.407
16.85	21.197	4.182
16.153	21.202	4.363
16.243	21.259	5.214
16.305	21.329	5.685
16.318	22.12	6.57
16.386	22.132	6.59
16.392	22.133	6.60
16.400	22.134	6.282
17.139	22.262	6.464
17.187	22.325	6.479
17.244	22.350	6.480
17.387	22.489	6.481
17.455	23.101	7.99
17.546	23.169	8.150
17.561	23.184	8.358
18.22	24.108	8.512
18.27	24.133	9.601
18.29	24.435	13.55
18.166	24.436	13.232
18.166		13.233
18.225		14.107
18.360	2.2 *Wish*	14.142
18.361		14.142
18.361	*Iliad*	15.82
18.415	1.18	15.476
19.294	1.20	16.30
19.348	1.42	16.247
19.569	2.259	17.341
19.579	2.260	17.417
19.598	2.340	17.640
20.323	2.418	18.98
20.326	3.102	18.107
20.392	3.102	18.121
21.77	3.160	18.124
21.113	3.255	18.125

19.264	8.340	18.79
20.121	8.341	18.112
20.121	8.342	18.122
21.274	8.409	18.141
21.360	8.411	18.142
21.429	8.413	18.147
22.286	8.414	18.147
22.304	8.465	20.79
23.91	9.534	20.80
23.650	9.535	20.117
24.139	11.613	20.119
24.139	12.106	20.199
24.226	13.42	20.236
24.246	13.43	20.344
24.556	13.44	21.201
24.556	13.45	21.201
	13.46	22.462
Odyssey	13.213	24.402
	13.229	24.461
1.47	14.53	24.491
1.265	14.172	
1.380	14.193	
1.387	14.195	
1.403	14.408	*2.3 Dynamic*
2.232	14.496	
2.232	14.503	*Iliad*
3.346	14.503	
4.668	15.112	1.100
4.685	15.128	1.272
4.699	15.180	1.301
4.735	15.359	2.12
5.10	17.243	2.29
5.10	17.243	2.66
6.180	17.355	3.66
6.181	17.399	3.223
7.148	17.476	3.235
7.149	17.597	3.235
7.224	18.79	4.539
7.316	18.79	5.192
		6.522

8.451	7.213	1.192
9.77	8.177	2.250
9.304	8.195	2.251
10.243	8.280	2.251
11.803	9.242	3.74
12.59	9.351	3.257
12.382	10.384	5.32
12.448	10.574	5.672
12.465	11.375	5.673
14.54	12.77	6.164
14.58	12.77	10.505
14.245	12.84	10.505
14.335	12.102	10.506
14.344	12.107	11.791
17.260	12.287	13.456
17.327	13.87	13.457
17.399	14.123	14.21
17.711	14.197	14.91
19.218	15.321	14.127
19.321	16.196	14.190
19.415	17.268	16.625
20.247	18.31	16.651
20.359	19.108	16.655
20.359	19.286	16.655
20.367	20.212	16.713
24.149	22.138	16.714
24.566	23.126	24.686
24.567	23.188	

Odyssey

Odyssey

1.402	*2.4 Objective*	2.335
1.402	*deontic*	2.336
3.114		3.170
4.64	*Iliad*	4.118
4.78		4.119
4.649	1.191	4.119
6.300	1.191	4.193
	1.192	6.142

6.144	3.281	9.255
10.52	3.284	9.278
10.52	3.289	9.359
15.24	4.98	9.359
15.300	4.170	9.362
17.236	4.170	9.393
17.237	4.353	9.393
18.91	4.353	9.412
18.92	4.363	9.414
18.92	4.416	9.429
20.11	4.416	9.604
20.135	5.129	9.692
21.193	5.132	10.55
22.335	5.225	10.107
22.337	5.232	10.346
23.86	5.258	10.449
23.87	5.260	10.449
24.238	5.351	10.452
24.238	5.763	11.315
	5.821	11.404
	6.94	11.405
3 Subjunctive in	6.260	11.455
conditional	6.275	12.71
protasis	6.309	12.71
	6.443	12.72
3.1 Specific	6.527	12.224
	7.77	12.245
Iliad	7.81	13.260
	7.81	13.380
1.90	7.118	13.743
1.129	7.173	13.829
1.137	8.142	14.110
1.324	8.287	14.311
1.341	8.471	14.369
1.580	8.478	15.499
2.364	8.482	15.504
2.364	9.136	16.32
3.26		

16.73	23.344	12.137
16.88	23.413	12.139
16.445	23.543	12.140
16.500	24.592	12.163
17.30	24.688	12.288
17.91	24.688	12.300
17.94		12.349
17.245	*Odyssey*	12.349
18.92	1.168	13.359
18.93	1.188	13.360
18.180	1.204	14.140
18.273	1.279	14.395
18.278	1.282	14.398
18.306	1.282	16.276
19.147	1.287	16.277
20.138	1.289	16.403
20.139	1.379	16.405
20.139	2.189	17.80
20.172	4.391	17.230
20.181	5.169	17.549
20.186	5.221	17.556
20.302	5.417	18.83
21.293	5.471	18.83
21.438	5.472	18.318
21.567	6.313	19.147
22.55	7.75	19.328
22.86	8.356	19.488
22.99	8.496	19.496
22.111	9.503	20.233
22.113	9.520	21.237
22.114	11.105	21.306
22.119	11.110	21.315
22.257	11.112	21.338
22.257	11.113	21.338
22.350	12.49	21.348
22.350	12.53	21.365
22.487	12.53	21.383
23.82	12.121	22.167

22.346	6.281	3.92
23.79	7.243	4.35
24.137	8.282	4.322
24.511	9.172	5.471
	11.791	12.96
	11.797	12.216
3.2 Iterative	11.799	13.182
	11.800	13.183
Iliad	12.275	15.312
1.81	13.236	17.51
1.166	14.78	17.60
4.262	14.165	20.225
9.481	15.297	22.77
10.225	16.39	22.253
11.116	16.41	
11.391	16.42	
12.239	16.725	*3.4 Complement*
12.302	16.725	
16.264	17.121	*Iliad*
21.576	17.652	4.249
21.576	17.692	7.375
22.191	18.143	7.394
	18.199	8.533
Odyssey	18.200	8.534
11.159	18.213	8.536
14.374	18.457	15.17
16.98	22.419	15.403
16.116	24.116	16.861
	24.116	18.601
	24.301	19.71
3.3 Hope	24.357	20.436
	24.357	22.245
Iliad		
1.67	*Odyssey*	*Odyssey*
1.207	1.94	2.333
1.408	2.144	14.118
1.420	2.186	22.07
5.279	2.216	22.07
6.277		

24.217	9.380	22.411
24.218	9.385	23.274
	9.389	23.346
4 Optative in	9.390	23.593
conditional	9.445	23.894
protasis	9.515	24.366
	9.515	24.653
4.1 Specific	9.516	
	10.190	*Odyssey*
Iliad	10.222	1.163
1.60	10.380	1.414
2.123	11.135	2.62
2.126	11.389	2.76
2.127	11.467	2.248
2.489	13.276	2.249
2.490	13.288	2.251
2.492	13.288	2.351
2.598	13.485	3.116
2.780	14.209	3.223
3.453	14.334	3.223
4.17	14.335	3.228
4.35	15.50	4.224
4.348	16.623	4.226
5.215	16.746	4.388
5.273	16.748	5.178
6.50	17.40	5.206
6.284	17.102	5.485
7.28	17.161	7.52
7.129	17.161	7.315
7.387	17.399	8.139
8.22	17.489	8.218
8.196	19.322	8.218
8.205	20.101	8.353
9.141	22.20	9.278
9.283	22.196	9.314
9.318	22.220	10.343
9.379	22.351	10.416

10.420	22.62	18.464
11.356	24.174	22.41
11.357		22.346
11.357	*4.2 Wish*	22.454
11.501		23.629
12.78	*Iliad*	23.629
12.88	2.372	24.74
12.345	4.178	
13.292	4.189	*Odyssey*
14.56	4.289	1.116
14.132	4.314	1.256
15.435	4.314	2.34
15.545	7.133	3.205
16.103	7.157	3.218
16.105	7.157	4.345
16.148	8.539	4.697
17.223	8.540	6.244
17.251	10.111	6.245
17.252	10.537	8.339
17.313	11.386	9.229
17.366	11.670	9.267
17.407	11.670	9.268
17.539	12.323	9.317
17.539	13.826	9.317
18.224	13.826	9.456
18.246	13.827	9.456
18.254	15.571	9.523
18.357	16.98	13.389
18.384	16.99	14.440
18.384	16.559	14.468
19.127	16.560	14.468
20.42	16.561	14.498
20.50	16.722	15.158
20.381	17.156	15.341
21.195	17.562	15.536
22.13	17.562	16.99
22.61	18.272	16.101

17.136
17.163
17.494
17.496
17.513
18.202
18.237
18.366
18.368
18.369
18.370
18.371
18.374
18.374
18.376
18.377
19.309
19.589
20.62
20.64
20.65
20.169
21.200
21.373
21.402

4.3 Hope

Iliad

2.98
2.98
3.450
4.88
5.168
10.206
10.207
12.123
12.333

13.760
13.807
14.163
17.104
17.681
18.322
20.464
20.464
20.465
22.246
23.40

Odyssey

1.117
1.117
2.343
4.317
5.439
6.144
6.144
9.350
9.418
9.422
10.147
10.147
11.480
11.628
12.113
12.114
12.334
13.415
14.460
14.461
15.316
20.327
22.77
22.91
22.382

4.4 Iterative

Iliad

24.768

5 Subjunctive in conditional apodosis

Iliad

1.137
1.324
2.365
9.394

Odyssey

4.389
17.137

6 Optative in conditional apodosis

Iliad

1.255
1.256
1.293
2.81
2.81
2.128
2.373
4.18
4.19
4.36

4.97	17.488	11.360
4.347	20.102	11.381
5.273	21.462	11.502
5.311	23.275	12.138
5.388	23.594	12.347
6.49	24.56	13.390
6.285	24.222	14.131
7.28	24.222	14.403
7.130	24.297	15.314
7.158	24.367	15.315
8.21	24.654	15.435
8.196	24.655	15.537
8.207	24.661	16.102
9.142		16.106
9.284	*Odyssey*	16.149
9.363	1.164	17.164
9.416	1.236	17.225
9.517	1.288	17.315
10.381	2.62	17.408
11.134	2.76	17.497
12.69	2.219	18.248
12.324	2.250	18.255
12.325	3.117	18.357
13.289	3.224	18.375
13.290	3.228	18.379
13.486	4.346	18.380
13.486	5.177	18.386
14.210	5.189	19.128
15.52	5.208	19.310
16.72	5.209	19.590
16.747	7.314	20.43
17.38	8.216	20.51
17.70	8.352	20.237
17.103	9.277	20.316
17.159	10.342	20.316
17.163	11.111	20.381
17.163	11.358	21.195
17.417	11.358	21.374

225

22.63	24.184	9.324
22.78	24.717	13.285
		15.363
7 Subjunctive in	*Odyssey*	21.575
subordinate	1.293	
clauses	1.293	*Odyssey*
	3.45	14.130
7.1 ἐπεί future	3.45	19.206
	4.412	19.515
Iliad	4.414	19.515
	4.494	20.86
4.239	5.363	20.202
6.83	6.262	24.7
6.412	6.297	
7.410	8.511	
9.358	10.526	*7.3 ὄφρα future*
9.707	11.120	
10.63	12.55	*Iliad*
11.192	14.153	
11.207	14.515	1.82
11.764	15.36	1.510
12.369	15.337	1.510
13.753	17.23	4.346
15.147	17.23	6.113
15.147	18.150	6.114
16.96	18.269	6.258
16.246	21.159	10.325
16.453	22.219	11.187
18.121	22.254	11.202
18.281	22.440	12.281
19.402		15.23
20.337		15.233
21.534	*7.2 ἐπεί simile*	16.10
22.68		17.186
22.125	*Iliad*	18.409
22.509	1.168	20.24
23.10	2.475	22.388
23.76	6.489	22.388
24.155	7.5	23.47

Odyssey	4.195	11.839
2.124	4.205	12.317
3.354	4.249	12.356
4.588	4.269	13.327
5.361	4.486	13.381
6.304	5.110	13.449
7.319	5.128	14.98
13.412	5.221	14.99
18.133	5.227	15.32
18.133	5.360	15.57
19.17	6.150	15.57
	6.231	15.59
7.4 ὄφρα *simile*	6.280	16.100
	6.361	16.243
Iliad	6.365	16.423
5.524	7.68	16.525
11.477	7.80	16.526
	7.85	16.568
7.5 ὄφρα *purpose*	7.86	17.480
	7.300	17.685
Iliad	7.349	18.63
1.119	7.369	18.114
1.133	8.6	19.102
1.158	8.105	19.144
1.185	8.191	19.191
1.186	8.376	19.191
1.411	8.406	19.232
1.515	8.420	20.185
1.524	9.258	20.213
1.579	9.370	20.303
1.579	9.423	21.61
2.237	9.428	21.61
2.299	9.691	21.487
2.359	10.97	21.558
2.440	10.146	22.56
3.105	10.425	22.57
3.163	10.444	22.58
3.353	10.444	22.282

22.343	7.187	17.11
22.382	7.317	17.52
23.52	8.27	17.469
23.53	8.42	17.509
23.210	8.242	18.43
23.737	8.395	18.183
24.075	8.432	18.352
24.295	8.477	18.364
24.313	8.556	19.45
24.431	9.13	19.98
24.636	9.17	19.98
24.658	9.18	20.292
24.658	9.280	20.297
	9.348	20.336
Odyssey	10.298	20.337
1.86	10.335	21.112
1.89	10.341	21.180
1.89	10.426	21.180
1.174	11.94	21.218
1.311	11.96	21.218
2.204	11.96	21.264
2.329	11.212	21.268
2.330	11.214	21.268
2.330	12.52	21.276
3.15	13.52	21.336
3.334	13.232	22.234
3.359	13.344	22.373
3.422	14.47	22.373
3.422	14.186	22.392
3.426	14.400	22.397
4.295	15.15	23.5
4.645	15.47	23.52
4.713	15.81	23.83
4.738	15.432	23.255
6.173	16.32	24.258
6.239	16.32	24.297
6.259	16.234	24.329
6.290	16.236	24.403

7.6 ἵνα *purpose*

Iliad

1.203	20.122	10.24
1.302	20.126	10.387
1.363	22.39	11.224
1.410	22.244	11.561
2.232	23.314	12.156
2.381	23.487	12.185
3.130	23.552	12.272
3.252	23.610	13.151
7.195	24.43	13.151
7.270	24.264	13.157
7.353?	24.382	13.303
8.180	24.467	13.304
8.515	24.555	13.306
9.99		13.327
9.495	*Odyssey*	13.364
9.512		13.418
9.614	1.95	15.219
11.290	1.302	15.309
12.435	1.373	16.184
14.274	2.111	16.369
14.365	2.112	17.175
14.365	2.307	17.529
14.484	3.78	18.30
15.31	3.200	18.54
15.402	3.327	18.204
16.19	3.361	18.339
17.445	3.361	20.267
17.522	3.476	22.168
18.387	4.591	
19.174	4.710	7.7 μή
19.174	5.91	
19.180	6.58	*Iliad*
19.275	6.311	
19.348	8.307	1.28
19.354	8.542	1.522
	8.580	1.555
	9.356	1.566
	9.517	1.587
	9.518	3.107

3.414	16.82	4.775
3.415	16.94	4.820
3.416	16.446	5.147
3.436	16.545	5.420
5.250	16.545	5.421
5.411	17.17	5.468
5.413	17.17	5.473
6.265	17.242	6.274
6.265	19.26	8.230
6.331	19.26	9.102
6.432	19.27	10.177
7.343	20.30	10.301
8.511	20.336	11.73
8.522	20.378	12.48
9.245	20.378	12.122
10.39	21.536	12.123
10.65	22.106	12.220
10.99	22.358	12.221
10.99	22.456	12.321
10.101	22.457	13.208
10.193	23.191	13.216
10.348	23.341	14.493
10.510	23.341	15.12
10.511	23.408	15.13
10.538	23.575	15.200
11.470	24.436	15.278
11.471	24.569	15.443
13.52	24.570	15.443
13.293	24.651	16.87
13.649		16.293
13.745	*Odyssey*	16.293
14.44	2.67	17.189
14.90	2.98	17.279
14.130	2.179	17.279
14.310	2.404	17.448
15.164	3.315	17.479
15.428	3.316	17.480
16.82	4.396	17.596

18.10	6.455	4.421
18.13	7.335	4.478
18.20	7.460	4.478
18.21	8.180	6.303
18.57	8.373	8.243
18.57	8.406	8.445
18.107	8.420	10.293
19.12	8.475	10.486
19.12	9.138	10.508
19.83	9.280	11.106
19.84	9.703	11.108
19.117	9.703	11.128
19.146	10.130	13.155
19.486	10.130	13.180
21.228	14.505	13.394
21.229	16.63	15.446
21.324	16.245	16.269
21.370	18.116	16.282
22.107	19.201	16.287
22.368	19.337	19.6
23.137	20.130	19.145
24.136	20.316	19.411
24.354	20.317	19.490
24.355	21.112	22.216
24.437	21.323	23.258
24.462	21.375	24.135
24.491	21.376	
	22.192	
7.8 ὅτε *future*	22.360	7.9 ὅτε *simile*
	22.366	
Iliad		*Iliad*
	Odyssey	1.80
1.519		1.164
1.567	1.41	2.147
4.41	2.100	2.395
4.53	2.358	2.397
4.164	2.358	4.131
4.167	2.374	4.141
6.448	4.420	5.91

231

5.501
5.598
6.507
10.5
11.155
11.269
11.293
11.305
11.325
11.415
12.451
13.334
13.572
13.589
14.414
15.80
15.170
15.207
15.210
15.264
15.359
15.382
15.606
15.624
15.681
16.53
16.212
16.298
16.365
16.386
16.642
16.690
17.62
17.390
17.522
17.756
18.207
19.183

19.375
20.168
20.495
21.199
21.258
21.347
21.522
22.75
22.189
24.369
24.417
24.480

Odyssey

3.238
4.337
4.400
6.183
7.72
8.147
13.101
14.60
15.409
16.72
17.472
17.520
18.134
19.567
20.196
21.133
22.469
23.233
23.235

7.10 ὅτε *iterative*

Iliad

2.782

4.230
4.260
4.344
6.225
9.501
9.501
12.286
13.271
14.522
17.98

Odyssey

9.6
9.8
9.10
10.217
10.411
11.17
11.18
11.218
14.170
14.374
20.84
20.85
23.275

7.11 *Relative future*

Iliad

1.139
1.549
2.231
2.347
2.361
2.366
3.71
3.71
3.92

3.92	17.100	2.161
3.287	17.230	2.193
3.354	17.230	2.213
3.460	18.271	2.229
4.191	18.467	3.355
4.306	19.72	4.29
5.033	19.110	4.756
5.421	19.235	6.28
7.171	20.250	6.37
8.34	20.308	6.202
8.405	20.363	8.549
8.419	20.454	9.356
8.430	21.127	10.288
8.465	21.296	10.539
9.75	21.484	11.135
9.101	22.130	11.149
9.102	23.248	13.400
9.146	23.345	14.139
9.166	23.345	15.21
9.288	23.554	15.311
9.397	23.805	15.448
9.424	23.806	15.453
9.615	23.855	16.350
10.67	23.857	17.11
10.235	24.92	17.19
10.282	24.119	17.559
10.306	24.147	18.46
11.367	24.176	18.46
12.227	24.196	18.47
13.234	24.335	18.63
14.127		18.86
14.190	*Odyssey*	18.270
15.46		18.286
15.109	1.158	18.336
15.148	1.316	19.28
15.148	1.389	19.323
15.495	2.25	19.378
17.93	2.43	19.403
	2.128	

19.406	1.294	15.580
19.577	1.527	16.54
20.115	1.543	16.387
20.335	1.554	16.388
20.342	2.294	16.590
21.75	3.62	16.622
21.76	3.66	17.134
21.280	3.109	17.631
22.66	3.279	17.658
23.140	4.483	17.726
23.282	5.6	18.208
24.454	5.138	18.209
	5.138	18.319
7.12 Relative	5.407	19.168
iterative	5.746	19.228
	6.228	19.230
Iliad	6.228	19.260
	6.229	21.24
8.408	9.117	21.104
8.422	9.140	21.158
9.510	9.282	21.283
9.510	9.313	21.347
11.409	9.313	22.23
12.48	10.185	22.73
13.229	11.559	23.322
16.260	13.64	23.518
17.110	13.138	23.761
	13.180	24.529
Odyssey	14.81	24.531
	14.81	24.759
1.416	14.376	
7.33	14.416	*Odyssey*
8.45	15.81	
	15.82	1.352
7.13 Relative	15.412	4.165
simile	15.491	4.196
	15.492	4.196
Iliad	15.492	4.208
		4.357
1.218		
1.230		

5.249	17.385	7.292
5.448	18.137	7.377
8.32	18.277	7.378
8.148	18.277	7.378
8.148	19.111	7.396
8.210	19.111	7.397
8.524	19.112	7.397
8.547	19.113	9.46
8.586	19.113	9.49
10.22	19.114	9.610
10.39	19.329	9.610
10.74	19.329	10.62
10.328	19.332	10.90
11.428	19.332	10.90
11.434	19.564	11.193
11.442	19.566	11.194
12.40	20.188	11.194
12.41	20.295	11.208
12.41	21.294	11.209
12.66	21.294	11.209
12.191	21.313	11.210
13.214	22.469	11.667
14.65	23.119	11.668
14.65	24.29	12.150
14.86	24.202	13.141
14.106	24.286	14.7
14.126		14.7
14.445		14.77
15.55	*7.14 εἰς ὅ future*	16.455
15.70		17.454
15.71	*Iliad*	17.622
15.281	2.332	21.128
15.345	3.291	21.231
15.401	5.466	21.232
15.401	7.31	21.532
15.422	7.71	23.244
16.77	7.72	24.154
16.228	7.292	24.183

235

Odyssey

5.378
6.296
6.296
8.318
9.139
9.139
10.461
11.122
13.60
15.26
15.51
15.53
15.75
15.76
15.76
15.543
17.56
19.143
22.59
22.73
22.444
22.444
23.269
23.358

7.15 εὖτε *future*

Iliad

1.243
2.34
19.158
19.159

7.16 εὖτε *iterative*

Iliad

2.228

Odyssey

7.202

7.17 εὖτε *simile*

Iliad

17.547

Odyssey

1.192
17.320
17.323
18.194

7.18 ὡς
complement

Iliad

1.559
1.559
4.67
4.72

7.19 ὡς *future*

Iliad

1.32
2.4
2.4
2.139
9.26
9.112
9.681
9.704
10.225
12.75

14.74
14.370
15.294
17.144
18.297
23.324

Odyssey

1.205
1.296
2.316
2.368
4.545
12.213
13.179
13.365
23.117

7.20 ὡς *simile*

Iliad

2.462
2.475
5.161
5.499
8.339
9.323
10.486
12.168
12.278
15.324
16.429
17.435
17.743
20.243
22.93

236

Odyssey

5.328
5.368
5.394
8.523
16.17
16.19

7.21 ὡς *purpose*

Iliad

2.363
2.385
3.110
3.166
6.69
6.96
6.143
6.259
6.358
6.364
7.294
7.335
7.463
8.37
8.182
8.509

8.509
8.513
9.311
15.235
16.083
16.84
16.86
16.86
16.273
17.635
17.636
17.713
17.714
19.151
20.429
21.459
23.339
24.76
24.76
24.337
24.337

Odyssey

1.77
1.87
2.376
3.19

4.749
5.26
5.27
5.31
5.144
5.164
5.168
7.193
7.195
8.101
8.251
13.402
14.181
16.84
19.319
19.321
22.177
24.360
24.532

7.22 πρίν *future*

Iliad

18.135
18.190
24.551
24.781

BIBLIOGRAPHY

Abbott, E. and Mansfield, E. D. 1977. *A Primer of Greek Grammar* (London: Duckworth).

Abraham, W. 1989. 'Futur-Typologie in den germanischen Sprachen', in Abraham and Janssen 1989: 345–89.

Abraham, W. and Janssen, T. (eds.). 1989. *Tempus – Aspekt – Modus: Die lexicalischen und grammatischen Formen in den Germanischen Sprachen* (Tübingen: Niemeyer).

Abraham, W., Givón T. and Thompson, S. A. (eds.). 1995. *Discourse Grammar and Typology* (Amsterdam: Benjamins).

Adamson, S. et al. (eds.). 1990. *Papers from the 5th International Conference on English Historical Linguistics* (Amsterdam: Benjamins).

Aijmer, K. 1985. 'The semantic development of will', in Fisiak 1985: 11–21.

Akatsuka, N. 1985. 'Conditionals and the epistemic scale', *Language,* 61.3: 624–39.

Allen, J. T. 1902. 'On the so-called Iterative Optative in Greek', *Transactions of the American Philological Association,* 33: 101–26.

Alpatov, V. M. 2001. 'Imperative in Modern Japanese', in Xrakovskij 2001b: 106–28.

Arbeitman, Y. L. (ed.). 1988. *A Linguistic Happening in memory of Ben Schwartz* (Louvain-la-Neuve: Peeters).

Asher, R. E. and Simpson, J. M. Y. (eds.). 1993. *Encyclopedia of Linguistics* (Oxford: Pergamon Press).

Athanasiadou, A. and Dirven, R. 1996. 'Typology of *if*-clauses', in Casad 1996: 609–54.

1997a. 'Conditionality, hypotheticality, counterfactuality', in Athanasiadou and Dirven 1997b: 61–96.

(eds). 1997b. *On Conditionals Again* (Amsterdam: Benjamins).

Austin, J. L. 1962. *How to do Things with Words* (Oxford: Clarendon Press).

Auwera, J. van der. 1983. 'Conditionals and antecedent possibilities', *Journal of Pragmatics,* 7: 297–309.

1986. 'The possibilities of *may* and *can*', in Kastovsky and Szwedek 1986 vol. II: 1067–76.

1997. 'Conditional perfection', in Athanasiadou and Dirven 1997b: 169–90.

Auwera, J. van der and Plungian, V. A. 1998. 'Modality's semantic map', *Linguistic Typology,* 2: 79–124.

Axmaker, S., Jaisser, A. and Singmaster, H. (eds.). 1988. *Proceedings of the Fourteenth Annual Meeting of the Berkeley Linguistics Society* (Berkeley: Berkeley Linguistics Society).

Bakker, E. J. 1988a. *Linguistics and Formulas in Homer: Scalarity and the Description of the Particle* περ (Amsterdam: Benjamins).

1988b. 'Restrictive conditionals', in Rijksbaron et al. 1988: 5–26.

Bakker, W. F. 1966. *The Greek Imperative: An Investigation into the Aspectual Differences between the Present and Aorist Imperatives in Greek Prayer from Homer up to the Present Day* (Amsterdam: Hakkert).

Bartsch, C. 1994. 'Translating the Lord's Prayer: are we telling God what to do?', *Notes on Translation*, 8: 1–3.

Basset, L. 1988. 'Valeurs et emplois de la particule dite modale en grec ancien', in Rijksbaron et al. 1988: 27–37.

1989. *La syntaxe de l'imaginaire: étude des modes et des négations dans l'Iliade et l'Odyssée* (Lyon: Maison de l'Orient Méditerranéen).

Bennett, C. E. 1910–14. *Syntax of Early Latin* (Boston: Allyn and Bacon).

Bennett, J. 1982. 'Even if', *Linguistics and Philosophy* 5: 403–18.

Benveniste, E. 1951. 'Prétérit et optatif en indo-européen', *Bulletin de la Societé Linguistique de Paris*, 47: 11–20.

1973. *Indo-European Language and Society*. Trans. by E. Palmer. Coral Gables, FL: University of Miami Press.

Biraud, M. 1985. 'La syntaxe de ὡς dans la langue Homérique: du subordonnant relatif au subordonnant conjonctif', in Braun 1985: 159–72.

Birjulin, L. A. and Xrakovskij, V. S. 2001. 'Imperative sentences: theoretical problems', in Xrakovskij 2001b: 3–54.

Boguslawski, A. 1985. 'The problem of the negated imperative in perfective verbs revisited', *Russian Linguistics*, 9: 225–39.

Bolkestein, A. M. 1980. *Problems in the Description of Modal Verbs in Latin* (Assen: Van Gorcum).

Bolling, G. M. 1949. 'ΟΦΡΑ in the Homeric poems', *Language*, 25: 379–87.

1960. 'Description of ἐπεί's syntax in Homer', *Glotta*, 38: 18–38.

Braun, R. (ed.). 1985. *Hommage à Jean Granarolo: Philologie, litteratures, et histoire anciennes* (Paris: Les Belles Lettres).

Bright, W. (ed.). 1992. *International Encyclopedia of Linguistics*, 4 vols. (New York: Oxford University Press).

Brisard, F. 1997. 'The English tense-system as an epistemic category: the case of futurity', in Verspoor et al. 1997: 271–85.

Brown, P. and Levinson, S. C. 1987. *Politeness: Some Universals in Language Usage* (Cambridge University Press).

Brugmann, K. 1916. *Grundriss der vergleichende Grammatik der indogermanische Sprachen* (Strasburg: Trübner).

Brunel, J. 1980. 'Les periodes conditionnelles du grec et le problème de l'optatif', *Bulletin de la Société Linguistique de Paris*, 75: 227–66.

Buck, C. D. 1933. *Comparative Greek and Latin Grammar* (University of Chicago Press).

1955. *The Greek Dialects* (University of Chicago Press).

Burrow, T. 1973. *Sanskrit Language* (London: Faber).

Bybee, J. L. 1985. *Morphology* (Amsterdam: Benjamins).

1988a. 'The diachronic dimension in explanation', in Hawkins 1988: 350–79.

1988b. 'Semantic substance vs. contrast in the development of grammatical meaning', in Axmaker et al. 1988: 247–64.

1995. 'The semantic development of past tense modals in English', in Bybee and Fleischman 1995: 503–70.

1998. '"Irrealis" as a grammatical category', *Anthropological Linguistics*, 40: 257–71.

Bybee, J. L. and Fleischman, S. (eds.). 1995. *Modality in Grammar and Discourse* (Amsterdam: Benjamins).

Bybee, J. L. and Pagliuca, W. 1985. 'Cross-linguistic comparison and the development of grammatical meaning', in Fisiak 1985: 59–83.

1987. 'The evolution of future meaning', in Ramat et al. 1987: 109–22.

Bybee, J. L., Pagliuca, W. and Perkins, R. D. 1991. 'Back to the future', in Traugott and Heine 1991 vol. II: 17–58.

1994. *The Evolution of Grammar: Tense, Aspect, and Modality in the Languages of the World* (University of Chicago Press).

Calboli, G. (ed.). 1989. *Subordination and Other Topics in Latin* (Amsterdam: Benjamins).

Casad, E. H. (ed.). 1996. *Cognitive Linguistics in the Redwoods: The Expansion of a New Paradigm in Linguistics* (Berlin: Mouton).

Chantraine, P. 1948. *Grammaire homérique*, 2 vols. (Paris: Klincksieck) (2nd edn).

1980. *Dictionnaire étymologique de la langue grecque: histoire des mots* (Paris: Klincksieck).

Chung, S. and Timberlake, A. 1985. 'Tense, aspect and mood', in Shopen 1985 vol. III: 202–58.

Coates, J. 1983. *The Semantics of the Modal Auxiliaries* (London: Croom Helm).

1995. 'The expression of root and epistemic possibility in English', in Bybee and Fleischman 1995: 55–66.

Cole, P. 1975. 'The synchronic and diachronic status of conversational implicature', in Cole and Morgan 1975: 257–88.

Cole, P. and Morgan, L. (eds.). 1975. *Syntax and Semantics vol. 3: Speech Acts* (New York: Academic Press).

Comrie, B. 1976. *Aspect* (Cambridge University Press).

1982. 'Future time reference in the conditional protasis', *Australian Journal of Linguistics*, 2: 143–52.

1985. *Tense* (Cambridge University Press).

1986a. 'Tense in indirect speech', *Folia Linguistica*, 20: 265–96.

1986b. 'Conditionals: a typology', in Traugott et al. 1986: 77–99.

1989. 'On identifying future tenses' in Abraham and Janssen 1989: 51–63.

Considine, P. and Hooker, J. T. (eds.). 1987. *Oswald Szemerényi Scripta Minora* (Innsbruck: Institut für Sprachwissenschaft der Universität Innsbruck).

Cristofaro, S. 1998. 'Grammaticalisation and clause linkage strategies', in Ramat and Hopper 1998: 59–88.

Crystal, D. 1985. *Dictionary of Linguistics and Phonetics* (Oxford: Blackwell).

Cuvalay, M. 1995. 'A classification of conditional satellites', in Devriendt et al. 1995: 149–75.

Dahl, O. 1979a. 'Review of Lyons *Semantics*', *Language*, 55: 199–206.

1985. *Tense and Aspect Systems* (Oxford: Blackwell).

1997. 'The relationship between past time reference and counterfactuality: a new look', in Athanasiadou and Dirven 1997b: 97–115.

Dancygier, B. 1998. *Conditionals and Prediction: Time, Knowledge, and Causation in Conditional Constructions* (Cambridge University Press).

Davies, E. 1986. *The English Imperative* (London: Croom Helm).

Delbrück, B. 1871. *Der Gebrauch der Conjunctivs und Optativs im Sanskrit und Griechischen* (Halle: Waisenhaus).

1879. *Die Grundlagen der griechischen Syntax* (Halle: Waisenhaus).

Dendale, P. and van der Auwera, J. (eds.). 2001. *Les verbes modaux* (Amsterdam: Rodopi).

Denniston, J. D. 1954. *The Greek Particles* (Oxford: Clarendon Press).

Devriendt, B., Goossens, L. and van der Auwera, J. (eds.). 1995. *Complex Structures: A functionalist perspective* (Berlin: Mouton).

Dik, S. C. 1990. 'On the semantics of conditionals', in Nuyts et al. 1990: 233–61.

Drubig, H. B. 2001. *On the Syntactic Form of Epistemic Modality.* MS., Univ. Tübingen, http://www.sfb441.uni-tuebingen.de/b2/papers/DrubigModality.pdf

Elmsley, P. 1825. *Oedipus Tyrannus* (London: Whittaker).

Enç, M. 1996. 'Tense and modality', in Lappin 1996: 345–58.

Etter, A. (ed.). 1986. *O-o-pe-ro-si: Festschrift fur Ernst Risch zum 75. Geburtstag* (Berlin: Mouton).

Faarland, J. T. 1985. 'Imperative and control. First person imperatives in Norwegian', *Nordic Journal of Linguistics,* 8: 149–60.

Fillmore, C. J. 1990. 'Epistemic stance and grammatical form in English conditional sentences', *Papers from the 26th Regional Meeting of the Chicago Linguistic Society*: 137–62.

Fisiak, J. (ed.). 1985. *Historical Semantics and Historical Word Formation* (Berlin: Mouton).

Fleischman, S. 1982. *The Future in Thought and Language* (Cambridge University Press).

1995. 'Imperfective and irrealis', in Bybee and Fleischman 1995: 519–51.

Flier, M. S. and Timberlake, A. (eds.). 1985. *The Scope of Slavic Aspect* (Columbus: Slavica).

Foley, W. A. and van Valin, R. D. 1984. *Functional Syntax and Universal Grammar* (Cambridge University Press).

Foolen, A. and Leek, F. (eds.). 2000. *Constructions in Cognitive Linguistics* (Amsterdam: Benjamins).

Fortescue, M., Harder, P. and Kristofferson, L. (eds.). 1992. *Layered Structure and Reference in a Functional Perspective* (Amsterdam: Benjamins).

Fortson, B. W. 1994. *Indo-European Language and Culture: an Introduction* (Oxford: Blackwell).

Friedrich, P. 1974. 'On aspect theory and Homeric aspect', *International Journal of Linguistics Memoir 28.*

Fries, C. C. 1927. 'The expression of the future', *Language,* 3: 87–95.

Geis, M. L. and Zwicky, A. M. 1971. 'On invited inferences', *Linguistic Inquiry,* 2: 561–6.

Gerø, E.-C. 2000. 'The usage of ἄν and κε in Ancient Greek: towards a unified description', *Glotta,* 76: 177–91.

Gilbert, E. 2001. 'A propos de *will*', in Dendale and van der Auwera 2001: 123–39.

Gildersleeve, B. L. 1882. 'Studies in Pindaric syntax I. The conditional sentence in Pindar', *American Journal of Philology,* 3: 434–45.

　1883. 'On the final sentence in Greek', *American Journal of Philology,* 4: 416–44.

　1906. 'Notes on the evolution of Oratio Obliqua', *American Journal of Philology,* 27: 200–8.

Givón, T. 1994. 'Irrealis and the subjunctive', *Studies in Language,* 18: 265–337.

Golovko, E. V. 2001. 'Imperatives in Aleut', in Xrakovskij 2001b: 300–14.

Gonda, J. 1956. *The Character of the Indo-European Moods* (Wiesbaden: Harrassowitz).

Goodwin, W. W. 1870. *A Greek Grammar* (London: Macmillan).

　1876. '*Shall* and *should* in Protasis, and their Greek equivalents', *Transactions of the American Philological Association,* 8: 87–107.

　1889. *Syntax of the Moods and Tenses of the Greek verb* (London: Macmillan).

Gordon, D. and Lakoff, G. 1975. 'Conversational postulates', in Cole and Morgan 1975: 83–104.

Greenberg, J. H. (ed.). 1978. *Universals of Human Language,* 4 vols. (Stanford University Press).

　1986. 'The realis-irrealis continuum in the Classical Greek conditional', in Traugott et al. 1986: 247–64.

Grice, H. P. 1975. 'Logic and conversation', in Cole and Morgan 1975: 41–58.

de Haan, F. 1998. 'Review of Bybee and Fleischman (eds.) 1995 *Modality in Grammar and Discourse*', *Linguistic Typology,* 2: 125–81.

Haegeman, L. 1989. '*Be going to* and *will:* a pragmatic account', *Journal of Linguistics,* 25: 291–317.

Hahn, E. A. 1951. 'Apollonius Dyscolus on mood', *Transactions of the American Philological Association,* 82: 29–48.

1953. *Subjunctive and Optative: Their origin as Futures* (New York: American Philological Association).

Haiman, J. (ed.). 1985. *Iconicity in Syntax* (Amsterdam: Benjamins).

Hainsworth, J. B. 1988. 'The epic dialect' in Heubeck et al. 1988 vol. I: 24–32.

Halliday, M. A. K. 1970. 'Functional diversity in language', *Foundations of Language*, 6: 322–61.

Hancher, M. 1979. 'The classification of cooperative illocutionary acts', *Language and Society*, 8: 1–14.

Handford, S. A. 1947. *The Latin Subjunctive* (London: Methuen & Co.).

Harris, A. C. and Campbell, L. 1995. *Historical Syntax in Cross-linguistic Perspective* (Cambridge University Press).

Harris, M. B. 1986. 'The historical development of si-clauses in Romance', in Traugott et al 1986: 265–84.

Haspelmath, M. et al. (eds.). 2001. *Language Typology and Language Universals: An International Handbook* (Berlin: Mouton).

Haverkate, H. 2002. *The Syntax, Semantics and Pragmatics of Spanish Mood* (Amsterdam: Benjamins).

Hawkins, J. A. 1978. *Definiteness and Indefiniteness* (London: Croom Helm).

(ed.). 1988. *Explaining Language Universals* (Oxford : Blackwell).

Heine, B. 1995a. 'Agent-oriented vs. epistemic modality: some observations on German modals', in Bybee and Fleischman 1995: 17–53.

1995b. 'On the German *werden* future', in Abraham et al. 1995: 119–38.

Heine, B., Claudi, U. and Hünnemeyer, F. 1991. *Grammaticalisation: A Conceptual Framework* (University of Chicago Press).

Hentze, C. 1909. 'Der Homerische Gebrauch der εἰ-Sätze mit dem Indikativ des Futurum', *Zeitschrift für Vergleichende Sprachforschung*, 42: 131–46.

Hettrich, H. 1992. 'Lateinische Konditionalsätze in sprachvergleichender Sicht', in Panagl and Krisch 1992: 263–84.

Heubeck, A. et al. 1988. *A Commentary on Homer's Odyssey*, 3 vols. (Oxford University Press).

Hewson, J. and Bubenik, V. 1997. *Tense and Aspect in Indo-European Languages* (Amsterdam: Benjamins).

Hoffman, K. 1967. *Der Injunktiv im Veda* (Heidelberg: Winter).

Hopper, P. J. and Traugott, E. C. 1993. *Grammaticalization* (Cambridge University Press).

Horrocks, G. 1980. 'The antiquity of the Greek epic tradition. Some new evidence', *Proceedings of the Cambridge Philological Society*, 26: 1–11.

1995. 'On condition . . .: aspect and modality in the history of Greek', *Proceedings of the Cambridge Philological Society*, 41: 153–73.

1997. 'Homer's dialect', in Morris and Powell 1997: 193–217.

Howorth, R. H. 1955. 'The origin of the use of ἄν and κε in indefinite clauses', *Classical Quarterly*, 5: 72–93.

Humbert, J. 1943. *Syntaxe grecque* (Paris: Klincksieck).

Jacobs, J. et al. (eds.). 1995. *Syntax: An International Handbook of Contemporary Research*, 2 vols. (Berlin: Walter de Gruyter).

Jacobsson, B. 1984. 'Notes on tense and modality in conditional *if*-clauses', *Studia Linguistica*, 38: 129–47.

JACT. 1978. *Reading Greek* (Cambridge University Press).

Jakobson, R. 1984. *Russian and Slavic Grammar: Studies 1931–1981* (Berlin: Mouton).

James, D. 1982. 'Past tense and the hypothetical. A cross-linguistic study', *Studies in Language*, 6: 375–403.

Janko, R. 1982. *Homer, Hesiod and the Hymns. Diachronic Development in Epic Diction* (Cambridge University Press).

1985. *The Iliad: a Commentary* (vol. IV of Kirk et al. 1985) (Cambridge University Press).

Janssen, T. A. J. M. and van der Wurff, W. (eds.). 1993. *Reported Speech* (Amsterdam: Benjamins).

Jebb, R. C. (ed.). 1885. *The Oedipus Coloneus* (Cambridge University Press).

1893. *The Oedipus Tyrannus* (Cambridge University Press) (3rd edn).

Jespersen, O. 1917. *Negation in English and Other Languages* (Copenhagen: Host).

1924. *The Philosophy of Grammar* (London: Allen and Unwin).

Joos, M. 1964. *The English Verb* (Madison: University of Wisconsin Press).

Justus, C F. 1993. 'Mood correspondences in older Indo-European prayer petitions', *General Linguistics,* 33: 129–61.

2000. 'Word order and the first person imperative', in Sornicola et al. 2000: 165–84.

Karttunen, L. 1971. 'Counterfactual conditionals', *Linguistic Inquiry,* 2: 566–69.

Kastovsky, D. and Szwedek, A. 1986. *Linguistics across Historical and Geographical boundaries*, 2 vols. (Berlin: Mouton).

Kibardina, S. M. 2001. 'Imperative constructions in German', in Xrakovskij 2001b: 315–28.

Kiefer, F. 1993. 'Modality' in Asher and Simpson 1993: 2515–20.

Kiparsky, P. 1968. 'Tense and mood in Indo-European syntax', *Foundations of Language,* 4: 30–57.

Kiparsky, P. and Kiparsky, C. 1971. 'Fact' in Steinberg and Jakobovits 1971: 345–69.

Kirk, G. S. et al. 1985. *The Iliad: A Commentary*, 6 vols. (Cambridge University Press).

Klein, F. 1975. 'Pragmatic constraints in distribution: the Spanish subjunctive', *Chicago Linguistic Society,* 11: 353–65.

Knünz, I. 1913. *De enuntiatis Graecorum finalibus* (Innsbruck).

König, E. 1986. 'Conditionals, concessive conditionals and concessives: areas of contrast, overlap and neutralization', in Traugott et al. 1986: 229–46.

Kozintseva, N. A. 2001. 'Imperative sentences in Armenian', in Xrakovskij 2001b: 245–67.

Kučera, H. 1985 'Aspect in negative imperatives' in Flier and Timberlake 1985: 118–28.

Kühner, R. and Gerth, B. 1898–1904. *Ausführliche Grammatik der griechischen Sprache* (Hannover/Leipzig: Hahn).

Kuryłowicz, J. 1956. 'Review of Gonda *The Character of the Indo-European moods*', *Kratylos*, 1: 123–30.

1964. *The Inflectional Categories of Indo-European* (Heidelberg: Carl Winter).

Lakoff, R. T. 1968. *Abstract Syntax and Latin Complementation* (Cambridge: MIT Press).

Lang, M. 1989. 'Unreal conditions in Homeric narrative', *Greek, Roman and Byzantine Studies*, 30: 5–26.

Langacker, R. W. 1991. *Foundations of Cognitive Grammar. Volume II. Descriptive Application* (Stanford University Press).

1997. 'Generics and habituals', in Athanasiadou and Dirven 1997b: 191–222.

Lappin, S. (ed.). 1996. *The Handbook of Contemporary Semantic Theory* (Oxford: Blackwell).

Leaf, W. 1900. *The Iliad* (London: Macmillan).

Leclerc, A. 2001. 'Verbal moods and sentence moods in the tradition of universal grammar', in Vanderveken and Kubo 2001: 63–84.

Lehmann, C. 1992. 'Relativization', in Bright 1992 vol. IV: 333–5.

1995. 'Relativsätze', in Jacobs et al. 1995 vol. II: 1199–1216.

Létoublon, F. (ed). 1992. *La langue et les textes en grec ancien* (Amsterdam: Gieben).

Leumann, M. 1953. '"Aoristi mixti" und Imperative vom Futurstamm im Griechischen', *Glotta*, 32: 204–13.

Lichtenberk, F. 1995. 'Apprehensional epistemics', in Bybee and Fleischman 1995: 293–327.

Liddell, H. G. and Scott, R. 1940. *A Greek – English Lexicon* (9th edn) (Oxford: Clarendon Press).

Lightfoot, D. 1975. *Natural Logic and the Greek Moods: The Nature of the Subjunctive and Optative in Classical Greek* (The Hague: Mouton).

Louw, J. P. 1959. 'On Greek prohibitions', *Acta Classica*, 2: 43–57.

Lunn, P. V. 1995. 'The evaluative function of the Spanish subjunctive', in Bybee and Fleischman 1995: 429–49.

Lyons, J. 1977. *Semantics* (Cambridge University Press).

Macdonell, A. A. 1917. *A Vedic Grammar for Students* (Oxford: Clarendon Press).

Magnien, V. 1912. *Emplois et origines du futur grec*, 2 vols. (Paris: Champion).

Malčukov, A. L. 2001. 'Imperative constructions in Even', in Xrakovskij 2001b: 159–80.

Malygina, L. V. 2001. 'Imperative sentences in Modern Hebrew', in Xrakovskij 2001b: 268–86.

Martinich, A. P. (ed.). 1985. *The Philosophy of Language* (Oxford University Press) (3rd edn).

McKay, K. L. 1981. 'Repeated action, the potential and reality in ancient Greek', *Antichthon*, 15: 36–46.

1986. 'Aspects of the imperative in Ancient Greek', *Antichthon*, 20: 41–58.

Meibauer, J. (ed.). 1987. *Satzmodus zwischen Grammatik und Pragmatik* (Tubingen: Niemeyer).

Meid, W. 1962. 'Die sprachliche Form des Prohibitivsatzes im Altirischen', *Zeitschrift für Celtische Philologie*, 29: 155–72.

1963. *Die Indogermanischen Grundlagen der Altirischen Absoluten und Konjunkten Verbalformen* (Wiesbaden: Harrassowitz).

1968. 'Remarks on the origin of Old Irish', *Studia Celtica* 3: 1–8.

Meillet, A. and Vendryes, J. 1927. *Traité de grammaire comparée des langues classiques* (Paris) (2nd edn).

Melo, C. J. de S. 2001. 'Possible directions of fit between mind, language and the world', in Vanderveken and Kubo 2001: 109–17.

Merry, W. W., Riddell, J. and Monro, D. B. 1886. *Commentary on the Odyssey* (Oxford: Clarendon Press).

ter Meulen, A. 1986. 'Generic information, conditional contexts and constraints', in Traugott et al. 1986: 123–45.

Mitchell, B. 1985. *Old English Syntax* (Oxford: Clarendon Press).

Mithun, M. 1995. 'On the relativity of Irreality', in Bybee and Fleischman 1995: 367–88.

Monro, D. B. 1891. *Homeric Grammar* (Oxford University Press).

Monteil, P. 1963. *La phrase relative en grec ancien* (Paris: Klincksieck).

Moore, R. W. 1934. *Comparative Greek and Latin Syntax* (London: Bell).

Moorhouse, A. C. 1959. *Studies in the Greek Negatives* (Cardiff: University of Wales Press).

Moreno de Alba, J. G. 1977. 'Vitalidad del futuro del indicativo en la norma culta del español hablada en México', *Anuario de Letras*, 8: 81–102.

Morris, I. and Powell, B. (eds). 1997. *A New Companion to Homer* (Leiden: Brill).

Mortelmans, T. 2000. 'Konjunktiv II and epistemic modals in German: a division of labour', in Foolen and Leek 2000: 191–215.

Moulton, J. H. 1908. *A Grammar of New Testament Greek* (Edinburgh: Clark) (3rd edn).

Myhill, J. 1998. 'A study of imperative usage in biblical Hebrew and English', *Studies in Language*, 22: 391–446.

Nagy, G. 2004. *Homer's Text and Language* (Champaign: University of Illinois Press).

Neuberger-Donath, R. 1980. 'The obligative infinitive in Homer and its relationship to the imperative', *Folia Linguistica*, 14: 65–82.

1982. 'Der Gebrauch von ὅτι und ὡς in Subjekt- und Objekt-Sätzen', *Rheinisches Museum*, 125: 252–74.

Nuyts, J. 2000. *Epistemic Modality, Language, and Conceptualisation* (Amsterdam: Benjamins).

Nuyts, J. et al. (eds.). 1990. *Layers and Levels of Representation in Language* (Amsterdam: Benjamins).

Palmer, F. R. 1983a. 'Future time reference in the conditional protasis: a comment on Comrie', *Australian Journal of Linguistics,* 3: 241–3.

1983b. 'Review of Coates *The Semantics of the Modal Auxiliaries'*, *Australian Journal of Linguistics,* 3: 287–93.

1986. *Mood and Modality* (Cambridge University Press) (1st edn).

1987. 'The typology of subordination: results, actual and potential', *Transactions of the Philological Society,* 85: 90–109.

1990. *Modality and the English Modals* (London: Longman) (2nd edn).

1995. 'Negation and the modals of possibility and necessity', in Bybee and Fleischman 1995: 453–71.

2000. *Mood and Modality* (Cambridge University Press) (2nd edn).

Palmer L. R. 1962. 'The language of Homer,' in Wace and Stubbings 1962: 75–178.

1980. *The Greek Language* (London: Faber).

Panagl, O. and Krisch, T. (eds.). 1992. *Latein und indogermanisch* (Innsbruck: Institut für Sprachwissenschaft der Universität Innsbruck).

Parry, M. 1928. *L'epithète traditionelle dans Homère* (Paris: Les belles lettres).

1930. 'Studies in the epic technique of oral verse making I: Homer and the Homeric style', *Harvard Studies in Classical Philology,* 41: 73–147.

1932. 'Studies in the epic technique of oral verse making II: the Homeric language as the language of an oral poetry', *Harvard Studies in Classical Philology,* 43: 1–50.

Podlesskaya, V. 2001. 'Conditional constructions', in Haspelmath et al. 2001: 998–1010.

Prior, A. N. 1967. *Past, Present and Future* (Oxford: Clarendon Press).

Quirk, R. et al. 1985. *A Comprehensive Grammar of the English Language* (London: Longman).

Ramat, A. G. (ed.). 1979. *Linguistic Reconstruction and Indo-European Syntax* (Amsterdam: Benjamins).

Ramat, A. G. and Hopper, P. J. (eds.). 1988. *Limits of Grammaticalisation* (Amsterdam: Benjamins).

Ramat, A. G. et al. (eds.). 1987. *Papers from the 7th International Conference on Historical Linguistics* (Amsterdam: Benjamins).

Rijksbaron, A. 1984. *The Syntax and Semantics of the Verb in Classical Greek* (Amsterdam: Gieben).

Rijksbaron, A. (ed.). 1997. *New Approaches to Greek Particles. Proceedings of the Colloquium Held in Amsterdam, January 4–6, 1996, to Honour C. J. Ruijgh on the Occasion of his Retirement* (Amsterdam: Gieben).

Rijksbaron, A., Mulder, H. A. and Wakker, G. C. (eds.). 1988. *In the Footsteps of Raphael Kühner* (Amsterdam: Gieben).

Risch, E. 1961. 'Review of Gonda *The Character of the Indo-European Moods'*, *Gnomon,* 33: 175–8.

Risselada, R. 1993. *Imperatives and Other Directive Expressions in Latin : a Study in the Pragmatics of a Dead Language* (Amsterdam: Gieben).

Rix, H. 1986. *Zur Entstehung des urindogermanischen Modussystem* (Innsbruck: Institut für Sprachwissenschaft der Universität Innsbruck).

Romaine, S. 1995 'The grammaticalization of irrealis in Tok Pisin', in Bybee and Fleischman 1995: 389–427.

Roth, C. P. 1974. 'More Homeric "Mixed Aorists"', *Glotta*, 52: 1–10.

Ruijgh, C. J. 1971. *Autour de 'τε épique'. Études sur la syntaxe greque* (Amsterdam: Hakkert).

1992. 'L'emploi le plus ancien et les emplois plus recents de la particule κε/ἄν', in Létoublon 1992: 75–84.

Sadock, J. M. and Zwicky, A. M. 1985. 'Speech act distinctions in syntax', in Shopen 1985 vol. I: 155–95.

Schmidt, G. 1986. 'Zum indogermanischen s-Futur', in Etter 1986: 33–59.

Scholz, U. 1987. 'Wunschsätze im Deutschen – formale und funktionale Beschreibung', in Meibauer 1987: 234–58.

Schwyzer, E. and Debrunner, A. 1950. *Griechische Grammatik* (Munich: Beck).

Searle, J. R. 1965. 'What is a speech act?', reprinted in Martinich 1985: 141–55.

1975. 'Indirect speech acts', reprinted in Martinich 1985: 168–82.

1979. 'A taxonomy of illocutionary acts', reprinted in Martinich 1985: 14–182.

Seiler, H. 1956. 'Review of Gonda *The Character of the Indo-European Moods*', *Kratylos*, I: 131–55.

1971. 'Abstract structures for moods in Greek', *Language*, 47: 78–9.

Serbat, G. 1975. 'Les temps du verbe en Latin II', *Revue des études latines*, 53: 390–405.

Shields, K. 1978. 'A Note on I.E. *tōt*', *Journal of Indo-European Studies*, 6: 133–40.

1988. 'Some thoughts about the origin of the Indo-European optative and subjunctive', in Arbeitman 1988: 543–57.

Shipp, G. P. 1972. *Studies in the language of Homer* (Cambridge University Press) (2nd edn).

Shopen, T. (ed.) 1985. *Language Typology and Syntactic Description*, 3 vols. (Cambridge University Press).

Sicking, C. M. J. 1991. 'The distribution of aorist and present tense stem forms in Greek, especially in the imperative (I and II)', *Glotta*, 69: 14–43; 154–70.

Sideri, C. 1996. 'L'Evolution de l'optatif en grec ancien', *Cahiers de l'Institut de Linguistique de Louvain*, 22: 205–9.

Sihler, A. L. 1995. *New Comparative Grammar of Greek and Latin* (New York; Oxford: Oxford University Press).

Skerrett, R. A. Q. 1971. 'Statement, command, question and wish', *Studia Celtica*, 6: 158–62.

Slotty, F. 1915. *Der Gebrauch des Konjunctivs und Optativs in den griechischen Dialekten* (Göttingen: Vandenhoeck & Ruprecht).

Smyth, H. W. 1956. *Greek Grammar* (Cambridge: Harvard University Press).

Sornicola, R. et al. (eds.). 2000. *Stability, Variation and Change of Word-Order Patterns over Time* (Amsterdam: Benjamins).

Stahl, J. M. 1907. *Kritisch-historische Syntax des Griechischen Verbums der klassischen Zeit* (Heidelberg: Winter).

Steele, S. 1975. 'Past and Irrealis: just what does it all mean?', *International Journal of American Linguistics*, 41: 200–17.

Steinberg, D. D. and Jakobovits, L. A. (eds.). 1971. *Semantics: an Interdisciplinary Reader in Philosophy, Linguistics and Psychology* (Cambridge University Press).

Stephens, L. 1983. 'The origins of a Homeric peculiarity: μή plus aorist imperative', *Transactions of the American Philological Association*, 113: 69–78.

Sweetser, E. E. 1990. *From Etymology to Pragmatics* (Cambridge University Press).

Szemerényi, O. 1954. 'The future imperative of Indo-European' reprinted in Considine and Hooker 1987: 5–23.

    1996. *Introduction to Indo-European Linguistics* (Oxford: Clarendon Press).

Tabachovitz, D. 1951. *Homerische εἰ Sätze* (Lund: Gleerup).

Thomas, F. 1938. *Recherches sur le subjonctif latin* (Paris: Klincksieck).

Traugott, E. C. 1985. 'Conditional markers', in Haiman 1985: 289–307.

    1989. 'On the rise of epistemic meanings in English: an example of subjectification in semantic change', *Language*, 65: 31–55.

    1990. 'From less to more situated in language: the unidirectionality of semantic change', in Adamson et al. 1990: 497–517.

    1997. 'Unless and but conditionals: a historical perspective' in Athanasiadou and Dirven 1997b: 145–67.

Traugott, E. C. and Dasher, R. B. 2002. *Regularity in Semantic Change* (Cambridge University Press).

Traugott, E. C. and Heine, B. (eds.). 1991. *Approaches to Grammaticalisation*, 2 vols. (Amsterdam: Benjamins).

Traugott, E. C. et al. (eds.). 1986. *On Conditionals* (Cambridge University Press).

Tynan, J. and Lavin, E. D. 1997. 'Mood, tense and the interpretation of conditionals', in Athanasiadou and Dirven 1997b: 115–42.

Ultan, R. 1978. 'The nature of future tenses', in Greenberg 1978 vol. III: 83–123.

Urdiales, J. M. 1966. *El habla de Villacidayo (Léon)* (Madrid Real Academia Española).

Vai, M. 1998. 'Imperativi negati, imperativi subordinati', *Acme: Annali della Facoltà dell'Università degli Studi di Milano*, 51: 51–71.

Vairel, H. 1979. 'Moindre actualité et moindre actualisation: sur l'emploi des formes verbales de passé en anglais, francais et latin; le problème de l'optatif grec', *Revue roumaine de linguistique*, 24: 578–84.

van der Wurff, W. 1993. 'Sequence of tenses in English and Bengali', in Janssen and van der Wurff 1993: 261–86.

Vandaele, H. 1897. *L'optatif grec: essai de syntaxe historique* (Paris: Bouillon).

Vanderveken, D. 1990. *Meaning and Speech Acts* (Cambridge University Press).

Vanderveken, D. and Kubo, S. (eds.). 2001. *Essays in Speech Act Theory* (Amsterdam: Benjamins).

Verspoor, M. et al. (eds.). 1997. *Lexical and Syntactical Constructions and the Construction of Meaning* (Amsterdam: Benjamins).

Verstraete, J.-C. 2001. 'Subjective and objective modality: interpersonal and ideational functions in the English modal auxiliary system', *Journal of Pragmatics*, 33: 1503–28.

Vester, E. 1989. 'Relative clauses: a description of the indicative-subjunctive opposition', in Calboli 1989: 327–50.

Wace, A. J. B. and Stubbings, F. H. 1962. *A Companion to Homer* (London: Macmillan).

Wackernagel, J. 1926. *Vorlesungen über Syntax, mit besonderer Berücksichtigkeit von Griechisch, Lateinisch und Deutsch* (Basel: Burkhäuser) (2nd edn).

Wakker, G. C. 1986. 'Potential and contrary-to-fact conditionals in Classical Greek', *Glotta*, 64: 222–46.

   1992a. 'Conditionals in the layered structure of functional grammar', in Fortescue et al. 1992: 369–86.

   1992b. 'Review of Basset *Syntaxe de l'imaginaire*', *Mnemosyne*, 45: 241–8.

   1994. *Conditions and Conditionals : an Investigation of Ancient Greek* (Amsterdam: Gieben).

Wathelet, P. 1997. 'Les particules ke(n) et an dans les formules de l'épopée homérique', in Rijksbaron 1997: 247–68.

West, M. L. 2001. *Studies in the Text and Transmission of the Iliad* (München: Saur).

Whitney, W. D. 1892. 'On Delbrück's Vedic Syntax', *American Journal of Philology*, 13: 271–306.

Wierzbicka, A. 1997. 'Conditionals and counterfactuals: conceptual primitives and linguistic universals', in Athanasiadou and Dirven 1997b: 15–59.

Wymann, A. T. 1996. 'The expression of mood in Korean' at www.wymann.info/Korean/atw_diss.pdf

Xrakovskij, V. S. (ed.). 1997. *Typology of Iterative Constructions* (Munich: LINCOM Europa).

   2001a. 'Hortative constructions', in Haspelmath et al. 2001: 1028–38.

   2001b. *Typology of Imperative Constructions* (Munich: LINCOM Europa).

Zycha, J. 1885. 'Gebrauch von ἐπεί ἐπείπερ; ἐπειδήπερ', *Wiener Studien* 7: 82–115.

Editions of works quoted from:

Homer *Iliad*

West, M. L. (ed.). 1998. *Homeri Ilias* (Stuttgart: Teubner).

Homer *Odyssey*

Allen, T. W. 1917. *Homeri Opera* (Oxford: Clarendon Press).

Sophocles *Philoctetes*

Lloyd-Jones, H. and Wilson, N. G. (eds.). 1990. *Sophoclis Fabulae* (Oxford: Clarendon Press).

Aeschylus *Eumenides*

Page, D. (ed.). 1972. *Aeschyli Tragoediae* (Oxford: Clarendon Press).

Aristophanes *Clouds*

Hall, F. W. and Geldart, W. M. (eds.). 1907. *Aristophanes Comoediae* (Oxford. Clarendon Press).

Thucydides *Histories*

Jones, H. S. (ed.). 1902. *Thucydides Historiae* (Oxford: Clarendon Press).

INDEX LOCORUM

Iliad

1.001	125
1.017	135
1.020	125, 130, 147
1.029	55
1.032	166
1.042	126
1.081	179
1.090	66
1.100	138
1.123	70
1.129	66
1.135	69
1.136	75, 76
1.137	66
1.158	168
1.166	153, 175
1.175	201
1.181	62
1.184	17, 30, 63
1.205	81
1.211	76
1.242	54, 72
1.255	31, 116
1.262	19, 64
1.272	138
1.301	138, 143
1.324	61, 66, 209
1.341	66, 74, 160, 164
1.363	104
1.510	73, 157
1.515	73, 157
1.518	76
1.564	40
1.580	66
1.610	180
2.003	76
2.012	138
2.029	138, 143
2.034	72
2.066	138
2.081	123
2.140	17
2.156	47, 121
2.231	76
2.236	81
2.250	145, 204
2.252	76
2.260	124
2.299	157
2.357	42, 44, 67
2.361	186
2.364	66
2.418	124
2.471	179
2.488	141
3.023	179
3.026	66
3.033	179
3.054	62
3.061	186
3.066	138
3.071	187
3.110	163
3.130	158
3.160	128, 129
3.216	176
3.220	118, 123
3.223	138, 139
3.235	138
3.281	66
3.283	85
3.284	66
3.289	31, 54, 65, 66, 67
3.300	131
4.014	76
4.018	19, 118
4.029	146

4.039	87	6.094	66
4.055	43	6.113	73, 157
4.093	17, 30, 136	6.141	118
4.095	116	6.163	146
4.098	66	6.173	14
4.160	178	6.260	66
4.170	66	6.275	66
4.191	73	6.282	19
4.220	73, 157	6.309	66
4.223	123	6.340	155
4.235	62	6.358	168
4.238	62	6.432	93, 156
4.262	176, 181	6.443	66
4.289	136	6.453	186
4.300	153	6.459	54, 64
4.304	127	6.462	64
4.305	63	6.464	17
4.353	66	6.521	189
4.363	66	6.522	138
4.416	66	6.527	66
4.429	123	7.048	136
4.486	169	7.104	50
4.539	123, 138, 141	7.132	135
5.006	183	7.157	135
5.024	155	7.270	168
5.034	84	7.286	127
5.085	123	7.294	159
5.127	168	7.340	164
5.129	66, 182	7.359	41
5.132	66	8.095	100
5.192	138	8.181	128
5.225	66	8.399	105
5.227	155	8.431	128
5.232	66	8.451	138
5.258	66	8.538	135
5.260	66	8.555	179
5.273	119, 120	8.556	179
5.301	153, 187	9.033	101
5.303	186	9.077	138
5.311	49, 121, 123	9.099	168
5.351	66	9.121	85, 86
5.388	123	9.304	138
5.411	128	9.312	188
5.684	104	9.318	181
5.763	66	9.337	128
5.788	179	9.495	166, 168
5.821	66	9.522	102
5.893	141	9.691	168
6.090	187	9.701	81

10.007	179	17.144	76
10.083	179	17.241	77
10.145	102	17.260	138
10.243	138	17.327	138
10.329	131	17.366	123
10.348	94, 156	17.398	123
10.386	179	17.399	138
10.571	160	17.418	66, 68
11.087	179	17.445	168
11.415	180	17.711	138
11.467	123	18.165	200
11.492	179	18.178	128
11.670	135	18.219	179
11.791	123	19.178	128
11.803	138	19.218	138
12.058	123	19.261	205, 207
12.059	138	19.321	138
12.216	94	19.332	164, 166
12.248	66, 68	19.354	170
12.279	179	19.415	138
12.356	168	20.121	147
12.382	138	20.122	128
12.448	138, 139	20.126	168
12.465	138	20.185	168
13.047	81	20.247	138
13.127	123	20.335	74
13.343	123	20.359	138
13.389	179	20.366	103
13.649	170	20.367	138
14.054	138	20.426	119
14.058	138	20.490	179
14.126	204	21.038	170
14.127	145	21.060	81
14.190	136	21.339	129
14.191	20	21.467	128
14.245	138	22.047	141
14.335	138, 143	22.071	76
14.344	138	22.282	168
14.397	179	22.339	104
15.023	172	22.416	85
15.115	101, 103	22.450	85
15.231	129	22.505	82
15.470	169	23.007	94
15.697	123	23.071	85
16.022	103	23.151	149
16.494	128	23.407	101
16.576	160	23.428	95, 102
16.617	49	23.629	135
17.070	123	24.053	95, 100

24.057	66, 69	7.333	118
24.140	147	8.138	181
24.145	143	8.177	138
24.149	138, 143	8.195	138
24.181	128	8.280	138
24.382	158	8.340	136
24.560	101	8.580	168
24.566	138	9.013	168
24.568	101	9.037	85
24.664	149	9.102	173
24.768	176	9.242	138, 142
24.779	101, 103	9.351	138
24.781	172	9.406	205, 208
		10.024	170
		10.384	138
		10.507.	81
	Odyssey	10.574	138
		11.111	143
1.133	156	11.251	102
1.396	81	11.349	200
1.402	138, 143	11.375	138
1.414	181	12.077	138, 140
2.052	160	12.084	138
2.053	164	12.102	138
2.054	164	12.107	138
2.222	86	12.156	166
2.287	138	12.157	164
3.015	168	12.383	86
3.055	101	13.086	123
3.078	170	13.087	138
3.114	138	13.215	85
4.064	138	13.303	168
4.078	138	13.304	168
4.080	81	13.306	168
4.163	75	13.364	158
4.193	136	13.376	76
4.391	81	13.401	160
4.637	149	13.418	168
4.649	138	14.056	181
4.713	168	14.071	160
4.735	130	14.123	138
4.749	168	14.155	118
5.356	109	14.156	187
5.484	181	14.197	138
6.126	85	14.373	209
6.173	168	14.408	165
6.300	138	14.468	135
7.051	181	14.503	135
7.213	138	15.024	148
7.293	123		

15.263	104	20.039	76
15.321	138	20.135	145, 205
15.537	165	20.212	138
15.538	165	20.294	7
16.196	138	20.326	149
16.234	168	20.383	160
16.297	164, 166	21.113	149
16.300	42, 71	22.138	138
16.301	109	22.139	81, 85,
16.369	170		89
16.437	63	22.262	149
17.139	122	22.301	179
17.165	165	22.325	119
17.250	160, 164	22.350	118
17.268	138	22.429	85
17.546	118, 207	23.073	85
18.027	119	23.126	138
18.031	138	23.134	160
18.367	179	23.135	164
18.369	165	23.188	138
19.017	157	23.269	172
19.108	138	24.436	149
19.286	138	24.485	85
19.311	165	24.491	130
20.028	76	24.532	160

GENERAL INDEX

Antecedent Possibility Theorem 44–5
assertion
    in definitions of modality 12, 14
Attic Greek
    see later Greek

classical Greek
    see later Greek
clause layers
    previous accounts 206
concessives
    compared with concessive
        conditionals 43
conditional modality 32, 194, 197
    compared with epistemic
        modality 31–2, 36, 46, 116
    different levels of probability 117,
        122
conditionals
    and wishes 135–7
    as non-assertive 38, 40, 41, 44, 51,
        57
    definition in previous accounts 38
    rarity of future markers in protases 66
    use of attitudinal modifiers 40, 41, 57,
        69, 70
conditionals, concessive 40, 42–3, 51
conditionals, counterfactual 46–50,
        121
    and modal particle 50
    meaning an implicature 47–8, 51
conditionals, iterative 175, 180–1
    compared with specific 175, 176–7,
        183–4
    meaning in apodosis 180
    with indicative 178–80
conditionals, obviously realised 40, 42, 51
    compared with causal clause 42
conditionals, open 44–6, 51, 67
    and positive epistemic stance 44, 45–6

in previous accounts 44
conditionals, real 67, 68, 78, 116, 117, 197
    and antecedent possibility
        theorem 44–5
    in previous accounts 45–6
conditionals, realis 40–3, 71
conditionals, resumptive 40–1, 45, 51,
        68–71, 78, 79
conditionals, unreal 116, 117, 118, 119,
        122, 124, 150–1, 197
    in previous accounts 45–6
conjunctions
    and modal particle 203, 204
    development of meaning 173
    development of ἵνα 158, 160
    development of ὡς 158
    development of ὄφρα 73–4, 156–8,
        159–60
    in purpose clauses 155, 156
consequences of the study 1, 124, 197
conventionalisation of conversational
        implicature 25–6, 34, 84, 86, 89, 90,
        136, 161–2
corpus 2, 5–9
cross-linguistic comparison
    distinction of preventive and
        prohibitive 95, 96–9, 108
    first person plural hortative expresses
        invitation 82
    future markers develop directive use 30,
        83, 90
    future markers express intention 87
    future markers used as gnomic 182
    intensional is irrealis 175
    negators defined in terms of scope 205
    of vivid subjunctive 168
    preventive markers have future
        reference 104
    rarity of future markers in protases 66
    remoteness of past tense 114, 115

cross-linguistic comparison: Aleut
  preventive and prohibitive 99
cross-linguistic comparison: Armenian
  preventive and prohibitive 97, 98, 99,
    105, 109
cross-linguistic comparison: Central
    Pomo
  distinction of realis and irrealis future
    60
cross-linguistic comparison: English
  'let's go' construction 34, 82
  'unless' 209
  'will' and its modal nature 58,
    59
  'will' explained by the theory of
    grammaticalisation 23–4, 193
  conventionalisation of conversational
    implicature 84
  future markers 59
  future markers are mature 66–7
  indicative with attitudinal modifiers in
    conditional clauses 37–8
  preventive and prohibitive 99
  sequence of tense 154, 168
  untrue resumptive conditionals 70
cross-linguistic comparison: French
  mood choice connected with non
    specificity 185
cross-linguistic comparison: German
  interaction of person and modality 88
  moods and modal verbs 32
  negative epistemic stance 120–1
cross-linguistic comparison: Hebrew
  future marker develops hortative
    meaning 83
cross-linguistic comparison: Hittite
  imperative morphology 133
  prayer petitions 131, 132
cross-linguistic comparison: Indo-Iranian
  future with desiderative meaning 80
cross-linguistic comparison: Japanese
  preventive and prohibitive 99
cross-linguistic comparison: Latin
  future developed from IE
    subjunctive 40, 41, 57
  future with desiderative meaning 80
  prayer petitions 132
cross-linguistic comparison:
    Proto-Indo-European

  negators
  prayer petitions 132
  subjunctive as future marker 57
  subjunctive endings 115
cross-linguistic comparison: Russian
  future markers in conditional
    protases 66
  preventive and prohibitive 99, 105,
    109
cross-linguistic comparison: Sanskrit
  rarity of aorist imperative 92
cross-linguistic comparison: Slavic
  negative directive and aspect 91
cross-linguistic comparison: Spanish
  continuing validity in indirect
    speech 168
  development of future markers 79
  distinction of realisable and non-
    realisable wishes 135
cross-linguistic comparison: Vedic
  imperative and aspect 92
  injunctive 92
  negators 206
  subjunctive endings 114
  subjunctive has future meaning 38,
    57

deontic modality
  see modality, deontic
diachronic perspective
  difference between *Iliad* and
    Odyssey 71
  different layers co-existing 91, 95–6,
    110
  in previous accounts 22
  later developments
    foreshadowed 190–1
  similes are late 183
  vivid subjunctives are late 8
  which use came first 30, 195
directives
  expressing auto-prescription 82, 85, 88,
    111
  expressing invitation 82, 83, 111
  in comparison with wishes 126
  less prototypical 127–30
  third person 126–7
dynamic modality
  see modality, dynamic

editing the text of Homer 19–20, 56, 74–5,
  76, 83, 84, 160, 164, 169, 172
epistemic markers
  expressing future 77
epistemic modality
  see Modality, epistemic
epistemic stance 32, 124, 194
epistemic stance, negative 120–1, 138,
  151
epistemic stance, positive 38–9, 44, 45,
  46, 48, 49, 51, 52, 121

formulae 5–7, 181, 188
future domain
  modal nature 13, 23, 57, 77, 78, 195
  more and less irrealis markers 53, 60–1,
    77
  potential reality 60, 62, 64, 65, 111,
    123, 195
  projected reality 60, 61, 62, 64, 66, 72,
    77, 78, 111, 122, 195
future indicative
  as more realis than the subjunctive 62,
    70, 76
  desiderative in origin 80–1
  difficulty of formally identifying 5,
    55–6, 58, 61, 74, 79–80, 81
  expressing intent 63, 87
  expressing prediction 62
  expressing threat 68
  in conditional protases 66, 68
  in other subordinate clauses 74–6, 77
  in purpose clauses 74–5
  in relative clauses 76–7
  in resumptive conditionals 68–1, 78,
    79
  in temporal clauses 74
future markers
  development 66–7, 79
  expressing 'gnomically true' 182
  expressing directive force 30, 83, 90
  expressing prediction 57, 77
  languages with more than one 59, 60
fuzzy set theory 33–4, 35, 85, 87–9, 111,
  196
  see also modality, as web

gnomic aorist 169, 178
grammarians

ancient views of moods 13, 106,
  137
grammaticalisation 1, 8, 10, 15–16,
  21–6, 35, 112, 192–3
  against finding an 'essential'
    meaning 22–4, 52, 142, 203
  against parallelism of subjunctive and
    optative 138, 193, 197
  and conventionalisation of
    conversational implicature 25–6
  and gradualness of development 154,
    157, 158, 159, 161, 162, 173, 189–90
  and negators 210
  and the development of the modal
    particle 201, 203, 204
  and the future tense in English 23–4,
    193
  importance for this study 26
  importance of construction 24–5, 183
Greenberg's irrealis continuum 16
Grice
  maxim of relevance in interpretation of
    indicative 38

Homeric language
  diachronic nature 6, 7–8
  interest 8–9, 192
  less mechanical than Attic Greek 8
  problems 5–6

imperative
  and aspect 90, 91, 92–3, 106–7, 108,
    109–10
  as prohibitive 103–4, 105
  compared with deontic modality 27, 28
  expressing unwanted order 146
  first person 82
  formation 133
  third person 127–30, 131, 132
  with agent 125, 129, 132, 137
indicative
  accompanied with attitudinal modifiers
    in conditional clauses 40, 41, 57, 69,
    70
  and subjectivity 193
  as real 49, 51
  as subjective 13, 37
  compared with optative in counterfactual
    conditionals 49–50, 52

indicative (*cont.*)
  expressing iterative meaning 178–80
  expressing positive epistemic
    stance 38–9, 44, 45, 46, 48, 49, 51,
    52, 121, 194
  in conditional sentences 38, 51,
    194
  in counterfactual conditionals 194
  in relative clauses 187–8
  in similes 179
  new map 193–4
  not realis 37–8, 51
  previous accounts 12, 37
  previously described as epistemically
    neutral/unmarked 38, 44, 51
  previously described as modal in
    counterfactual conditionals 47,
    48–50, 51, 194
  previously described as non modal
    193
  previously described as realis 16, 37,
    51, 53, 93–6
  reasons to discuss 37
injunctive 92, 95, 96–9, 110
irrealis 14, 28, 55, 57, 61, 63, 66, 67, 111,
  155, 161–2, 188, 189
  and intensional meaning 175
  as controversial term 14
irrealis continuum 14, 16, 20, 51, 52, 53,
  55, 72, 73, 113, 134–5
iterative
  definition 175
  meaning in relative clauses 183

later Greek
  differences from Homeric Greek 8, 61,
    71, 79, 107, 110, 132, 167, 174, 176,
    178, 196, 203

metre
  effects on language 6
mixed aorists 80
modal particle
  and grammaticalisation 201, 203,
    204
  corrected to fit theories 5, 19–20
  dialectal differentiation 200
  formed from missegmentation 200
  in conditional clauses 176, 202–3

  in counterfactual conditionals 50
  in purpose clauses 203, 204
  marker of type of modality in previous
    accounts 19–20, 139
  previous accounts 201–3
  previously described as having lexical
    meaning 201
  two treated as one 199
  unreliable marker of modality 19–20,
    200–1, 204
  with future indicative 200–1
  with indicative 200
  with indicative in counterfactual
    conditionals 200
modal verbs
  bias towards in previous studies 2,
    32–3, 194
  in comparison with moods 15, 31, 114,
    123, 195
  with negation 18
modality 1
  and assertion 12, 14
  and future domain 13
  and subjectivity 12–13, 50, 193
  as non factual 12
  as web 33, 34, 35, 85, 88–9, 112,
    136–7, 142, 151, 154, 196, 197–8
  deontic 17–18, 27–8, 87
  deontic, compared with imperative 27,
    28
  deontic, compared with speaker-oriented
    modality 27–8, 36, 195
  deontic, compared with wishes 133–4
  dynamic 140–1, 142–3
  dynamic, as ability 150
  dynamic, expressed by modal verbs in
    English 138, 139, 142, 143
  dynamic, expressing permission 142,
    143
  dynamic, expressing root
    possibility 143
  dynamic, other ways of expressing in
    Greek 141
  dynamic, relationship to other types of
    modality 140–1
  epistemic 17–18
  epistemic, compared to conditional
    modality 30–2, 36
  epistemic, future reference 58

epistemic, overlap with future
   markers 58
formal distinction of deontic and
   epistemic in previous
   accounts 18–19, 20, 199
in modern theoretical studies 10,
   27–34, 35, 140
interest 192
of wishes 133–4
performative 28–30
speaker oriented 27–30, 34, 125, 133,
   195, 197
speaker oriented, importance for a
   diachronic approach 30, 195
subjective and objective 29, 144
moods in Homeric Greek
interest 1
previous accounts 1, 10, 11, 16–20, 35,
   155
morphology
aorist subjunctive 79–80
formal confusion of subjunctive and
   future indicative 55–6, 58, 61, 79–80,
   81
formation of optative 8
formation of subjunctive 55
primary endings on optative 115
relationship between subjunctive and
   optative 15–16
remoteness of the optative 113,
   114–15
secondary endings 113, 114, 115
secondary endings on the optative 150
short vowel subjunctive 55, 56
speculative origins of the moods 24
third-person imperative 133
primary endings 113, 114, 115

negative directive 90, 112
and aspect 90, 91, 92–3, 106–7, 108,
   109–10
comparison of subjunctive and
   imperative 102–5
distribution of preventive and
   prohibitive 105–6, 108
metrical evidence 95–6
preventive 96, 97, 98, 108, 109
preventive and prohibitive in
   Homer 99–106

previous accounts 91
prohibitive 96, 97, 98, 108
negator μή 90
development 156
not only with prohibitions 205
with speaker-oriented modality 205
negator οὐ
in wishes 207
negators
and grammaticalisation 210
explained in terms of scope 205–10
in conditional clauses 208–10
markers of type of modality in previous
   accounts 19–20, 145, 199, 204
unexpected with optative 145–6
New Testament Greek
   see later Greek
non-specific
in relative clauses 190
of moods in subordinate clauses 184–9

objective modality
as constative, non-performative 149
optative
after primary main verbs 161
as timeless 123, 163, 174, 181, 184
as unreal 120, 124, 142, 150–1, 171,
   173, 174, 181
compared with the imperative 27,
   125–33, 137, 146, 147, 151
compared with the indicative 49–50,
   52, 120
development of meaning in iterative
   clauses 184
development of meaning in subordinate
   clauses 180–1
distribution in subordinate
   clauses 163–4
dynamic 138–42, 144, 150
dynamic, permission 143
dynamic, root possibility 143
expressing delayed imperative 148
expressing negative epistemic
   stance 120–1, 124, 138, 150–1, 197
expressing objective desire 149
expressing reported imperative 147
expressing speaker oriented
   modality 197
formation 8, 115

optative (*cont.*)
  in comparison with English modal
    verbs 138, 139, 142, 143
  in conditionals 116, 150–1, 197
  in counterfactual conditionals 48–50,
    121
  in primary sequence 164–5, 174
  in purpose clauses 159–61
  in relative clauses with specific
    antecedent 185–6
  in secondary sequence 16, 155
  in subordinate clauses 197
  in wishes 151, 197
  more polite 126, 130, 137
  morphological foundation for
    remoteness 113, 114–15
  new map 197–8
  not grammatically required in
    subordinate clauses 197
  not less likely 197
  not less vivid 120
  not more remote 116, 117–18, 119,
    120, 124
  not most irrealis 134–5, 151
  objective deontic 144–9, 150
  obsolescent in later Greek 191
  of attraction 165
  origin 24
  previous accounts 113, 138, 139
  previously described as future 122–3
  previously described as grammatically
    required in subordinate clauses 159
  previously described as less vivid 119
  previously described as most
    irrealis 16, 113, 155
  previously described as past time variant
    of subjunctive 114, 150, 154
  previously described as polite 146, 147,
    148
  previously described as remote 15, 113,
    114, 117, 123, 124, 150
  secondary endings 150
  significance of name 137
  web of modality 135–8, 144, 147,
    148–9, 150, 151, 152, 154, 197–8
  wish 124, 148
  wish, in conditionals 117–18
  wish, indirect 130–1
  wish, with agent 126, 130, 136
  wish, without agent 126, 130
  wishes, realisable and non
    realisable 151
  with ἵνα 160
  with ὄφρα 159–60

past tense
  and irrealis 24
  and remoteness 25, 114, 115
performativity
  and modality 28, 111, 133, 144, 145,
    195
person
  interaction with meaning 84, 85, 87–8,
    89, 111, 166, 174, 196
politeness 126, 130, 131–3, 137, 146, 147
positive epistemic stance 38–9, 44, 45, 46,
  48, 49, 51, 52
prayers 131, 132
preventive 96, 97, 98, 108, 109, 195
  and future reference 104, 109
  and tense 106–7
  difficult to differentiate from
    prohibitive 98–9
  first person 95
  in previous accounts 106–8
  second person 95
primary endings 113, 114, 115
prohibitive 96, 97, 98, 108
purpose clauses 73–4, 189–90
  and modal particle 203
  compared to conditionals 165
  conjunctions 73–4, 155, 156–8,
    159–60, 173
  development of meaning of the
    moods 189–90
  origin in parataxis 155
  real and unreal 165
  with future indicative 74–5

relative clauses
  mood choice 184–9, 190
  moods chosen independently of the
    specificity of the antecedent 188, 189
  non-restrictive 185
  restrictive 186
  with indicative and non-specific
    antecedent 187–8
  with indicative in previous accounts 187

with iterative meaning 183
with singular subject pronoun but plural antecedent 7
with specific antecedent 185–6
remoteness
and past tense 25

secondary endings 113, 114
semantic map 192–3
of the indicative 193–4
of the optative 197–8
of the subjunctive 194–7
sequence of moods
compared with sequence of tenses 154
short-vowel subjunctive 55, 56, 74
similes
as latest chronological slice 183
speaker-oriented modality
see modality, speaker-oriented
speech acts 13, 132
expressives 134
indirect 130–1, 134
wishes 134
structuralist approaches and their problems 10, 21, 23, 35, 54
subjunctive
as emphatic 68
as real 171, 172, 173, 181
as realis 76
compared with the future indicative 53, 54–5, 61–3, 64, 65, 66, 67–8, 72–6, 77, 111, 195
compared with the future indicative, developing differently 53
compared with the future indicative, different distribution 68–71, 78, 79, 111, 195
compared with the future indicative, formal confusion 5, 55–6, 58, 61, 74–5, 77, 111
compared with the future indicative, functional difference 56, 57, 77
compared with the imperative 27, 54, 80, 81, 90, 94, 100, 108, 125
deontic intent 54, 63, 83, 86–9, 111, 196
development in purpose clauses 156–9
development of meaning 111, 195

development of meaning in subordinate clauses 73–4, 163, 171, 174, 180–3, 184, 196
epistemic uses 53, 54–5, 111
expressing speaker oriented, performative modality 16, 53, 81, 90, 93–6, 195
formed with primary endings 113
formed with secondary endings 114
future marker 53, 54, 58–60, 64–5, 72, 73, 78–9, 83, 87, 110, 111, 159, 162–3, 165–6, 173, 196
future meaning in apodoses 61
future meaning in conditionals 66–7, 72, 78
future meaning in main clauses 61–6, 77
future meaning in relative clauses 72–3, 185–6
future meaning in subordinate clauses 55, 72–7
future meaning in temporal clauses 72
future meaning, expressing prediction 194–5
hortative 53
hortative derived from future 83–5
hortative in the negative 94–5
hortative in the plural 83
hortative, putative examples in second and third person 81–2
in fear clauses 93
in primary sequence 155, 162, 165–6
in similes 183
more mature 67, 71, 79, 111
negative directive 90, 112, 195
negative directive in previous accounts 91
negative directive, comparison of subjunctive and imperative 90, 102–5
negative directive, expressing preventive in first person 100
negative directive, expressing preventive in second person 100–1, 102, 103, 104, 105
negative directive, expressing preventive with controllable verbs 101
negative directive, expressing preventive with emotions 101

subjunctive (*cont.*)
  negative directive, expressing preventive
    with warning 101–2
  negative directive, interaction with
    aspect 90–3, 107, 108, 109–10, 112,
    195
  negative directive, not purely
    aspectual 16, 53, 93–6
  new map 194–7
  origin 24
  previous accounts 53, 196–7
  previous accounts of iterative
    meaning 182
  previously described as more
    irrealis 16, 53, 55, 57, 111, 194, 195
  previously described as more vivid 119
  short-vowel 55, 56, 74
  significance of name 153
  vivid 8, 164, 166–8, 172–4
subjunctive and optative
  as parallel 162, 174
  deontic and epistemic meanings 17, 20
  not grammatically required 173, 181
  not grammatically required in relative
    clauses 188, 189
  not parallel 138, 150, 152, 177–8, 184,
    197
  parallelism has morphological
    support 15–16
  previous accounts 11–12, 192
  previously described as expressing
    iterative meaning 184, 190
  previously described as grammatically
    required in subordinate clauses 154,
    155, 173–4, 185, 189

  previously described as parallel 15–16,
    21–6, 154, 189
  relationship compared to modal verbs in
    English 15, 31
subordinate clauses
  as irrealis 155
  development of meaning 175
  examples 153

tense
  definitions 57

vivid subjunctive
  and lateness of passage 8
  in other subordinate clauses 172–3
  in past time 170–2
  not Homeric in previous accounts 169
  of continuing validity 167–8, 173, 174
vividness 119, 120, 166–7
  and cross linguistic comparison 168

wishes 124
  and conditional sentences 135–7
  and the irrealis continuum 134–5
  as expressives 134
  as performative 145
  as performative desire 137, 148
  as speech acts 134
  compared with deontic modality 133–4,
    137
  compared with directives 126, 137, 151,
    197
  optative and desiderative 135
  realised and non realised 135, 137
  without agent 137